DRIVE

DRIVE

How Vince Carter Conquered the NBA

CHRIS YOUNG

DOUBLEDAY CANADA

Doubleday Canada and colophon are trademarks.

National Library of Canada Cataloguing in Publication Data
Young, Chris
        Drive : how Vince Carter conquered the NBA

ISBN 0-385-25998-0

1. Carter, Vince   2. Basketball players — United States — Biography.   I. Title.

GV884.C377Y68 2001   796.323'092   C2001-901033-8

Jacket design: Carol Moskot
Printed and bound in Canada

Published in Canada by Doubleday Canada,
a division of Random House of Canada Limited

Visit Random House of Canada Limited's website: www.randomhouse.ca

FRI 10 9 8 7 6 5 4 3 2 1

To. G.L.Y, who loved writing, sports and justice

contents

INTRODUCTION
Vinsanity   1

CHAPTER ONE
June 2000: The Storm Before the Calm   15

CHAPTER TWO
July 2000: Goodbye, Tracy   33

CHAPTER THREE
September 2000: Wizard of Oz   53

CHAPTER FOUR
October 2000: Say It Ain't So   77

CHAPTER FIVE
November 2000: Selling Product   103

CHAPTER SIX
December 2000: Getting Younger   127

CHAPTER SEVEN
January 2001: Escape to Florida   149

CHAPTER EIGHT
February 2001: Making a Point   171

CHAPTER NINE
March 2001: Bland Is Beautiful   199

CHAPTER TEN
April 2001: In the Mecca   227

EPILOGUE
Time and Distance   245

Acknowledgments   257

Vinsanity

H e has a nice smile and an easy manner, especially with young people. He can do things with a basketball that amaze and astonish. He makes a good living, and figures to make more. But maybe the luckiest thing about the lucky fellow named Vince Carter is that he wasn't around to watch the original Toronto Raptors.

Luck and design — and don't forget sheer, hide-your-eyes, bum-numbing horror — brought Carter to Canada to pull on the garish uniform of the Raptors, a franchise barely out of diapers and without history or credibility. Oh yes, at one time there was plenty of horror. Too many nights of Oliver Miller, Vincenzo Esposito, Benoit Benjamin and all the other marginal players, which according to pro sports' unique system of reward put the Raptors in a position to acquire Carter's supernova act in the first place. Too many Isiah Thomas promises gone unfulfilled. Too many arenas gone unbuilt, topped off by a nightmarish third season directly preceding Carter's arrival.

The luck came in with the National Basketball Association's "lottery" system for its annual draft, wherein the losers from the season just completed are called out like bingo numbers in the chase for next year's top incoming young players. The irony of May 1998 was that the Raptors groaned when their ball popped out at no. 4, despite having the NBA's second-worst record. It would turn out to be a lucky drop down, steering them away from bigger players who were more prized at the time.

Then there was the design, a shrewd draft-night trade engineered by a pair of NBA greenhorns that sent Carter from the Golden State Warriors, picking right behind the Raptors, to Toronto in exchange for the no. 4 pick. It wasn't exactly Manhattan for a bag of beads all over again — Antawn Jamison, Carter's teammate at the University of North Carolina, went to the Warriors — but it was close. And it was the most important deal general manager Glen Grunwald and coach Butch Carter could ever hope to make.

Those earlier names of Miller and Benjamin and Acie Earl and, oh yeah, Isiah Thomas, too, belong to a prehistory from which the Raptors have emerged with Carter as their saviour. Only in the world of pro basketball can one player turn around the fortunes of an entire team — and, occasionally, an entire franchise. And in the rarest of cases, an entire league.

In his three years around the post-Jordan NBA block, Carter has done some of that. He has managed the neatest of paradoxes, turning mundane nights memorable as he made the extraordinary look ordinary. Try as he might to downplay it, his package of skills — the gravity-challenging levitations, the power and élan of a dunk, the twisting body control — has turned him into one of pro sports' rarest of performers: an irresistible, bankable superstar. For a franchise just gaining a toehold, he *is* the franchise. As Vince goes, so go the Raptors and the NBA in Canada.

It wasn't always this way. Officially, the franchise's short and inglorious life began in 1993, at the St. Regis Hotel in New York, when 27 NBA owners voted unanimously to bring Toronto into their exclusive club. All that the Raptors had to do in return was give them US$125 million, a record high at the time for an expansion team, and agree to a passel of conditions virtually guaranteeing the new club to at least three years of ineptitude on the basketball court. It could have been worse. The NBA had been kicking around a price tag of a daunting US$140 million as an entry fee until Vancouver came along to turn it into a two-pronged money grab from the league and its first serious presence outside the United States.

They got their three years, and then it was Carter's arrival in time for year four that signalled "time beginning" in Toronto, as opposed to time B.C. From there, you can choose your own date for the coming-out party: perhaps the February '99 opening of the Air Canada Centre, the arena the Raptors share with the Maple Leafs, the new and the old of Canadian pro sports in the country's largest market, under one corporate umbrella and one steel roof. Or maybe it was the night Carter was drafted into the pros, or even before that, the day he worked out for the Raptors and left one team official literally shaking with anticipation.

One such moment came on a snowy February 1999 night in Indianapolis, at old Market Square Arena. A palace when Elvis Presley opened it a quarter-century earlier, Market Square was a down-at-the-heels bandbox that the current climate of professional sports, with its mix of money and bullshit and balls, was in the process of closing and burying.

Vince Carter came into this night as just another talented pro basketball rookie. At the time, he wasn't even considered the best rookie in the league. According to the NBA's first monthly set of awards, Paul Pierce of Boston was February's finest, in the early days of a demi-season that almost didn't happen.

February 1999 was the cruellest month for the NBA. Michael Jordan had just retired, and if the NBA was not exactly teetering on the brink of total collapse, as it was painted in some quarters, then it was at least going through a kind of mid-life crisis. For a decade and a half, it had been on a joyride with NBA commissioner David Stern at the wheel, going from rags to filthy rich. In a span of less than a year, though, it was showing signs of running down.

Jordan, its most marketable and recognizable star, was gone from the stage. He had taken the last shot of the previous June's championship final and walked off with a sixth championship ring. The shoe companies that had marched alongside, hyping NBA stars and helping to fuel this power surge, had cut back their endorsement budgets as their profits dropped and the fashion appeal of basketball shoes took a dip. Increasingly, NBA players appeared out of touch, unaccountable and out of control: think of Dennis Rodman kicking a courtside cameraman, or Latrell Sprewell choking his coach. (Never mind that the owners were in some cases just as bad, Larry Miller of Utah going into the stands to fight, and Charlotte's George Shinn involved in a sordid sexual harassment case.) At a number of levels, around a lot of corners, the NBA looked overdone.

More than any other development, though, the most ominous sign of an overdue market correction was a bitter labour dispute that everyone knew was coming. Still, it very nearly killed the 1998–99 season — at least that's what the poker-faced Stern wanted everyone to believe. After a management lockout of the players dragged from the summer into October, November, December and early 1999, a settlement was finally reached just as the window for getting in some kind of a season was closing. A breakneck season was scheduled — 50 games in 90 nights — and thus Vince Carter and the Raptors were, like the rest of the league, trotted out, ready or not.

The public yawned. They'd seen this before. For the first time in its history, the NBA had in effect become just like all the other pro leagues in North America, losing games (along with money, and the support and trust of some of its customers) because of labour troubles. Major-league baseball had suffered an estimated $150-million operating loss in the wake of its 1994–95 labour stoppage, its attendance diving 15 per cent. That ground had not quite been regained by the end of the decade, as baseball fans proved slow to forgive, growing more cynical and remote. Wasn't this just another example of millionaires fighting among themselves? How could it be any different for basketball?

TV ratings began to slide, and no wonder. Michael Jordan had been as adept at selling as he was at winning. He brought casual, non-basketball fans to the arenas and the television sets. Without him around, broad swathes of empty seats greeted the players on their return. With no transcendent talent, no unassailable superstar to carry the NBA through the aftermath of the lockout, there appeared to be a vacuum at the top.

On that high plateau, breathing that rarefied air, were instead mere pretenders. Jordan's contemporaries had grown old and prospered in his shadow, but few had any gas left in the tank for a run at greatness. Meantime, the younger generation coming along was eclipsed in so many ways, from championship rings to jump-shooting prowess to other fundamental skills

— in just about every way but at the pay window. The Chicago Bulls, Jordan's old team, were immediately broken up, in a few short months going from the group of Jordan, Scottie Pippen, Phil Jackson and a host of role players who had won six championships in the 1990s to god-awful no-names. In short, the NBA had changed over, and most everybody was thinking for the worse.

But in February 1999 the games began marching again, creating at least the illusion of being back to normal. Which brings us back to Market Square Arena in Indianapolis, capital of the basketball-mad state of Indiana. A crowd of 14,700 showed up to watch the hometown Pacers against the Toronto Raptors — well below the 16,530-plus capacity, and the second-lowest crowd of Indiana's season — and even if they were among the most boisterous and smartest of NBA crowds, the downturn was more than a little depressing for Pacers officials, or anyone checking the NBA's suddenly erratic pulse. Then again, their opponents in the freaky purple uniforms weren't exactly a hit road show.

When Vince Carter was ordered out by coach Butch Carter for 20 extra minutes of pregame shooting, barely anyone in the early-arriving crowd paid any heed at all. Carter's introduction on the P.A. was virtually ignored. About the only visitor to provoke any kind of reaction was former Knick and current Raptor Charles Oakley, a survivor of many Pacers–New York playoff battles. He elicited a few half-hearted boos.

Nothing more could have been expected. The Raptors were under a dark cloud heading into a sort-of season. In their home market, they had become synonymous with tumult — here was their fourth season just beginning, and they were into their third head coach and under their third owner. To the rest of the league, the Raptors and their expansion mates, the Vancouver Grizzlies, were the NBA's version of Siberia. "I'd chain myself to this locker if I got traded there," Boston's Kenny Anderson said of Toronto, and he was by no means alone in his opinion. "I'd retire first," said New Jersey's Kendall Gill when his name came up in trade rumours involving Toronto.

So there wasn't much optimism when the mists from the lockout cleared and the Raptors reconvened for this '99 interlude. The best that general manager Glen Grunwald was hoping for was an end to the convulsions that had become the norm. Ticket sales had flatlined and expectations were low — in essence, Toronto had tuned them out.

And then it was February 24, 1999, Game 10. Late in the first quarter, Vince Carter is on the left side of the floor in Indianapolis, clearing for a takeoff. He is by himself with the ball, his teammates backing off to the other side of the court — in the lingo of the game, the Raptors are running a clearout for Carter. Chris Mullin, old school all the way — thirteenth-year pro, flat-top haircut, harsh Brooklyn accent, original Dream Teamer, the kind of guy who looks allergic to tanning — comes a half-step closer out to cover him.

The old meets the new, but instead of an embrace, Carter is gone in a blur. Mullin is left half-turned, half-leaning, reaching with his left hand and grasping nothing, his eyes widening, looking like a man who has just felt a bullet graze by as Carter drives toward the baseline, pushing the ball with his left hand. Now Carter is putting the ball on the floor. One dribble. Jump stop, right foot planting just inside the painted area extending out from the basket.

Mullin tries to follow, going up with his right hand from behind as Carter uncoils and begins to extend, but he is unable to reach the ball — it's too far, he's too late, and Carter's body is up there shielding him. Suddenly Carter is off the ground, the ball held two-handed out in front of him.

A pair of Pacers half-heartedly move into the vicinity to help, but like Mullin they are a step slow. Dale Davis stops, stands and watches almost in admiration, a slight "oh" forming on his lips. Rik Smits, nearly a foot taller than the six-foot-six Carter, comes from the opposite baseline but merely raises his arms like a hapless robbery victim.

It's all Carter, floating now. A flashbulb from a sideline photographer briefly illuminates him and casts everyone else in a dimmer light. He pumps once as he glides by Smits, and then he is pumping again, bringing the ball down, down, down to his knees — "down to his ankles!" one excited Market Square customer will gush to his friend two hours later as they walk out into the night — and then the ball is suddenly coming up, faster and faster, Carter's head just below the basket, his eyes looking straight through the nylon netting as he brings the ball up higher and over his head and behind his head and over the rim and finally he reverse flushes it down through the cylinder.

It is only two points. It unfolds in just a couple of seconds. There is no rim-hanging or other styling added for punctuation — none is necessary. Carter drops to earth on his left foot, his right leg extended like a dancer's at Radio City. He looks nonchalantly toward the other end of the floor, away from the basket he has just ravaged. All is quiet, as if there's been a collective intake of breath throughout the arena.

Then the Market Square crowd is reacting. It starts with open-mouthed surprise, then a turn to your neighbour for confirmation, then a drone that becomes a buzz that sounds very much like 14,700 saying ...

"I just went 'whoa,'" said Indiana's Antonio Davis. A few months later, he would be traded to the Raptors to play alongside Carter.

"Man, that was sick. Sick!" said Tracy McGrady later. "I told him, he's gotta stop that, man. That's just nasty."

On the Toronto bench, Carter's teammates are up on their feet at once, punching the air and cheering. Negele Knight, an injured guard in civvies on the end of the bench, is dressed in one of his usual sharp suits, the ones that earn him the nickname Billy Bathgate, and with his gold chains glinting and winking, he grabs a towel and excitedly fans the air with it.

The bigger game continues, the Pacers walking the ball up to the other end, Mullin jogging by Indiana head coach Larry Bird. We'll need help on him, Mullin's look seems to say as he makes eye contact with Bird and slightly shakes his head. Bird nods back. The audience continues to buzz away, oblivious for one moment to the scoreboard. Which was, all in all, a good thing for the two teams. This was a mismatch, the more experienced Pacers beating up on the young Raptors.

But it is not your ordinary winter pummel. Market Square Arena has seen much in 25 years of use. Many in the building have seen basketball's most electrifying performers in their prime, going back to the flamboyant and freewheeling days of the old Pacers, charter members of the defunct American Basketball Association, to the dime-a-dozen dunk masters of this post-postmodern NBA. Julius Erving. David Thompson. Dominique Wilkins. Michael Jordan. And now this. On a blowout night, a new star.

"I've seen some good dunks," says Bill York, a Pacers original game-night employee for 32 years. "But I have never seen an in-game dunk like that one."

Sure, there had been signs it was coming. The hard core had been waiting patiently, following Carter from as far back as his years on the team at Daytona Mainland High and later at the University of North Carolina.

Three days earlier, he'd christened the Raptors' brand-new home, the Air Canada Centre, with a 32-point performance against the Grizzlies. It had earned him a new nickname, Air Canada, partly a recognition of his NBA home floor but also referring to Michael (Air) Jordan — just the sort of comparison that Carter detested.

Carter's dunk in Indiana — a baseline, double-pump, reverse two-hander in NBA shorthand — was featured on the TV sports highlights, where the largest gathering of sporting eyes are fixed. It would become a staple in the weekly and even yearly best-of compilations and via Internet downloads.

It was not the best dunk of the year for Carter. On rare occasions, he would talk of others that he rated higher. But it certainly was the last time that Carter's act would surprise, the last time that he could sneak in under the radar screen unnoticed. Mullin wouldn't be the last to wave for help. Market Square wouldn't be the last crowd to gasp. But it would be the last time that a Carter swoop would occur without any sense of anticipation. Carter played the game with a rare flair and a sky-scraping 41-inch vertical leap — it was finesse and power and charisma all wrapped up in a wholesome package.

Yes, there was a wholesome element to Carter, as old-fashioned as that sounds. No tattoos, no piercings, no gangsta posing, no entourage, just a middle-class background and that blue-ribbon Carolina pedigree. In a league brimming over with attitude, here was a newcomer who addressed coaches as "sir."

What he served up had the look of a streetball assault — the quick first step, the treading-air levitations, the double-pump fakes, the quick elevations (and, just as quick, back up again for the second time), the finishes, sometimes silky and sometimes raw — and here it was being executed by a sheltered and protected kid from Florida. Two-handers, reverses, windmills, tomahawks, not to mention the otherworldly contortions that looked more like something out of the Cirque du Soleil. The basketball rim is 18 inches in diameter and stands an imposing 10 feet off the ground, but Carter joined the select few — from Elgin Baylor and Connie Hawkins to Jordan and Wilkins — to whom length and distance and the laws of physics seemed nothing but irrelevancies.

It wouldn't take long for this high-wire act to earn a name of its own — "Vinsanity." The ESPN network in the U.S. pinned that tag on its almost nightly highlight packages of the latest from Carter. Quickly, he had gone from undercover to over the top. His game would become the centre of nearly non-stop attention, his moves on the floor accompanied, always now, by a sense of gleeful anticipation. Crowds would arrive early, pens and programs in hand, and a growing number of fans would hang around late.

Whenever Carter approached the basket, it seemed the temperature in the arena would rise, the buzz grow a little louder. Flashbulbs popped. By his second NBA season, when Carter went into visiting cities and the slam-dunks were slow in coming, he would hear the fans yell out: "Hey, Vince, I bought this ticket to see you dunk!"

Some nights, he would turn and acknowledge the comment with a half-smile, half-grimace. In season or out, Carter heard it. More often than not, he delivered. At New York's summertime institution, the venerable Rucker Tournament, he showed up unannounced and dunked in an alley-oop with such majesty that observers called it the greatest they'd ever seen. In Miami in the summer of 2000, he finished another stupefying slam with both elbows ending up inside the rim. It was a reprise, and then some, of the elbow-hanging, hand-caught-in-the-cookie-jar jam that was part of his winning tour de force at the NBA's slam-dunk championship in February 2000, nearly a year to the day after that opening salvo in Indianapolis.

But the one-dunk-pony tag — and the inevitable comparisons to Jordan that had followed him around since the day he arrived on campus in Chapel Hill, North Carolina — was something Carter was eager to shed. He could joke as he went back over a particularly eye-popping move, but almost immediately he would catch himself and shift away, appearing a little uncomfortable, as if he'd just caught himself out.

Carter's lament was not exactly original. He was like the dancer who yearns to sing, the singer who pines to act — the performer who wants to be taken seriously, even as everyone waits in anticipation for just that one thing.

"Everybody sees me as a dunker," he said more than once during his rookie season, as the highlight reel grew longer and word began to spread about the Raptors' young, phenomenal talent. "I want to be seen as a basketball player. I want that respect more."

That respect would come in time. By the end of his first season, Carter had transformed the Raptors, taking them to the edge of the playoff hunt, only to fall short. Individually, he polled 115 of a possible 119 votes to win the NBA Rookie of the Year award. Paul Pierce, the one-time leader in that race, got the other four. He was as well liked by his NBA peers — including many of the harder-to-please veterans — as he was by the fans.

"Part of my routine is to get to practice early and watch ESPN *Sportscenter* in the locker room," says 76ers coach Larry Brown. "When the players start filing in, they'll see it on and ask, 'Oh, what did he do today?' They don't have to mention him by name. I know who they mean."

"He does things that we probably never thought anybody could do," said Ray Allen, a close friend of Carter's who plays for the Milwaukee Bucks.

Back in February 1999 at Market Square Arena, just days into Vince Carter's pro career, Larry Bird saw what was coming. "If he gets to the point where he can make that 18-footer," Bird mused later that night, "he may be impossible to stop."

CHAPTER ONE

June 2000:

The Storm Before the Calm

It takes the average NBA expansion team starting from ground zero about five years to reach bare competence, otherwise known as the playoffs. So the Raptors arrived right on schedule in the spring of 2000, at the end of their fifth season. They got there on Vince Carter's clock, too, Carter delivering as he'd promised one year earlier, when he stood on the Air Canada Centre floor and told the departing crowd that he guaranteed a playoff berth in the coming season.

In an age of diluted product and bloated playoff grid — 16 of the NBA's 29 teams make the playoffs — this was a modest milestone to reach. Under normal circumstances, it calls for some backslapping and celebrations. Champagne, ticket price hikes and dreams of contract extensions yet to come.

This is a franchise, however, that has rarely gone the normal route. Playing at Indiana with a week to go in the schedule, the Raptors lost a tough four-point game to the Pacers and figured they'd have to wait till the next game to assure a playoff berth. An Orlando loss, though, had put them in — no one realized it until an hour after they'd finished the game. Butch Carter, the last out of the locker room, was stopped and informed of the situation by a reporter. "Really," Carter said with a falling intonation, as if half-pleased, half-exasperated. This set the tone for their playoff performance: bundled in and out with three successive losses to the New York Knicks.

All the playoffs and their aftermath did was provide Toronto general manager Glen Grunwald with two vexing problems that wouldn't go away until they went away for good: his head coach, Butch Carter, and young Toronto free agent Tracy McGrady.

Until then, the pair had seemed to be the cornerstones of the team. The coach had signed a four-year contract extension in December of 1999 and at the time was regarded in some quarters as one of the NBA's bright young sideline minds. McGrady, Vince Carter's distant cousin, was a 21-year-old just coming into his own and carrying an eye-catching bag of tricks.

By June of 2000, however, just one month after the Knicks ended the Raptors' playoff lives in the shortest of orders, they had both become millstones. Butch Carter seemed determined to commit professional suicide. McGrady was preparing to leave the Raptors for Orlando and thus escape the lengthening shadow of one Vince Carter.

So while Vince Carter was back at the University of North Carolina attending summer classes to finish up his college degree, Grunwald was putting out fires back at the Raptors offices on the fourth floor of the Air Canada Centre.

It was a job the 42-year-old Chicago-born lawyer had grown accustomed to since taking over by default from Isiah Thomas, even if it wasn't exactly what he'd expected. True, the Raptors had lurched through their 1999–2000 season, occasionally looking forceful but as often not. They puzzled as much as they dazzled. With a pair of young studs like Carter and McGrady at their core, there was bound to be a mercurial element to their fortunes.

But they were winning more than they lost for the first time in their brief history. And off the floor, the Raptors had earned a touch of something perhaps far more elusive than wins and losses: credibility. Carter's arrival and the acquisition of established players Charles Oakley, Antonio Davis and Kevin Willis had turned the Raptors into a much more serious, and seriously regarded, NBA team.

And now it was all flying apart.

The first item for Grunwald was Butch Carter, his act gathering its own kind of bizarre momentum as it grew thinner with each passing day. Carter had always been something of a maverick in the NBA coaching ranks. A journeyman pro player, his coaching career seemed to have stalled when Isiah Thomas hired him as an assistant coach in charge of the Toronto offence, such as it was, in the fall of 1997. Carter immediately drew the scorn of Raptors guard Damon Stoudamire, Toronto's first hardwood star but like Thomas on his way out shortly thereafter.

"He had his eye on the big job right from the start," Stoudamire would say later. "I never trusted the guy."

Butch Carter had crossed paths with the Raptors before, way back in the early days. As a Milwaukee Bucks assistant, he'd buttonholed the Raptors' original owner, John Bitove, at the hotel headquarters of the 1994 All-Star weekend in Minneapolis. The Raptors were more than a year away from deciding on their first head coach, but Butch Carter wanted the job. It was enough to send Bitove, just confirmed in the lodge but unsure of his status, over to NBA vice-president Russ Granik for a ruling.

"That's Butch Carter over there, looking for a job," Bitove explained to Granik. "Am I allowed to talk to him? Or is it still a matter of we can talk, but we can't *talk*?"

Thomas, Butch Carter and Grunwald had played together nearly two decades earlier at the University of Indiana under Bobby Knight, the loud, loutish and sometimes out-of-control Hoosiers head coach. Thomas and Grunwald shared an NCAA championship in 1981, the year after Carter graduated.

But it was Grunwald and Carter who survived Thomas with the Raptors. They shared a bond that was severely tested as the season developed, but it was a bond that looked unbreakable for a time. The two men were separated in age by only a year and were both Midwesterners — Carter hailing from a poor background in Columbus, Ohio, and Grunwald growing up in the Chicago suburbs. Carter was street, Grunwald corporate. They found themselves side by side in a nearly impossible situation after Thomas left. Not much was expected of them, they knew it, and they were actually able to take advantage of it.

As a team, they worked well together. Carter was an adept coach in games. He preached discipline, and reached out to McGrady after Darrell Walker had been so cavalier with the youngster's development. For a while, Butch Carter managed the thorny veterans-youngsters equation that had undone so many pro coaches before him. He also did his share of schmoozing free agents and was vocal with his personnel suggestions.

Grunwald, who tended to keep his own counsel, sometimes acted on those suggestions. The Vince Carter draft-night deal in 1998 was a combined effort. The push to trade for Charles Oakley came from Grunwald. The signing of free agent Dell Curry was almost entirely a Carter production.

"It was no surprise they got on so well," said one team official. "Glen and Isiah were the same way together. Glen was able to see the good in Isiah, same as he was able to see the good in Butch. Isiah and Butch are very much alike. They're both people who came from the streets. They both manipulate."

But by the spring of 2000, the Grunwald–Carter relationship was fraying. In a book written by Butch Carter and his brother Chris, a receiver for the NFL Minnesota Vikings, the Raptors coach accused Knight of directing a racial epithet at a player widely assumed to be Thomas. The allegation, never confirmed by anyone involved, provoked a brief firestorm. Knight was in the midst of other troubles at Indiana that would eventually result in his dismissal. Grunwald, still loyal, flew down to Bloomington, Indiana, to show his support at a rally for his old coach. The situation drove a rather large wedge between Grunwald and Carter, after the two had begun the season trumpeting their close relationship. At the office, the two rarely spoke to each other. Carter felt betrayed by Grunwald for not backing up his story; Grunwald felt his coach was being attacked unjustly.

Grunwald was growing leery of Butch Carter's outbursts, wondering privately about his agenda. It wasn't the first time that Carter had invited controversy. Earlier in the season, he had brought rap star and NBA wannabe Master P (Percy Miller) into training camp, figuring he could give him the last spot on the injured list for the season. Carter's grand plan was for Miller to take some of the spotlight and pressure off of Vince Carter and Tracy McGrady, but Grunwald cut Miller before the season began. Later, Butch Carter talked at length about an NBA conspiracy to get Vince Carter out of Canada and into the U.S. market. He refused a league request to wear an in-game microphone for television purposes and was threatened with a $100,000 fine. Privately, he railed about how some of the players' wives had it in for him.

But most disturbing to management was Carter's repeated questioning of Maple Leaf Sports and Entertainment's board of directors. Carter was particularly upset with Bill Waters, the Maple Leafs assistant GM. He mused that the six-man board favoured the established hockey Leafs and wasn't willing to spend the kind of money necessary to build a winner in the NBA.

On the face of it, there was some truth in the latter charge. Toronto's US$34.7-million player payroll was twenty-seventh of twenty-nine in the league in 1999–2000, with Portland ($73 million) and New York ($62 million) at the top. And it was also true that the Leafs board was hardly positive toward basketball when they first bought the NBA team and the Air Canada Centre. Gradually, though, they had warmed to the game and especially to its ability to generate big money. The coach's criticism was particularly galling for board members, given the $8-million extension they had just given him and the large deals Charles Oakley and Michael Stewart had agreed to with the club.

It also threw Grunwald into another awkward spot, as he was charged with the often delicate task of explaining the NBA's bigger player salaries to a board schooled in the smaller economies of the NHL. The NBA's average player salary was US$3.522 million, while the NHL's stood at $1.194 million. Besides, from the board's standpoint, the Raptors were doing well on a value-added basis, their bargain-basement roster outperforming most of the higher-priced outfits around them. What Carter called cheap, they saw as fiscally sound. Some board members were livid. Grunwald wasn't that happy either, calling the coach on the carpet and ordering him to shut up.

But it was behind the closed doors of the Toronto dressing room where Butch Carter was having the most serious problems. Grunwald had assembled a team that relied on veteran players around the youthful core of Carter and McGrady. Those older players weren't impressed with this neophyte coach. "He's a control freak who's losing control," said Oakley.

Toward the end of the season the Raptors roster was deeply torn, with Butch Carter desperately hanging on to the kids (Vince Carter and McGrady) on one side, the veterans on the other, and everyone slowly sliding into an ocean of troubles. "The ship is sinking, man," McGrady drawled. Some veteran players threatened to boycott the team's annual Rap-Up dinner and charity auction, a normally lighthearted event that key sponsors and supporters of the team pay upwards of $250 each to attend, until Carter promised them he would leave after a half-hour. When the coach stayed longer, they began walking out.

At a team meeting, Carter was the target of three hours of venting from the players. Doug Christie and Alvin Williams were the loudest, belying their normally placid demeanours. Williams, one of Grunwald's projects, was among the quietest and most hard working of the players in the room, but he had always been Carter's personal yo-yo, one day appearing in the rotation, the next day parked anonymously at the end of the bench.

The biggest and most bizarre bombshell of all dropped just before the Raptors and Knicks began their best-of-five playoff series. Former Raptor Marcus Camby, dealt to New York for Oakley in the summer of '98, started it by calling Butch Carter a liar in a newspaper article. Camby asserted that Carter had reneged on a promise that he wouldn't be traded. "No one likes him, and no one wants to play for him," Camby said.

Over dinner three nights before the series started, Butch Carter startled Grunwald by saying he was considering suing Camby for defamation.

Grunwald and others in the organization urged Carter not to bother, and the GM thought he had talked the coach off that particular ledge — until the next day's news of a $5-million lawsuit filed in suburban New York's Westchester County.

"I'm responding to an article of untruths in the only way I can," explained Carter, "and that's through the courts." The suit contended that Carter had been "damaged and suffered great pain and mental anguish, and has been held up to ridicule and contempt by his friends, acquaintances and the public."

It's not uncommon for rival coaches in the playoffs to indulge in gamesmanship, partly to get inside their opponents' heads or under their skins, and partly to deflect attention away from their own players. But a lawsuit? When Knicks coach Jeff Van Gundy called the team together at the start of practice to tell them the news, they literally laughed.

"Out of a two-hour-and-15-minute practice," Van Gundy said, "we spent 12 seconds on this and 8 of those were laughing. It's of no importance. I know how it's going to be played. The story's already written. If they win, it fired them up. If they lose, it distracted their team. And you know what? None of that is true."

Raptors management, most notably president Richard Peddie, were furious with Butch Carter. The players rolled their eyes and no-commented when asked about the lawsuit. (Later in the series, when NBC wanted to interview Vince Carter, he agreed with one proviso: no questions could be asked about his coach.)

Camby, who still had a few friends on the Toronto side — including Vince Carter — took the opportunity to take a shot at Butch Carter, while pointing out the obvious regarding the Raptors' team troubles. "I really don't trust him, and I think that's what is going on with that team right now," said Camby. "I think a lot of guys don't really trust him, and they're going to play hard just for themselves."

Camby had more to say in the privacy of sold-out Madison Square Garden. During the second quarter of Game 1, he sidled over to the Toronto coach and, sotto voce, delivered his own rebuttal: "You fuck." All around the Garden, in typical full-throated playoff yell, the fans rained epithets down on the coach. "Liar!" and "See you in court!" were among the PG-rated.

NBA commissioner David Stern, a lawyer, laughed off the suit as being the product of a rookie in over his head: "There's a certain kind of pressure and publicity that comes from being in the spotlight that you just don't know about until you've been there. That's true for players, commissioners and coaches. It gets to be like it's the time of the year when the moon is full 24 hours a day. [A lawsuit] is a new weapon in the playoff assault arsenal. Imagine the backlog in the courts if this were routine."

That was Stern in his Easy Dave, joking persona. He left the role of heavy to his long-time deputy Russ Granik, who called the lawsuit "unprecedented and highly inappropriate." Carter was soon fielding telephone calls from the league office, from Granik and from NBA legal chief Joel Litvin urging him to drop the lawsuit and for pete's sake stick to coaching.

It might have been new to the NBA, but Carter had gone this route before. Six years after serving as an assistant coach at Dayton University from 1989 to 1991, he sued former Dayton head coach Jim O'Brien and athletic director Elaine Dredaime, contending the pair made false statements that defamed him, cost him a chance to become the school's head basketball coach and forced him to leave college coaching. The suit was eventually dismissed after an out-of-court settlement was reached. "It makes people tell the truth," Carter said of the strategy. "In the past for me, it's been highly successful."

Even the more charitable among league executives were stunned. If it was a ploy to draw attention away from Vince Carter and Tracy McGrady in their playoff debut — under the hot glare of New York's lights, too — then there was one caveat. It had to work. You've got to win. Then you can take credit for it.

Instead, Butch Carter just looked ... dumb. It failed. The Raptors lost, and there was no credit to be taken. After six days of being hammered in the media as a buffoon and counselled by the league to drop the suit, the coach finally backed down.

With the lawsuit at least technically out of the way, Butch Carter couldn't stop losing, whether it was a basketball game or in the court of public opinion. The Raptors trailed 2–0 when he again brought up the subject of team payroll and contract, saying the Knicks were winning because all their players were signed to long-term deals. He also said there was no dressing-room leadership and that it was he himself who had taken on that mantle.

"Right now is not a time to even be talking about contracts, this and that," said a grumpy Charles Oakley. "We're trying to win a playoff game, man."

Indeed, given Butch Carter's troubles with his older players, his comments on leadership were akin to turning a hose on a wasp nest. That Carter had lost the veterans completely became clear when he replaced Doug Christie with Muggsy Bogues in the starting lineup prior to Game 2. The move upset not only Christie but many of the other veterans as well. "He's killing us," Dee Brown said.

Carter's changing rotation had been a subject of grumbles and grouses all season long, and here he was at it again. Vince Carter again refused to answer any questions about the coach, and spent most of his time in media interviews repeating that plea. Yes, this was some distraction his coach had provided.

After Game 2, one team insider said, "it was pretty clear that most everybody just wanted the season to end. You had Dee and Butch, Oak and Butch, and the Doug Christie situation. There was so much crap going on. It was like, why bother extending this beyond today?"

In one final act of nose-thumbing defiance, Christie and Brown wore black headbands for Game 3. Butch Carter hated headbands, figuring they belonged at lunchtime games at the local Y and not in the NBA. Predictably, the Raptors collapsed down the stretch of a reasonably close game, and their season was over. Van Gundy didn't bother to shake Butch Carter's hand, a snub that illustrated the contempt left in the wake of the failed lawsuit. But for Butch Carter, there would be no off-season.

Reports soon surfaced that the coach wanted to add the general manager title to his own and to push Grunwald upstairs into some sort of undefined, über-boss position. During a meeting in Florida with Tracy McGrady and others, Butch Carter apparently suggested that McGrady support him in his bid for the GM's job.

In an interview with the Toronto *Sun*, Oakley said the coach should be fired. Others in the organization were finally beginning to feel the same way. Grunwald and Robin Brudner, the team's general counsel, urged Peddie to cut him loose. But Peddie had been among the most vocal supporters of a long-term extension for Carter and was loath to eat the final three years of the coach's contract. Peddie also contended that Carter could change, and that the Raptors could continue to build on what they'd accomplished in the last season.

The pre-draft camp in Chicago in early June, during which prospects for the draft worked out in front of every team in the league, was as much a gossip mill as a talent show. Within the kibitzing and the shop talk, the Raptors were being held up to worse than ridicule. It was affecting their ability to get any work done. Some players and agents told team officials that they wouldn't come to Toronto for private workouts, many of them wondering about the future direction of a coach who was so volatile and unpredictable, and a team that seemed unwilling to fire him or even publicly admit that anything was wrong.

At a promotional appearance in Los Angeles during the NBA finals, McGrady weighed in. Taking five minutes out of his schedule, he told a trio of Toronto reporters in his strongest language yet that returning to the Raptors was a long shot, if not impossible for him. While neither defending nor repudiating his controversial coach back in Toronto, McGrady deemed it "very tough" for the Raptors to re-sign him. It was no surprise to anyone but the Raptors, who had held out hope that McGrady would stay.

"Here we are in the off-season, we're supposed to be talking about re-signing Tracy McGrady, but we have all this other stuff going on in the organization," said McGrady. "It's not the time to be going through that right now. I mean the Butch stuff, I mean all of that."

Even the NBA commissioner was wondering. He approached a Toronto reporter at the league's finals between the Los Angeles Lakers and Indiana. "What's going on with Butch and Tracy?" Stern asked.

Peddie returned from his vacation a few days later. After pondering the headlines, he quickly agreed with the others at the top of the team hierarchy. It wasn't so much what McGrady had said as what he didn't say. There had been no vote of confidence in Carter from the last man who could perhaps have saved him — or at least offered him a stay of execution. Now that it was clear that the young free agent wouldn't be back, there was no reason to keep the coach around. Butch Carter was alone, and he had to go.

Even Vince Carter showed no inclination to save him, although he would later offer a lukewarm thank-you. "He gave me an opportunity," he said during the summer. "He didn't have to do that." For Vince, who was fastidious in skirting controversy, it was about as expansive as he would get. He did have a point, however. The coach had shown an uncommon trust in his no-relation star, putting him into the starting lineup before he had played a single NBA game. And just a few games into that first season, after Christie had struggled and missed a couple of chances at the end of games, Butch Carter revamped the offence and designated Vince Carter as the primary option.

But this had long ceased to be a decision based on Carter's coaching and his record — which, in terms of wins and losses, hadn't been that bad since he inherited the hopeless squad of February 1998. It had been a mere six months since Carter was signed to a contract extension. True, Grunwald had pushed for less than the four years given to Carter, figuring that a short interim term and one lockout-shortened season wasn't enough to warrant such a deal. Going that long had been Peddie's idea, and Grunwald eventually agreed, wanting to send out a message of long-term stability and give the coach a firmer footing in the locker room. "It was supposed to be stability," said Grunwald. "It turned out to be anything but."

Grunwald had vouched for Carter and now he was firing him. Carter showed no real enthusiasm for the job any more, nor did he ever adopt the low profile that Peddie demanded at the end of the season. Within a day of one of their meetings at which Carter assured him he would be "invisible" from them on, Peddie was dismayed to turn on the television and see Butch Carter on a local station flogging his book and defending himself against the arrows the players and media were firing at him.

That Butch Carter may have wanted to leave was apparent — he had asked Toronto management about the possibility of doing just that as early as two days after the season had ended. Now that it was happening, Carter seemed relieved.

"In my perception of things that have gone on, it would have been in the best interest for everyone involved that something change," he said. "I didn't want out of Toronto. I wanted out of a bad situation ... I wasn't troubled, but I could see trouble coming for the group."

The two sides met briefly, agreeing to a settlement of $4 million to tear up the contract, although finalizing the deal would drag on into the winter. It was a bitter pill for an organization that always seemed to be fighting to establish credibility.

Carter would cast himself as a victim. Two days after his farewell press conference, he was at a downtown Toronto bookstore signing copies of the book that had created such a chasm between him and Grunwald. He gave a little talk, then asked whether there were any questions. One man shot up his hand and shouted: "Is $4 million for five months' work a fair severance package?"

"Yes, it is," Carter answered. "For what I had to go through, it is."

So in early June, a whirlwind week of damage control loomed for Grunwald. In the span of less than an hour, and on his forty-second birthday yet, he announced the firing of Butch Carter and boarded a plane for Seattle to meet with Lenny Wilkens, released by the Atlanta Hawks at the end of the season.

Wilkens had been contacted by the Washington Wizards, New Jersey Nets and Vancouver Grizzlies about their vacant coaching positions, but he wasn't interested. He had done some television work during the play-offs and thought he might pursue that for a year or so. Television is the usual holding cell for NBA coaching hopefuls, and Wilkens, even at 62, still felt he had some sideline life in him.

"I thought there was a serious possibility that I wouldn't coach this year, and I told my wife that," said Wilkens. "Then Glen Grunwald called. He came out the very next day, and that impressed me. I'm not a phone person."

The two had lunch in town. Perfect strangers beforehand, they found out they liked one another. More to the point, Wilkens liked the Toronto roster.

Grunwald returned to Toronto to continue preparations for the upcoming draft. A scant few days after that, Wilkens met with the Toronto board, found there was mutual good feeling, and then turned over the negotiations to his agent, Lonnie Cooper. A four-year, $19-million contract was drawn — the Hawks, still owing Wilkens $11 million from his previous contract in Atlanta, paying about half the Raptors' tab.

It was all very quick and clean and thorough, a stark contrast to the previous months of chaos under Carter. Wilkens appeared to have everything Butch Carter had squandered — respect, a glowing reputation as a winner, the ability to communicate with veteran players, as well as some things the former coach could only dream of acquiring.

As far as Isiah Thomas was concerned, Carter was the worst legacy he could have left to the Raptors. "I made a big mistake," Thomas said later. "He was a former teammate, and just on that I gave him a chance. I had no idea it would work out the way it did. I never in a million years thought he had a chance of becoming the head coach."

Within the organization, there was some relief. Butch Carter had burned more than just a few bridges in the locker room and throughout the NBA. He had also alienated many team officials with his bullying and mind games.

"It got so bad, nobody knew what was coming," said a long-time staffer. "Every day it seemed he'd be picking on somebody different than the day before. It got so you just accepted this bunker mentality and didn't trust anyone. After he was gone a bunch of us were sitting around in the office talking about things, and we all discovered that what had happened to each one of us had happened to everyone in the room. That was Butch. He would divide, divide, divide."

Wilkens carried no such baggage. He had been in the league in one capacity or another for 40 years, winning more games (1,179) than any other coach in NBA history. He was one of just two individuals to be inducted twice to the Basketball Hall of Fame, going in as a player and as a coach. (The only other two-time inductee was John Wooden, the former UCLA coach.) He'd won an NBA championship and an Olympic gold medal.

Despite all the acrimony surrounding his final days, the Raptors weren't seeing the last of Butch Carter. The former coach remained close friends with Vince Carter, Vince's mother, Michelle, and Vince's agent, Merle Scott. Butch Carter stayed around Toronto during the winter of 2000–01 to work on some business ventures. It was an arrangement that would be cause for some uneasiness, but at least the Raptors star appeared to be on the right page about a replacement. When Grunwald asked Vince to name his favourite candidates for the job, Wilkens appeared at the top of the list.

"We're very lucky," said Grunwald. "For the job, we had two lists — Lenny Wilkens, and all the other candidates. In my wildest dreams, I didn't think we could get a coach of Lenny's qualities and character. Sometimes, the obvious choice is the right choice."

"Butch was a happy-go-lucky guy — just happy to have a job," said Oakley. "And it showed in the way he did a lot of things. Lenny's won a championship. He's been around. He's like a down-home meal. And it's hard to get a good down-home meal."

From Butch Carter to Lenny Wilkens. It wasn't exactly the promised land, but it was as if the Raptors had replaced Benny Hill with Alistair Cooke.

If only Tracy McGrady had been so simple.

CHAPTER 2

July 2000:

Goodbye, Tracy

In the Raptors hierarchy, there was Vince Carter, the franchise player. And there was Tracy McGrady, the "other" franchise player, the sidekick, the yang to Carter's yin. As far as McGrady was concerned, it wasn't going to change. So *he* decided to change.

These two had grown up four counties apart in Florida, not knowing each other. But the basketball pipeline that transports young talents into one high-testosterone pool would bring them together. One went to the basketball factory at the University of North Carolina, lending his locker to the other, who was fast-tracking through high school and readying to leap directly into the pros.

That was where they would find each other. Together at Carter's first Toronto training camp in January of '99, it looked like one of those beautiful friendships as well as a dynamic partnership. They were distant cousins, which added another element to their story together.

"Related?" chuckled teammate Dee Brown. "More like Siamese twins."

McGrady had come to the Raptors out of Mount Zion Christian Academy in Durham, North Carolina, in the summer of 1997. He was Isiah Thomas's last first-round draft pick as Raptors GM, and like NBA counterparts Jerry Krause in Chicago, John Gabriel in Orlando and Jerry West in Los Angeles, Thomas regarded McGrady as a player with a Scottie Pippen–like package. Possessing a 40-inch vertical leap and a 44-inch sleeve, the six-foot-eight McGrady had the hops and the wingspan and was a better than average passer. A fabulous dunker, he could do more than that.

"I like his game, I like his versatility," said Thomas. "And in this kind of draft, he might be the best talent."

The '97 draft was not regarded as all that deep, but in hindsight, Thomas was not far off. Wake Forest senior Tim Duncan, a multiskilled seven-footer, was a lock at the no. 1 spot and would prove to be a genuine superstar. After that, it was a riddle and would remain so. For a team like Toronto, looking for help just about anywhere as it headed into its third season, McGrady's all-round arsenal was irresistible.

"Special and rare — he's got skills you can't teach," was Raptors scout Craig Neal's assessment. It was Neal, Toronto's scout in the southeastern U.S., who saw McGrady nine times, sometimes in the damnedest places.

But John Gabriel was a particularly ardent admirer, too, with Orlando just a 40-minute drive from McGrady's home in Auburndale, Florida. NBA talent spotters love to tell "snowstorm stories" about arduous journeys through difficult conditions to watch a player they like, and Gabriel had one he trotted out regarding McGrady.

"I drove three hours through a snowstorm to some middle school in North Carolina," he recalled. "There was a photographer from *Sports Illustrated* with me for the ride, and when we got there the gym was one of those 1950s gyms, built up on the second or third floor, and the place was locked up. We had to throw snowballs against the windows until someone heard us and let us in. Then we finally get in there, and the coach is calling an end to the practice. They're running laps, and we're thinking, jeez, what a trip for this! Then someone isn't running fast enough, so the coach is ordering a half-hour more of practice. At least we had something to show for it then."

But McGrady was going to be long gone by the time the Magic made its pick at no. 17. They'd have to wait three years for their next chance.

Isiah Thomas had his hopes pinned on McGrady being available when Toronto's name was called but didn't think that would come to pass. He spent the day of the draft on the phone, looking to trade away the pick. The talk making the rounds said that McGrady would be taken at no. 6 by Boston. Golden State coach P.J. Carlesimo told McGrady he would be chosen by the Warriors with the eighth pick if he had the chance.

"I think I shopped that no. 9 pick to almost everybody in the league," Thomas recalled. "We were trying to trade out of the draft."

Duncan, the only sure thing, was taken at no. 1. Boston's new coach and basketball boss Rick Pitino, who had tried to recruit McGrady for Kentucky the previous winter, had staked much on winning the lottery and getting Duncan. The Celtics instead ended up with nos. 3 and 6, and took Chauncey Billups and Ron Mercer. Three and a half years later, the entire trio — Billups, Mercer, Pitino — were gone from Boston, along with the Celtics' fabled mystique and Pitino's miracle-worker reputation. (It's no stretch to say that Pitino could well still be in Boston if he had gone the other way and taken McGrady with one of those picks.) The Warriors, drafting just in front of the Raptors, took Adonai Foyle in spite of what Carlesimo had said earlier. Foyle would spend the next three seasons struggling for minimal playing time on a bad Golden State team.

So the Raptors got McGrady at no. 9, and gushed about their luck. In truth, it was by no means a sure thing. He would turn out to be Isiah Thomas's last and perhaps best draft gamble as the Raptors GM. Just a couple of years later, the consensus among NBA scouts had McGrady at no. 2 behind Duncan in that game of where they would fall if the same draft were to be held today. That was saying something. Duncan was the central figure in the Spurs' NBA championship win during the 1998–99 lockout season. Like Vince Carter with the Raptors, Duncan was the Spurs' franchise player.

McGrady was all of that hazy word "potential" — just a month past his eighteenth birthday when he was drafted and not so much a classic late bloomer as one who had fallen through the cracks a touch. Baseball was McGrady's first love growing up in Auburndale, a town in Florida's flat and featureless interior. But it was basketball where he excelled, catching the eye of AAU coach Alvis Smith, who eventually facilitated his move to Mount Zion and helped deliver him to Adidas.

McGrady had come a long way from Florida to North Carolina. At Auburndale he had put up big numbers, but the school's 2-A program was so lowly regarded (6-A is the highest in the state) that he went unnoticed by the scouting services. In 1995, the year before he moved to Mount Zion, McGrady was not even ranked among the top 100 high-school players in the United States.

By the time of the 1996 Adidas ABCD camp, though, he was on his way to becoming a first-team all-American. Everyone was talking about

McGrady, who finished among the leaders in just about every category that mattered at the annual meat market and was the top shot-blocker in a group of future pros that included Lamar Odom, Dion Glover and Ricky Davis.

"The last player to transform himself from total obscurity into a consensus national top-five player — the way Tracy McGrady did at the Adidas ABCD camp this summer — was Shaquille O'Neal in 1989," wrote Clark Francis in the *Hoop Scoop* newsletter, which chronicles the comings and goings of the prep basketball world. "Not only was McGrady the obvious choice as the best player at ABCD, but he totally dominated the camp statistically."

During the all-star game portion of the camp, McGrady did just about everything — he hit three-point shots, ran the offence from the point position, posted up his opposite and finished with an eye-catching windmill dunk that became the signature moment of the entire weekend. "I had chills run through my body," McGrady said of the slam. "It was like the moment I knew I had finally arrived."

"He was a virtual one-man highlight film," wrote Dave Schultz, another *Hoop Scoop* contributor. "At times he looked like the next Anfernee Hardaway, while at other times his game resembled Scottie Pippen's."

Among the crowd in the stands was Neal. If anyone was responsible for tipping the Raptors on McGrady, it was Neal, an engaging 32-year-old Georgian getting his first chance at NBA scouting.

"He was like a young colt," Neal said of McGrady, lapsing into a scout's shorthand. "He had the body, the length, nice build. Skinny, but he was so young, you know he's going to fill out. Long arms. Huge wingspan. If you follow these kids long enough, he was always going to stand out because of his athletic ability."

Scouting is a business fraught with difficulty, and when the subjects are high-school kids, projections become that much more difficult. The fundamental questions are the same as they always are: How athletic is he? Does he or will he have an NBA body? Does he have a feel, an intuition, for the game? What skills does he have? Can he do one or two things really well (to a scout, that's good), or is he one of those players who can do everything good but not one thing great (to a scout, that's not a good sign)? Does he remind you of any established player? Is he a winner? What's his work ethic like? How tough is he, and how much heart does he have?

Neal couldn't answer some of these questions, which is normal. All he could do was keep watching, and everyone in the Raptors scouting department was of the same mind. After McGrady's show-stopping turn at ABCD, the Raptors put a circle around his name. Even if he was playing high-school ball, he would be watched closely.

Neal travelled to Virginia to watch Mount Zion play three games in a holiday tournament. There were two at Mount Zion, one at Chapel Hill, a couple more in the state tournament, then an all-star game after graduation. The crowds swelled as the season went along. With McGrady not yet declaring for college, the NBA could see he might come out early.

"Everybody was there to see him," said Neal. "Everybody knew his talent. But it was still considered a far-fetched thing, high-school kids making the jump. At the time, Kevin Garnett was the rarity, the exception. Now there's two or three a year, it seems."

By the end of his senior year at Mount Zion, McGrady was named *USA Today*'s high-school player of the year and had the usual blizzard of scholarship offers to consider. Pitino, then at the University of Kentucky, made a big pitch for him, but McGrady cooled just as he was about to commit when the UK duo of Derek Anderson and Ron Mercer told him they were coming out early for the NBA draft. Closer to home, Florida State was also in the running, McGrady's mother wanting her son to stay close to home and go to Tallahassee. In the wings were North Carolina, Florida and Miami.

They were all blue-chip, top-drawer basketball factories. And none of them had a chance. McGrady and his advisors looked at the steep drop-off in talent beyond Duncan and decided that a top-10 lottery spot was guaranteed. There was the matter of Adidas, too, which had noticed McGrady and had their own stake in him. Mount Zion's program was tied in with the shoe company, and Smith was one of their talent-spotters. It came as no surprise that after he announced at a press conference that he was going to declare for the NBA draft, McGrady signed a $12-million deal to wear Adidas shoes. It was something of a coup. The year before, Kobe Bryant had come straight out of high school and signed with the same company, which was targeting the youngest incoming NBAers in its ongoing tussle with industry leader Nike. McGrady hadn't played a single real game against college or professional players, yet he was already being anointed as one of the chosen.

All this led to the larger question facing all of these youngsters stepping into a man's job. True, McGrady was an unpolished diamond. But just out of high school, would polish be possible, or would this be another case of a kid being asked to grow up too fast, too soon? Those were high schoolers he was averaging 25 points, eight rebounds and seven assists against. Those were high schoolers he was being judged alongside in the camps. Everything else was projection. Could he handle the routine, physically and mentally? Would the Raptors give him the proper environment and support?

Kevin Garnett was the model for the high schooler turned pro. Drafted at no. 5 by Minnesota in 1995 — the Raptors, picking seventh in their first NBA draft, coveted Garnett but settled for Damon Stoudamire — Garnett had become a pro's pro, blossoming midway through his first year after a tepid start. "It's a league full of old guys who foul a lot" was Garnett's deadpan early take on the NBA; by his third season, he was an all-star. The Timberwolves rewarded him with a record $126-million contract, which would indirectly set the stage for the 1999 lockout.

But Garnett was the exception. Some others who made the leap struggled mightily. Kobe Bryant and Jermaine O'Neal were the big names of the '96 draft to follow Garnett and precede McGrady in bypassing college — Bryant, starting out slowly, would eventually turn into one of the NBA's bright young stars, while O'Neal would never crack the deep Portland lineup and ended up as one of incoming Indiana coach Isiah Thomas's first additions in the summer of 2000.

How green this McGrady kid was when he first arrived in Toronto! For his first exhibition appearance as a Raptor, he somehow forgot to tie his shorts. Trying to cover Gary Payton is hard enough on its own. Doing it with your britches in danger of falling down adds a whole new excitement.

McGrady wasn't exactly in his element in Toronto. On his first night out with Raptors management in his new city, at an upscale Italian restaurant, McGrady asked for ketchup to put on his fettuccine. His waterfront condo was furnished "minimally." There was a stereo, complete with turntable — he'd rarely seen one of those before. Resting on it, ready to play, was a dusty Anne Murray record. "Canada's snowbird" was just another mystifying custom he couldn't get his head around.

All that was easy compared to McGrady's first year with the Raptors. Instead of a gentle transition — or at least as gentle as it could be going from high school to playing against men in their twenties and thirties — the team imploded around him. Thomas, who was mentor and guru to the likes of Damon Stoudamire, Marcus Camby and many of the club's young players, resigned his GM position. After he announced to the team that he was leaving, Thomas made a point of turning to McGrady, sitting even more wide-eyed than usual at his locker. "Welcome to the NBA," he told him with a shrug.

"We really let him down," said Thomas, who had talked of putting McGrady into some correspondence courses during his rookie year. "The business end of it became so much bigger than anything else that the basketball was really neglected at the start of that year, and I think there's no question it hurt Tracy's development."

Without Thomas's presence, the locker room turned mutinous. It wasn't just Raptor players who behaved badly and wanted out, though. Head coach Darrell Walker, flapping like a lame duck, ripped into McGrady for a poor work ethic — as if a kid coming into such a chaotic and negative environment was going to be any different. Hell, this was a team that rarely had enough players healthy or willing enough to get up a practice quorum.

McGrady loathed Walker, who had never been much more than Thomas's bench alter ego. With Thomas gone, Walker had given up even the semblance of trying to coach. The Raptors lost 19 in a row and no one seemed to care, half the room beset by injuries real or imagined, and still McGrady hardly got off the bench to play.

"He was sort of an old-school coach, or at least he was trying to be that way," said McGrady. "He used me as a scapegoat because we didn't have a very good team. ... My first year, the organization was junk. It was nothing."

He survived, honing an inner toughness and discipline that had been awakened during his year at Mount Zion, an ultra-conservative school that featured a high-powered prep basketball program. Head coach Joel Hopkins's lengthy rulebook included 4:45 a.m. wakeup calls, lights out at 10, no swearing, no tattoos or piercings, no rap music, church attendance twice a week, no dating — actually, no contact at all with the opposite sex, although the resourceful McGrady managed to find a girlfriend. It was austere and rigorous.

Mount Zion did not even have its own gym at the time, which put them level with the Raptors, still paying rent to play out of the SkyDome. The joke went that McGrady had made a lateral move from the previous year. He had few friends on the team or around the league and spent most of his time in his condo — lonely, far from home, enduring the Canadian winter by sleeping the days away. A couple of friends moved to Toronto to stay with him through parts of the season, which seemed to drag on like a never-ending soap opera. Once Walker quit in February, his successor, Butch Carter, immediately increased McGrady's role, and he responded well. If there was one bright light still on at the end of that long season, it was Tracy McGrady.

Through it all, though, McGrady was thinking about an escape route, telling friends privately about a yearning for other NBA locales, like Florida or the Los Angeles Lakers. Florida was home. L.A. was the bright lights, where his Adidas shoe pal Kobe Bryant was developing into a player worth watching.

But all that history and yearning and talk mattered a whole lot less once Vince Carter arrived on the scene for McGrady's second season. Here was a dynamic complement. They were the sort the Raptors could build around, and with them the team could thrive over the next decade.

McGrady and Carter knew each other — they were distant cousins by marriage, McGrady learning of the connection via his grandmother and Carter's grandfather at a family barbecue when he was eighteen. And wasn't that perfect. When McGrady had played in summer pickup games at Chapel Hill against many of Carter's teammates and alumni during his year at Mount Zion, he'd borrowed his cousin's locker to store his gear.

The pair compared themselves to a young Jordan-and-Pippen act, and it was easy to see why. Just two years apart in age — Carter was born in January of 1977 and McGrady in May of '79 — they were the fast-beating young heart of the Raptors' hopes for entry into the NBA's upper echelon. Growing up and maturing together, McGrady and Carter were regarded by scouts as the best young 1–2 wing combination around.

They were also reasonably tight, closer than might be expected for a duo so similar in talent, position and age. McGrady was a slightly better ball handler than Carter, considered a Pippen or Penny Hardaway or Jalen Rose type, a versatile player capable of playing both backcourt spots and small forward. Carter, playing out of position at small forward for the Raptors his first two seasons, was a better outside shooter and more dynamic scorer. Carter was the better one-on-one defender of the two, but McGrady was closing that gap rapidly by his third year in Toronto, and as for consistent attention to defence, McGrady had the clear edge. Both could jump through the roof and run all day, quick enough to outrun their own mistakes, athletic and charming enough that both were invited to compete in the revamped slam-dunk competition at the 2000 All-Star game in Oakland.

But there was also a potential downside. Put athletes like this together on a team, with only one basketball on the floor and only one spotlight to share, and full-scale conflagrations are not uncommon in the ego-driven

NBA. In the mid-1990s, the Dallas Mavericks thought they had the finest young backcourt/wing trio in the league with Jason Kidd, Jimmy Jackson and Jamal Mashburn, but they were long gone in a couple of years, scattered and torn by their own rivalries and jealousies. The Philadelphia 76ers dealt away first Jerry Stackhouse and then Larry Hughes because they weren't happy sharing the ball with Allen Iverson.

Garnett's big contract tore the Timberwolves apart, young point guard Stephon Marbury forcing the club to deal him when he made it clear he wasn't coming back after his third year. Marbury and Garnett were the sort of outside-inside, small-big combo that would have made the Timberwolves into perennial title contenders, but Marbury said he yearned for New York's brighter lights and bigger endorsement dollars. (Instead, he ended up in New Jersey. Be careful what you wish for, indeed.)

"All these young teams, they fell apart because too many guys were trying to be the Man," said Orlando head coach Doc Rivers. "It seems that in this day and age, there are always those kinds of issues with every team."

Perhaps the most ominous example for the Raptors was the 1995 Orlando Magic. The Magic reached the NBA Finals that year with Shaquille O'Neal jumping centre and Penny Hardaway a budding and versatile backcourt star. O'Neal was in his third pro season and was already regarded as one of the finest big men to ever play the game. Hardaway, in his second year, was being hailed as another Magic Johnson. Among his legion of admirers was a Floridian named Tracy McGrady who would later wear his no. 1. The Magic were young — some thought too young — yet here they were on the edge of a title. When the Rockets spanked them out in four games straight, just about everybody watching figured the Magic would be back soon.

But a year later, O'Neal had reached the end of his first NBA contract and promptly bolted for the Los Angeles Lakers, signing for a then-record $121 million. The Magic were suddenly just another team, wondering what went wrong. O'Neal's parting shot stung: "A dried-up mud pond," he called his old NBA city. The community lost its taste for NBA basketball, attendance for the game never again reaching that 1995 level.

"It didn't really sneak up on us," John Gabriel recalled later, "but there was no real solid reason for him to go. We had just been to the finals. There were the rap records and the movies he was making, and there was a large agent influence [Leonard Armato, based in Los Angeles]. The message was that this town was too small for him. He wanted the spotlight. Even back then, he wasn't willing to admit to sharing the spotlight [with Hardaway]. In that way, it might have been similar to what happened in Toronto."

The parallels weren't all that exact, but the Raptors shared with the '95 Magic and the '98 Timberwolves one item: they had a single player contract to take care of that meant the difference between a promising future and a disappointing step back. Coming into the league in 1997, McGrady was in the last group of incoming players subject to a collective bargaining agreement that ended in the 1998 lockout. As such, he was bound to the Raptors for just three seasons, after which he could become a free agent and go wherever he pleased, to whoever could afford his asking price.

Glen Grunwald knew of McGrady's early dreams of moving on. He heard the talk of McGrady's determination to leave. But he held out hope, even after McGrady and his agent, Arn Tellem, told him in the summer of 1999 that they wouldn't sign an extension. That summer, after McGrady's second season, was the one window the Raptors had open that was denied other teams. It was the same window that the Timberwolves had used to sign Kevin Garnett to his huge deal. But McGrady and Tellem were adamant. They would wait and test free agency. They said Toronto would get full consideration.

It was McGrady's continued development as a player earning starter's minutes and the Carter–McGrady relationship that Grunwald figured could be the clincher in Toronto's favour. The pair seemed close because they *were* close, separated by only three floors in their waterfront condo building, meeting up to play video games or listen to music or just talk the evening away.

In the dressing room, they needled one another incessantly. McGrady teased Carter for his defence, sometimes mocking him in a good-natured but nevertheless pointed way. McGrady also wondered about Carter's toughness. One night, after McGrady had been smacked in the face by a New Jersey Net and left wincing, he was asked if he was hurt.

"Naw," he said, as ever delivering the barb with a sleepy smile. "I be faking. Like Vince."

Carter fired back in his own fashion, but he was not quite as quick with a quip or as sardonic and cutting as McGrady could be. When McGrady dove to the floor for a loose ball, Carter's eyes widened and he figured, "There must've been a blue moon out there tonight."

The jabs seemed to be more love taps than poison darts. But as their second season together continued, McGrady began to assert himself on the floor, forcing Butch Carter's hand.

By February, McGrady was inserted full time into the starting lineup. He would finish the season with 34 starts and average 15.4 points — second only to Carter's 25.7 on the team's list. And on a team sorely lacking an intimidating stopper at the back of the defence, McGrady led in blocked shots, averaging 1.91 a game.

In the playoffs, with the Knicks concentrating most of their defensive strategy on stopping Carter, McGrady was the Raptors' best player, despite a sore ankle — and to the Knicks, nothing less than a revelation. Allan Houston in particular had trouble defending McGrady's unique combination of length, athleticism and ability. "I probably didn't give him the respect I should have," mused Houston.

Then that series was over in the blink of an eye, it seemed, and McGrady was waving to the Air Canada Centre crowd after the Knicks had completed their sweep — waving goodbye, as it turns out, although he refused to admit anything of the sort.

Despite all the talk of the certainty of his impending departure, the Raptors had spent most of the season trying to change McGrady's mind. They had brought in a mentor: Washington, D.C.–based DeNita Turner moved to Toronto for four months to work with him. He had earned and received a steady increase in playing time. They talked about getting endorsement opportunities for him. Customers at the Air Canada Centre waved "Come Back T-Mac" placards they designed themselves as part of a contest. The Raptors seemed to have a monetary advantage, too — under the rules, he could re-sign with Toronto for a maximum of $93 million, but with any other team the limit was $72 million. The NBA is no different than real life in one aspect: it's money that usually decides these matters, and the Raptors figured this would be no different.

But professional sports does not work like a fairy tale, or like real life for that matter, and by mid-season most everyone around the Raptors figured McGrady was on the way out — everyone except Grunwald, that is, who would later be left wondering what happened when McGrady left the Raptors for Orlando. Now, Grunwald is nobody's fool, but he admitted to one rather large mistake over the course of the 1999–2000 season that would have a huge effect on his team's fortunes: he believed McGrady, who later admitted he never had any intention of re-signing. Most of all, McGrady wanted to go home.

"I wonder about the people around him," Grunwald said ruefully, much later, still bitter about it. "I talked to Tracy maybe six times over the season. I'd say, 'Tracy, tell me if you're thinking of leaving. Let me know, you're not doing me any favours if you don't.' And all the time it was the same answer: 'I like playing here. I like playing with Vince.'

"Turns out he didn't want to play with Vince. Turns out he was lying all along. He's a decent enough kid, but he's very immature. I think it was the people around him, like that Alvis Smith guy, maybe telling him that he had to be deceitful in all this, that that was the way it was done."

Indeed, Smith, along with McGrady, had assured Toronto management and reporters at season's end that the player's intentions included giving the Raptors their due when the free-agent dance began. Smith had been courted and coddled by Butch Carter, and the coach thought he had made headway. It all turned out to mean very little. It was Smith, based in Ocala, who had discovered McGrady in Florida and who had remained a constant companion and advisor as he made the transition to the pro ranks. In their book *Sole Influence,* Dan Wetzel and Don Yaeger detailed the relationship, reporting that Smith received $150,000 annually out of the player's Adidas shoe contract, as does McGrady's old head coach at Mount Zion, Joel Hopkins. (One of McGrady's first moves after being drafted by the Raptors was to give Mount Zion a $300,000 cheque for improvements, his way of saying thanks to the school and the people who had got him to the NBA.)

Such deals are not common, but they're not exactly rare either. In the murky pool of basketball recruiting, the players are ever younger, the territory is split along shoe company lines, and the payoffs are large for the very few at the top of the pyramid. The Raptors had invested three years in developing McGrady from a phenom to a more well rounded basketball player and grown-up, and now they were watching him go. As far as they were concerned, their agenda didn't match his agenda, nor the agenda of the people around him.

The new Raptors coach, Lenny Wilkens, tried a couple of times to meet with McGrady, once in Atlanta, once in Toronto, but each time the plans fell through. Vince Carter's new agent, Merle Scott, met with McGrady in Orlando during the final days of the Butch Carter meltdown but never afterward, and with the July 1 beginning of the NBA's free-agency period, McGrady was not looking back.

The Magic, the Bulls and the Heat all made their best pitches at McGrady. One of the few points of contact between his camp and his old boss Grunwald came with a phone call from Smith urging the GM to make a sign-and-trade deal that would send McGrady to the Miami Heat — this, a few days after McGrady had declared publicly he was going to the Magic. (Sign-and-trades had become a common, albeit difficult-to-execute, part of the NBA landscape in the era of the salary cap. In effect, they allowed teams to sign their own free agents, then immediately trade them away, allowing the departed players to reap the benefit of the Larry Bird exception and be paid the same higher salary they would have received by staying with their old team.) Not only was the double-talk making Grunwald's head spin and his blood pressure rise, but the Magic and the Heat were wondering just what was going on with McGrady as well.

In the end, McGrady committed to Orlando after all. Like the Pistons with Grant Hill, the Raptors had lost a key piece to the Magic. There was one major difference, though. The Pistons picked up a couple of players in exchange for the all-star Hill. Grunwald was not able to work a sign-and-trade deal of any magnitude with the Magic, who had little left to give up. The Raptors got a draft pick — a conditional one at that, and one that they would trade away before the season was out. McGrady cashed in large, with the maximum allowable contract totalling $92.9 million over the next seven years.

The loss was doubly hard to take for Grunwald, whose entire off-season plan had changed. The Raptors have had a tough time in the NBA's free-agency wars, successful in attracting older players near the end of their careers (Dell Curry, Muggsy Bogues) but unable to sign young studs, which was one reason McGrady would use for his departure. Yogi Stewart was an expensive bust, Grunwald's worst move, while Alvin Williams hadn't progressed into a dependable starting guard.

In most cases, the Raptors had served mostly as a bargaining chip for players on the market. Seattle's Rashard Lewis, Austin Croshere of Indiana and Houston's Cuttino Mobley and Maurice Taylor were no different in the summer of 2000, each pursued in turn by Grunwald but re-signing with their respective teams despite bigger offers from Toronto. Vince Carter got involved in the Mobley pursuit — the two were friends, having hit it off at their NBA rookie orientation sessions, and Carter called Mobley often to plead Toronto's case — but to no avail.

Without a young free agent, Grunwald went to McGrady contingency plan B. He signed Mark Jackson to the largest deal ever given by the Raptors to a free agent switching teams: four years and a maximum $16.4 million. And he traded away Doug Christie, the longest-serving Raptor, thus freeing a spot for Vince Carter to move to his natural shooting guard position. Corliss Williamson, out of favour in Sacramento, came in the trade for Christie.

Truthfully, though, no one remaining on the free-agent or trade market could equal the loss of McGrady. Only the loss of Vince Carter could hurt more — and preventing that had immediately moved to the top of Grunwald's to-do list. It wouldn't be easy. Heading into their most important season yet, with expectations set higher than ever before, the Raptors had been dealt a huge blow.

CHAPTER 3

September 2000:

Wizard of Oz

Vince Carter was ready to howl at the world. Back at Chapel Hill for two final summer school courses toward his degree in African American studies, Carter closed the book on his university education only to find another kind of learning curve ahead. His cousin Tracy McGrady had left Toronto for good, the *coup de grâce* coming in an *ESPN* magazine article in August in which McGrady had called their relationship overrated. Carter could understand McGrady's departure. He could even understand McGrady feeling confident, freshened and emboldened by his newfound independence and a $93-million contract. But these shots at him in the media came from nowhere. He was hurt and confused.

The business side — which he tried to keep at arm's length, his mother, Michelle, in charge down in Florida — was going no better. In July, Carter had been hit with a $13.5-million judgment for breach of contract with Puma, the shoe company he had signed with before his rookie season. And just a few months before that, the Tank Black situation had reached its depressing conclusion, Carter being the last pro athlete to abandon his agent's rapidly sinking ship. Finally, he had watched from afar as another man he trusted, his first pro coach, Butch Carter, was fired.

Then there were the Raptors, swinging and missing in their free-agent search, including his buddy Cuttino Mobley. With the Olympics on the horizon, Carter's closest friend on the Raptors, Muggsy Bogues, was telling him he didn't think he'd get a deal to be back in Toronto for the coming season. Just thinking about that, and the nightmare finish to the previous season, made Carter gulp. Bogues's talks with the Raptors had bogged down by early August, and there was concern that the team wouldn't have enough money left in the budget to accommodate him. In town for his annual fantasy camp, Carter pitched a unique offer at Grunwald: he would pay Bogues's salary, or at least $1 million a year of it, if it would help get the five-foot-three guard back into a Raptors uniform. Carter was feeling a little desperate, and Grunwald, normally an unflappable sort, was feeling a little stunned.

On the home front, there was more bad news. Just before Vince set off for the Sydney 2000 Olympics, his mother told him that she and her husband, Carter's stepfather Harry Robinson, were filing for divorce after 16 years of marriage. And while he was away, his brother Chris was charged with possession of cocaine for the second time.

No wonder that this Olympic adventure would turn into something of a Jekyll-and-Hyde story for Vince Carter. No matter how far away he was going, no matter how high he would soar, his troubles were right there at his back.

"It got to be so bad, I would wonder — did I step in something bad here? Did I do something wrong?" he recalled in an interview. "It was like there was a string of things going on, one after the other, right in a row. After I'd try to get over one thing, there was something else, then something else, it was just ongoing and never-ending.

"I was trying to leave it hanging, so to speak. But I don't care how far you go, it's always going to be there, right behind you, closing in on you."

In the unofficial Vince Carter Olympic scrapbook, two pictures catch the eye. One is astounding; the other merely confounds. Study them closely and it's hard to believe that the fellow in both photos is the Vince Carter we've come to know here in North America, the one who is equal parts style and smile. Study them closely and you begin to understand exactly what Carter is talking about.

He went to Australia and the Olympic Games as a spectacular NBA performer on the rise, but also the youngest on the American team. "I just go with the flow," he said in describing his outlook heading in, and such a deferential attitude seemed like the usual Vince. At times beforehand, there had been a certain passivity to his nature, an unwillingness to rock the boat and an avoidance of any sort of confrontation. His insistence on joining into opposing teams' prayer circles and his laughing banter with those same opponents during heated contests were at times detested by his Toronto teammates. "When Vince is here, trouble is over there," says Michelle Carter, and given Carter's squeaky-clean rep, it sounded like more than a mother's love talking.

But on this trip, it was as if he had changed more than just hemispheres. He was ostensibly just one of 12 marvellous players, albeit one who had been assigned uniform no. 9, much to his irritation. It was Jordan's old number, and for a fellow who had long grown tired of the comparisons, it was galling. He did what he usually does: shut up and put up with it, even if it was about the last time he would take such an approach. And he became, like it or not, Jordanesque: the leading man, the brightest and most glittering of these jewel-encrusted millionaire Olympians, the one who was not just taking the last shot but demanding it. He also became a marked man, and an angry man. When the Americans needed something — good or bad, at the start or at the finish, something mesmerizing, irresistible or exasperating — it seemed that Vince Carter was there to provide it. The sum of all those summer frustrations and reversals had settled in, a rather large chip bearing down on his slender frame.

Picture no. 1 in that scrapbook is Carter's dunk over French centre Frederic Weis, which looks like a triumph of man over matter, or at least a suspension of physics. The photo that was carried in more than 200 newspapers and magazines around the world catches him frozen at the apex of his ascent. His legs are splayed just above Weis's face, his knees are in Weis's chest, while the ball in his outstretched right hand is being stuffed in the basket. When it occurred, it was as if time stood still for a couple of beats at the Dome inside Sydney's Olympic Park, just as it had 19 months earlier in Indianapolis, just as it had in the team's first practice together in Hawaii a month before.

Weis is seven foot three inches tall, and there's Carter — a mere six foot six — dunking *over* him as if he were some giant Gallic vaulting horse, a mere prop for the act. On the American bench, coach Rudy Tomjanovich thought Carter had left the ground too early. "And he just kept going and going and going higher," Tomjanovich marvelled. For Carter, whose toughest audience is at times himself, even this one was nothing special.

"It was just reaction," he insisted. "I was just playing the game." And then he continued, almost apologizing. "I don't do them for my enjoyment, believe me, I don't. I just do them because that's what happens."

On the world's biggest stage, Vince Carter had gone up and up and out of this world. Even if he was the only one unable or unwilling to enjoy the view — until much later, when he would call it "one of the first slams I've done in my career that I've watched more than once or twice."

"Le facial," drawled one French reporter.

"I knew he could jump," said a bemused Weis, dubbed "the Eyeful Tower" by the *Toronto Star*'s Mary Ormsby. "I didn't know he could jump like that. I was trying to take a charge, but he didn't even touch me."

Back in Carter's hometown of Daytona Beach, boyhood friend Joe Giddens was watching. "I had to get up and turn the TV off," said Giddens. "I've known Vince since elementary school, I've seen him dunk with two elbows inside the basket, I talk to him every day and I've seen just about everything. But I couldn't believe what I had just seen."

Back in Carter's hometown of Daytona Beach, boyhood friend Joe Giddens was watching. "I had to get up and turn the TV off," said Giddens. "I've known Vince since elementary school, I've seen him dunk with two elbows inside the basket, I talk to him every day and I've seen just about everything. But I couldn't believe what I had just seen."

"That was probably the greatest play in basketball I've ever seen," said Jason Kidd, Carter's teammate who dubbed him "the Next Coming" during the Americans' brief training camp.

This had certainly been something of a welcome party for Carter. He was not even among the originals selected for the Dream Team, as the assemblage of U.S. talent had always been called. In truth, it was a group that represented an abrupt shift for the Americans, with not one NBA championship ring adorning the 12 pairs of hands on the roster. (The host Australians had three, Luc Longley having been part of two Bulls' titles and Andrew Gaze a bit player during the Spurs' championship year.)

Instead of elders, youth defined them, and none was younger than the 23-year-old Carter. Perhaps it was inevitable, then, that instead of a grizzled benevolence, their most marked characteristic was a grim sense of their own importance. This was no vacation. "We're on a mission," Carter said beforehand, with a touch of weariness, as if the Olympics carried no cross-cultural importance at all but were just another road trip.

It was that way from the very start, when they gathered in San Diego in mid-August for a shopping spree at the United States Olympic Committee's outfitting centre. "It was the last time for 42 days that all of them looked happy," said Associated Press basketball writer Chris Sheridan.

After two earlier incarnations of the Dream Team, these players didn't exactly relish that nickname and all it hearkened back to — the originals of 1992, when the NBA pros made their Olympic debut in Barcelona. That team had included Jordan and Bird and Magic, the holy trinity of the NBA's rise through the 1980s and into the early '90s, a time of unprecedented and explosive growth for the league. That team was the first, and in some minds the only — so exotic that opponents clamoured for pictures and autographs after being soundly beaten, so untouchable and above reproach that Charles Barkley could joke about an Angolan "spearthrower" after elbowing him in the throat, and everyone standing around listening would laugh and say, "Oh, Charles!"

Almost inevitably, the teams that followed were viewed as lesser copies, each of them losing a little more sharpness and lustre than the last. The '96 team played on home ground in Atlanta, and even if the margins weren't as lopsided as four years earlier, it wasn't as if they were ever pushed. Lenny Wilkens, the '96 team head coach, would later say that the only time he had to raise his voice with the players was halftime of the very first exhibition game they played. After that, he could have coached from a Barcalounger.

Given that history, and given the USA's 16–0 record in Olympic play since the '92 tournament, a been-there, done-that attitude prevailed, at least among the public. Shaquille O'Neal, Kobe Bryant, Tim Duncan and Grant Hill turned down invites because of either injuries or indifference. This group wasn't even regarded as the NBA's best. NBC, the official network for the Olympics and also the NBA's U.S. network, was bracing for a ratings hit in Australia before it even happened.

But that was all someone else's problem. The Americans went from San Diego to Lahaina, a tiny whaling town on the west coast of Hawaii's Maui island paradise, and went at it. For five days, a sleepy place where the sun shines and the August surf is calm and silky was transformed into the place to be if you were in the basketball world.

Inside the Lahaina Civic Center, a couple of giant fans moved the sultry air around. The NBA had invited along several heavyweight coaches and officials from past U.S. teams to schmooze with their sponsors — basketball in the mornings, golf in the afternoon, barbecue luau at night. Along with the selection committee that had chosen the dozen working out on the floor, these were all recognizable names, some legends of the game, some merely legends in their own minds.

So there was Wilkens, Carter's new coach in Toronto, parking himself alongside Mike Krzyzewski, coach of Carter's college arch-rival, Duke University. Sitting baseline, neither of the two took their eyes off the court as they talked sotto voce. What did they see?

"The whole court," explained Wilkens. "Not just what's in front of me or who has the ball, but what's off to the side, what's going to happen and when — whether that guy's going to cut through the lane for the pass, when the defender is going to slide over, stuff that people might not see …"

In other words, the technical and arcane, anything but the sort of exclamation points that show up on the TV highlight shows. Clyde Drexler, P.J. Carlesimo, Chuck Daly, Quinn Buckner, Stu Jackson, Russ Granik — all of them watched, all of them with solid, sometimes spectacular NBA credentials.

Vince Carter had come for their approval as well as for something else — a place at their tight little table. TV highlights didn't seem to matter so much here. Carter was just another live body, even going unrecognized at first glance, his hair having grown long over the summer for a new look that required some getting used to.

At times, it's as if there are two kinds of approaches rubbing up against each other within the NBA world: the playground game and the team game. They are rarely in perfect sync, but when they do mesh — as in the precision and solidity of a well-timed, oft-rehearsed screen that frees a Vince Carter for an alley-oop feed and a rim-rattling dunk — coaches breathe easier and dream of championships.

Carter could walk into any playground, into the Rucker tournament or Alonzo Mourning's summer clambake and dunkfest, and dazzle without even breaking a sweat. The trick here, in this more demanding environment, was to wait for the right moment. The showman in him is always lurking, ready to bust out whenever the opportunity should arise. Like it did on the very first morning.

Tomjanovich had his perimeter players working through back picks and coming out the other side to either take a lob pass or post up a defender. It was Carter's turn. An errant pass was sailing out of bounds, and he was airborne, stretching and stretching to get it as it sailed away.

Catch.

Dunk!

"The practice just stopped," said Jackson. "It was like, wow."

"It was just a terrible pass, but Vince caught it at his shoe tops and made the play," said Larry Brown, one of Tomjanovich's assistants. "It was such a unique thing, and it happened so early in our first practice. That was the start. Ray Allen and [Antonio] McDyess and [Kevin] Garnett would make spectacular plays, too, but Vince's were just a little different."

It became a bit of a game for his teammates. Jason Kidd or Gary Payton, the eldest on the team at age 32 and the only Olympic holdover from '96, would spot Carter on the break and throw a parabolic pass. Each one went higher than the last, and each one Carter would meet up with and dunk. It was as if they were testing his limits and finding them somewhere up in the stratosphere.

Tomjanovich and the rest of the coaching staff noticed and immediately added into their offensive sets a couple of plays designed to put Carter on the finishing end of lob passes. But there was more he was seeing, too. Tomjanovich had always liked Carter's makeup and figured he should have been named to the U.S. team earlier than he had been. But this fellow he was seeing in practice, with his eagerness to work hard, was surpassing his expectations. The Americans would finish each practice with a one-on-one tournament, and it would be no surprise to the coach that Carter would end up winning it, or that he would throw a wrench into his original plan of splitting up the minutes between all 12 players as closely as he could. "He just rose to a level of excellence where he had to get a little more," said Tomjanovich. "He earned it."

Carter had come here to find out if he belonged with the best, and he worked at it. He conned from Gary Payton for tips on playing defence. He sat with Kevin Garnett in his hotel room, picking his brain about the pitfalls of making it in the NBA. He stayed late after practice.

"I always knew he was a gym rat, but this was the first time I'd really seen it, with our forty-something days together," said Brown. "You couldn't get him off the court. Him and Kevin would play one-on-one, or if you wanted them to stay out there and work on something extra, they'd do it, no problem."

But even if he wanted to keep his feet planted firmly on the ground in the metaphorical sense, there was no way he could do that in reality. Or in games, for that matter. Carter brought the house down with his acrobatic play in the U.S. team's first two exhibition games in Honolulu, where the adoring fans outside the University of Hawaii's Stan Sherrif Center sent the team bus off carrying signs that read "Marry Me, Vince!" and throwing kisses.

"I knew this kid was big," said Brown. "But in Hawaii or Japan, he surprised me. He was getting the biggest hand, all the time."

It was after one of his slam-dunks and the ensuing frenzy in the stands that Alonzo Mourning dared to voice what many in the room were thinking about Carter. "He is the next Jordan ..."

When told of Mourning's comment, Carter fixed a hard look. "Don't even go there," he said.

In Japan, where the Americans went next to play the host country's national team in an exhibition, the sunny atmosphere continued. They were the gold-medal favourites, and the locals were treating them that way. No one received more attention than Carter, the NBA's reigning slam-dunk champion. Wilkens and Krzyzewski could debate the merits of college's match-up zone versus the pros' switching man-to-man, they could watch for the cutter moving at just the right time down the lane, but a slam-dunk doesn't require any subtitles.

Carter gave it right back, too. When the anchor for the NHK network's morning show interviewed him, he played right along till the end, making a couple of acrobatic dunks on the fly, then lifting her up so that she could sign off with a dunk of the basketball.

"It was like a coronation from Hawaii to Japan for Vince," said Terry Lyons of the NBA. "It was almost a lovefest in Japan, with the media requests, the scrums and the fan interest."

Once the Americans touched down in Australia, however, everything changed. Their timing and choice of accommodation couldn't have been worse. They arrived in Melbourne a week before the Games began, nothing on their schedule other than a final exhibition game with the host country, some practice, a little acclimatization and lots of quiet time before the flame was lit and the real work began.

Instead, their downtown Crown Casino hotel was the venue for the World Economic Forum in the coming days. As such, it had become the focus for ten thousand protestors. The hotel was barricaded from the outside world, security at each checkpoint, and inside the lobby a "bizarre and at times frightening scene," according to U.S. player Allan Houston.

"We were prisoners in our own hotel," said Carter. "It was like clearing customs every time you wanted to get on a bus to get out of there. They were talking about putting us on boats, with big sheets on the side to hide us so we could just get out of there and go to practice."

But first there was a game to be played, a game that carried its own sense of foreboding. The United States was playing Australia, which was feeling very good about itself as a medal hopeful after winning a tournament in Hong Kong. The Melbourne Park arena sold out in 55 minutes for the game, 15,114 watching and cheering Carter and Kevin Garnett's thunderous warm-up dunks.

Such matches are called "friendlies" overseas, but that didn't fit the U.S. team's mood. Out of public view, in the tunnel between the locker room and the floor, they met up for the usual pregame huddle. "Let's bury these motherfuckers!" one of them cried. This zeal for what was actually a rather meaningless game came from the most unlikely of sources. When they had arrived at Sydney airport in transit to Melbourne, a copy of *The Australian* newspaper had been passed around, its cover story about this U.S. team carrying the headline "Dream On: Basketball's New Generation of Nobodies."

It was fairly innocuous stuff under that bold headline, a touch overstated but much the same sort of comment the team had received back home — "Jason Who? Unlike the 1992 team, the Dream Team of 2000 contains names that will mean nothing to all but devoted fans," wrote Cameron Stewart. Indeed, the article in *The Australian* included an excerpt from the *Chicago Tribune*.

Perhaps the most tiresome of sports clichés at the turn of the millennium is the one that pro teams and athletes manufacture about being "disrespected," and this inexperienced group, along with supposedly more mature old hands such as Tomjanovich, couldn't resist. This was the same Tomjanovich who had talked earlier about "doing this the right way ... we not only represent our country, but we represent the game of basketball itself." That is, until they saw the newspaper.

"Some people might see it another way, but we looked at it as a challenge," said Houston.

"How would you like to be called second-rate?" Tomjanovich sniffed months later, the sting still in his voice. "That's what the article said, that they didn't belong. It was real. It hurt a lot of guys."

Stewart was no stranger to North America or its professional athletes, having spent four years as *The Australian*'s New York–based correspondent. But he was surprised to find that the article he wrote resonated so deeply with this team. When he showed up to cover the U.S. team's practice the next day, Garnett swore at him. Payton managed to outdo his teammate, directing five profanities at Stewart wedged into his two-sentence two-cents' worth.

Carter's turn was coming. And it unfolded so fast.

Thirty-six seconds into a game that had begun with passion and intensity and plenty of X-rated yakking, Australia's Andrew Gaze put up a three-point shot that missed, and suddenly Carter was headed the other way to receive a breakaway pass. Gaze hooked him down by the arm. They rolled on top of each other, Gaze grabbing with his hands, Carter headlocking Gaze.

"You could feel the intensity in the air at the beginning of the game, so I'm not surprised something like that happened," said Alonzo Mourning. "Vince is a very emotional player out there, and I think they got a little tangled up."

Tangled up? If the Weis dunk was the hit record of the Olympics, then this is its B side. Picture no. 2: Vince Carter standing over Andrew Gaze, snarling down at the ancient Aussie like a young Ali. And just like that, Carter had gone from lightning to lightning rod, the very face of the Ugly American cliché.

"You can be physical and intense without having a blue with someone," Gaze told Australian reporters later. "There's a certain Olympic spirit you have that doesn't include going out and hitting someone."

Carter was incensed. "It was a dirty play," he said. "What bugged me the most was the way he was saying one thing to one person after and another to someone else. If I had let him pull me all the way down, I was going face first into the floor. It would've broken my nose. There were no punches thrown. I'd forgotten about it pretty quickly."

Even if he did, though, the customers in the stands could not. Purely by accident, Carter couldn't have come up with a worse choice to get stroppy with than Gaze. At 37, Gaze was the éminence gris of the Aussies, playing in his fifth and final Olympics, and at home in Melbourne yet. "In Australia, Andrew Gaze is Mother Teresa," said Stewart. The confrontation got the crowd going, and then Aussie Shane Heal, a blonde-headed pit bull, was barking in Carter's face to stoke it further.

When order was finally restored, Gaze and Kidd and Luc Longley playing peacemakers among the milling fray on the floor, Carter was almost immediately involved in another controversial play. As he turned upcourt, he bowled over referee Billy Mildenhall, sending him off his feet. The crowd turned harsh, some laughing at the sight of the referee sitting down holding his dislocated elbow, others booing Carter. Mildenhall had to retire, and Carolyn Gillespie, who had officiated the preceding women's game, came down from the stands to take his place after a 10-minute delay.

"I was turned away from him, and all of a sudden I felt an elbow to my jaw," Carter recalled of the collision. "I thought it was somebody punching me in the face. This was getting crazy. Thank God for the delay. I had some time to relax. That frustration, that anger was *that close* to boiling over, but the delay gave it a chance to go away."

The game proceeded relatively incident-free from there — Mourning ranted into Gillespie's face after she whistled him for a foul and was booed lustily by a crowd that normally loves to bait officials — but Carter was clearly rattled. He missed two free throws badly and was held without a point in the first half. Worse, the audience got on his case early in the second half, unveiling a "Carter is a wanker" chant reserved for the opponents Australians truly regard as poor sports or overblown posers.

As Larry Brown walked Carter away after the collision with Gaze, he'd warned him: "Hey, this is something that might happen in your career, when a guy tries to get inside your head or an arena gets on you."

"Vince never had any crowd on him like that before," said Brown. "He'd never been considered a bad guy. The immediate effect really bothered him. He was really shook up."

This was new for Carter. For the rest of the time in Australia, he didn't really care about what the crowd was doing. He ignored the media critics that were castigating him, and there were many. "As far as I was concerned, I thought I handled it pretty well," he said later. "When things like that happened, like the Gaze situation, for all that was built up inside me, I could have very easily thrown a punch. I had this great chance to let all that frustration go. But I didn't. I stayed under control."

The Americans would win the game 89–64, Carter managing but seven points and saying very little afterward to the media or to his teammates other than to note the "brutal" crowd. Something had definitely changed, and it wouldn't get any better for these visitors.

"So much happened in the first five minutes of that game — enough to last a whole season," said Kidd. "We knew we were going to a country where people are very friendly. But they're the host country. This was going to be a test of wills and understanding what was really going to take place. That whole Melbourne trip put things in sharp perspective."

Back at their hotel, it became clear that getting around was going to be a problem. With the roads and entrance points blocked off, the only way out was via ferry, up the Yarra River. The American coaches went that route to attend a scheduled clinic, but some of the U.S. players were having none of that.

The pure tension surrounding their whole environment was becoming extreme. Security cordons established to keep protestors away were beefed up. The lobby was more gloomy and expansive than usual, with sentinels "standing like Easter Island monoliths," according to *The Age* newspaper. Hotel guests, including the U.S. players, wore I.D. badges issued by the police. Anyone who did get inside the hotel was frisked and sent through metal detectors.

Outside, there were clashes between police and protestors that were replayed on the televisions in their hotel rooms. By Monday night, two days after the exhibition game, the casino in the hotel closed, the hotel staff was ordered home, and traffic around the hotel complex was being disrupted. Protestors trapped the premier of Western Australia in his car and managed to block a third of the 850 delegates from attending.

"When you're on a Dream Team, you expect that people are going to be trying to see you — but we couldn't even get out of the hotel," said Houston. "It put a lot into perspective. We were there to take part in world history, but there was another kind of more important history swirling around us."

"I'm from Berkeley," said Kidd, "so I've seen a lot in terms of protest. It reminded me of school. It opened up a lot of eyes on the team. It could've got very ugly."

The Americans cancelled their practice and left early. Their team bus headed out in predawn darkness, travelling deserted streets to the airport and a flight to Sydney — but not before one last security check. "They were looking to see if there were any delegates on board," said Lyons. Everyone in the bus cracked up, and Carter recorded the departure from the deserted lobby and out through the empty streets on his digital camera, giggling at the irony of it — these pampered basketball players, bringing down their own luggage, stealing away under cover of darkness. It was the perfect, surreal ending to this leg of their trip.

Carter had essentially played his way onto this American team, passed over until Tom Gugliotta's injury opened up a spot in March, but by this time it was clear that he belonged. With Vancouver's Shareef Abdur-Rahim also on the American team, the pair became the first from a Canadian-based club to wear the USA jersey.

This was regarded as a great credibility coup for both the Grizzlies and the Raptors. But while Abdur-Rahim went about his business as perhaps the most anonymous of the so-called Dream Teamers, Carter would emerge as something larger than life, depending on your point of view and home address: either the villain or the hero. Or, more accurately, both personas at once. He was a young man testing his limits, showing both startling maturity and his own full measure of this team's bravado and arrogance on the basketball floor.

In the background, too, there was a different kind of business to be taken care of. Carter had bounced from the Puma judgment to a new deal with Nike, but the changeover wasn't official until the day before the Olympics began.

Michelle Carter was the only mother on the entire trip from Hawaii to Australia. Even before the Games began, she was exhausted.

"I thought it was going to be a five-week vacation, but it wasn't, not at all," she said. Along with agent Merle Scott, she would be up and on the phone at 4 a.m. in Hawaii attending to the business and continued to keep on top of things in Australia on even more challenging time-zone differences. "There was so much that needed to be done. Vince had a heel that was blistering, too, and that was bothering him. Nothing could be fixed fast enough. It became like a business trip. After the Gaze thing, and the

Puma-Nike thing, I was ready to go home."

There were some good times, though. Marching in the opening ceremonies, Carter rekindled a friendship from his North Carolina days, chatting with fellow Tar Heel alumnus and American multi-gold-medallist Marion Jones. At Chapel Hill, they had played pickup basketball together. Staying in a hotel outside the city and the Olympic village, the Americans had little opportunity to absorb the "Olympic experience" or tour the city, so these moments would be the ones they would remember.

"After all that stuff leading up to it," Carter said, "it was a tremendous relief to realize that this was what we were here for, and to feel the chill across my body when you saw all those people in the stands, and the cameras flashing, and heard the yelling. All these countries, too, countries that I'd never heard of, and people were coming over and wanting to take a picture or get an autograph, or just say hello. It was wonderful. And I found my mom in the stands, somehow. I had no idea where she was sitting, but I found her."

Carter wasn't one for seeing any sights. He stayed mostly in his hotel room. When he ventured out, it would be with his teammate Antonio McDyess, with whom he had developed a good rapport. On her birthday, Michelle Carter was taken to a nearby nightclub for a celebration, with 11 members of the U.S. team. The only one who begged off was her son Vince.

"He said he was tired and needed to rest, and besides, according to the time back home it wasn't my birthday yet, he said." We celebrated it the next day, and for the present he got me, we went directly to the store to pick it up, then came right back to the hotel.

"It's sort of sad to me. He was such an outgoing person. Now he's kind of like Clark Kent offstage, and when he gets on the basketball court it's like he puts on the Superman uniform."

When it came to the basketball tournament, perhaps it was no surprise that the Americans developed a tiresome us-against-them mentality, much like Carter already had. They were winning, which was expected. But the margins were closer than they'd ever been before. The world was catching up and almost beating them, but all they could do was grouse about the international game (different than the NBA, therefore not as good as the NBA), their opponents (different, therefore not as good), the rules and referees (different, therefore not as good), and so on.

"We invented the sport, we created it and we perfected it," Mourning said early on, showing a knack for revisionism to go with the usual hubris.

"The best games to play in were the ones we had in practice," said Carter. "Those games we played against those national teams, they'd look at us like we're NBA superstars and it was like we had a target on our backs. The games we had, we knew who we were, we knew we all had the success, the money, the cars. Every possession was just about playing basketball."

Now and then, though, whenever something new would appear in the way of Vinsanity, they assessed Carter. Take him away from this team, and it's hard to imagine how dreary it would have been. This was a basketball butterfly emerging with new brightness and flair and, yes, the preening and look-at-me posing to go with it.

"Athletic-wise and jumping-wise, he's probably ahead of Jordan at this stage," said Antonio McDyess. "I feel like he's going to be the next Jordan. You can really see the raw talent in him. He's still learning the game, but he can really play."

"That's the Next Coming. Michael Jordan hasn't done that, nobody's done that," Kidd said after the dunk over Weis. "I think everybody sitting here, even myself as a teammate, enjoyed watching a player like that — and for him to be so young! He's going to put people in the seats."

All Carter wanted to talk about, though, was playing defence and fitting into the team. Making big shots when he wanted to, when he was asked to. Even playing some defence. He led the tournament in scoring at 14.8 points a game. There were dunks and jumpers, and shots when they counted — including an impossible-looking floater over two seven-foot Lithuanian defenders to seal a tight first-round victory and a reverse dunk to seal the gold-medal game.

"People talk about the Weis dunk, but that was just as spectacular," Brown said of the shot against Lithuania, a high, soft banker off the glass with 41 seconds remaining. "It was hard [for the coaches] sometimes. We're sitting there trying to be fair to everyone, with 12 superstars on the bench but only one can take the shot. I think Rudy felt all along that Vince was one guy you could go to. He wanted the ball. Not too many guys are like that."

"As a coach, you wish you were a puppeteer," said Tomjanovich. "You know, telling guys to do this, or go there, or get that shot. It never works that way. It always breaks down in a way you don't expect. Vince got himself into these situations where he tried to create these shots. And he made them, or at least made them happen."

But that was also Carter, locking up his opposite, France's top player, Antoine Rigaudeau, in the final. Carter and Garnett teamed up to short-circuit France's pick-and-roll plays after Gary Payton wanted no part of the assignment, and that made all the difference for the U.S. And finally, that was Carter going after a Russian opponent, snarling and angry after he had been undercut on a drive to the basket. Dunking, shooting, defending, talking trash to the Lithuanians after the final buzzer of a razor-close game, and blowing a taunting kiss to the crowd after dunking the last dunk of the gold-medal final, Carter ran up and down the scale from incandescent to infuriating.

The enmity from the crowds toward Carter would continue throughout, a hangover from Melbourne. He was the lightning rod, and the entire U.S. team fell in place to receive the same treatment as they took Carter's lead. All in all, they were a hard bunch to like.

"Australians love their sport, and they love to see the great plays and will react to them," said Cameron Stewart. "But it seemed that whenever there was a great play, something else would happen that would work the crowd the other way. There was something about this Dream Team that meant the fans just couldn't get behind them."

Carter wasn't the only one showing off. Mourning glared at anyone who dared enter his personal space. The coaches routinely screamed at referees, and after beating Lithuania in the semifinal, LarryBrown had to be restrained after he went out on the floor to berate an official. At times like these, it was equal parts pout and petulance. "Win or Lose, NBAers Are Embarrassment," read a headline in the *New York Post*, and underneath came the kicker: "Unbecoming, unsportsmanlike and, if we still have any self-respect as a country, un-American. This was the Nightmare Team."

NBA commissioner David Stern's interpretation was hardly an endorsement. "They're learning," he said. "It's been a long six weeks for them, and when everyone in the building is against you, no wonder there's a bit of a circle-the-wagons mentality."

In the end, this American team would be known as the ones who nearly lost, a four-point win over Lithuania in the semis the tightest fit in Dream Team history. That gold-medal game had a 10-point margin; it was never in doubt, but it wasn't entirely comfortable either. They were in something of a no-win situation — damned if they did win, damned if they didn't — but sure of one thing: they didn't want to lose.

"I don't think we'd want to go home," Kidd said. "We would definitely be the ghosts of the Olympics."

At the final buzzer, after Carter had made his reverse dunk and blown that kiss for the exclamation point, after they received their gold medals, he found his mother in the stands at Sydney's Superdome and climbed up the rows to get to her. The medal hung from his neck. They cried as they embraced, appreciating the moment and its weight like no one else in the arena could ever imagine.

"I was shocked by Vince's demeanour," Michelle Carter recalled. "It wasn't at all like him, and it wasn't something he talked about. But then I sat back and started to think about all the things that had happened to him, and I understood."

"I never told anybody about what was going on inside me," said Carter. "Finally, something good had happened that I was proud of and I appreciated. All through the Olympics — the boos, the people giving us a hard time because we weren't the Dream Team, the idea that we might actually be the first [U.S.] team to lose a game — and then we had the gold medal. I was just happy to be a part of something I'd seen on TV for years, something that when I have kids I can show them and they'll be proud of me for it.

"I felt on top of the world. Winning washed a lot of the pain away, a lot of the aggravation. It helped the situation."

He skipped off the floor, a digicam in hand, taking it all in, chanting, "They said we couldn't do it, but we did!" over and over.

From the sublime to Buffalo, Carter would return to the Raptors and their training camp just across the Canada–U.S. border five days later. In his hotel room, he shot the breeze with Muggsy Bogues and Dell Curry while he unpacked. Then it was down to the first order of business:

Bogues got out his razor and shaved Carter's head. It was a calculated move that Carter had thought through beforehand, as if the Australia persona — the brass that had at times eclipsed the brash — would end up with the cuttings on the floor, ready to be swept away.

In at least one sense, it sure looked like Vince Carter had changed. Heading into his third NBA season, he had proved a rather large point in Australia, grown a thicker skin, showed a side of himself he had never shown before and perhaps that he had never known was there. He was indisputably the Man, whether you were talking about the Raptors, the NBA's future in Canada, or perhaps even the entire league if he wanted it to be.

CHAPTER 4

October 2000:

Say It Ain't So

For the Raptors, it was the present meeting the past: Vince Carter standing along the sideline, Isiah Thomas, the former Raptors GM, taking a couple steps over to him, talking so low no one else can hear. Up in the stands, Glen Grunwald noticed and wondered. Thomas was his old friend, true. But he was also one to grab an edge wherever he could. What was this all about?

"I told him he had some great years in front of him," said Thomas. "I think he's got it very good here in Toronto."

After the game, Thomas is standing in the corridor outside the visitors' dressing room at the Air Canada Centre, surrounded by reporters. He knows some, makes sure to call them by name. But even the ones he's never met will get the same direct look, the same measured answer delivered in an earnest tone and, every now and then, a hearty laugh and a hand on the shoulder. Six tape recorders are rolling and half a dozen more notepads are out; later, there will be no doubt about what he said.

What he really *believes* is anyone's guess. Isiah Thomas is a politician of the street, playing an old game. He is the living, breathing, Hugo Boss–wrapped proof of the well-worn axiom that says almost any kind of talk goes on the eve of a new season, before a single game has been played. Hopeless optimism, shameless revisionism, unadulterated bullshit — they are all part of the routine, and the rule is that no one calls you out. It's the pre-season, silly. It's not supposed to be real.

In the early days of the Raptors, Thomas's voice was the only one that mattered. And three years after passing from this scene, his voice can still command a room. It's like old times again: Isiah Thomas is talking, and everyone listens. His hands lightly chop the air as he speaks, then stir, then go into his pockets as he puffs out his chest and looks up toward the ceiling to consider his words. "Urgency pulls at the seams of his tailored exterior" was how an early chronicler of his Toronto period put it, and there is assuredly an urgency to his message, and to his method. It is all about mending a reputation that was nearly as tattered as the franchise he left behind.

"Everything we talked about, everything we diagrammed, it's all here today," he says. "Even though we're not in charge of it, we can be proud of it."

Just a few paces down the hall are pictures of before and after — Marcus Camby and John Wallace, two of Thomas's pickups, now long departed to other NBA outposts; Kevin Willis and Charles Oakley, a pair who came along after his exit and have endured. A little farther down the hall and the directors of Maple Leaf Gardens stare out from beneath their glass frames: 81 middle-aged white males dating back to that hockey arena's inception in 1931, a group that Thomas once aspired to. And across the way, the hockey team ownership that was once the bitterest and haughtiest of establishment enemies for Thomas's upstart Raptors is gathered in the Air Canada Centre's directors' lounge, nibbling on hors d'oeuvres and sipping beverages. He has not been invited.

Sure, it's all here today. The Raptors and the Leafs under one roof was, loosely speaking, what Thomas had in mind at one time when he worked as the team's original general manager, and later as an owner with a 9 per cent stake and trying for more. And just as he envisioned it half a decade ago, Thomas heads up a roster sprinkled with versatile young whippets.

After that, it's about as clear as mud. Instead of names like Rogers and Camby and McGrady as the interchangeable parts, he has Bender and Harrington and Foster. Yes, there is a diminutive, left-handed point guard who likes to shoot the ball first — not Stoudamire, but Travis Best.

Instead of the Raptors' GM, Isiah Thomas is an Indiana Pacer. A visitor. Once he had tried to sell this game here, his pronouncements as important as his personnel decisions. Now it is far more difficult. He's dependent on wins for his survival and, if the job consumes him the way it has so many others, for his sense of self-worth as well. The gift of gab, a charismatic smile — none of that is particularly important now. And everything has changed.

The new position, this huddle in the hallway, the audience filing into the Air Canada Centre, they're all part of the fallout from his three and a half years as Toronto's first basketball architect. But just like he planned it? No, Thomas lost that war, and there are fewer and fewer links from those days. He still talks occasionally with Steve Stavro, the chairman of the ownership group that oversees the Raptors, Maple Leafs and Air Canada Centre and the man with whom he tried to forge an alliance way back when. The Raptor, the team's effervescent mascot in the red dinosaur suit, provides another blast from the past as he wanders by. "You're still the best in the league," Thomas calls out and they are shaking, hand meeting claw.

When Isiah Thomas was named general manager of the Raptors, it was a far different world up here — more forgiving, more trusting. In a scene that's ironic in hindsight, he hobbled rather than burst his way through a giant paper logo in May of 1994, still suffering from the Achilles tendon injury that had ended his NBA career. The Raptors, just christened with the nickname the week before, were at the time apparently all set to build their new home eight blocks north, snuggled up next to the Eaton Centre. That was the site John Bitove had sold the NBA on, the site for which he printed up tickets, handing them out to reporters and onlookers — "Admit One" to opening night of a place called Centre Court Stadium.

In fact, the site was far too small, and Centre Court Stadium never had a chance. It served its purpose, though, as the focal point of Bitove's aggressive and winning campaign to gain the Toronto expansion franchise in the first place. A year and a half later, his group eventually landed at Toronto's old Postal Services Building. The phantom Centre Court Stadium was the beginning of a pattern for the Bitove–Thomas union. They brought the NBA to Toronto. They put a face on it. But they never really took it anywhere. To turn around the old cliché, when the going got tough, they got out. Bitove was full of energy, but ultimately more of a deal maker and a salesman than a builder — "He was Mark Cuban before Mark Cuban," Thomas later said, comparing his old boss to the Dallas

Mavericks' energetic present-day owner — and was viewed as more manageable by the NBA, an organization that runs its franchises as if they were McDonald's hamburger stands.

"John and I were both very young, very wide-eyed kids almost, in the business world," Thomas said. "I think we had great ideas, but we were just naïve about some aspects of business."

(In a final bit of comeuppance on the arena, it would not be until March of 1997 that ground was broken at the new postal site, 17 months behind schedule. By then, Allan Slaight had bought out his partner John Bitove and the days of free spending were over. Thomas and Slaight wore hard hats and stood with their arms around each other's shoulders, smiling broadly for the cameras. Within months, Thomas was gone, too, after trying without success to craft a deal that would make him majority owner, forge an alliance with the Leafs, and bring them into an arena together. As he left, Thomas claimed that he would never have built the Air Canada Centre, that he would have preferred to stay in the SkyDome, pay the NBA penalties of $20 million a year, and wait for the Leafs to join them.)

That was then, this was now, and none of it was disturbing Thomas's sunny view from the hallway. In this autumn of 2000, he had put his ownership of the Continental Basketball Association into a blind trust while he tried to sell it and salvage some of his $8-million investment in the 40-year-old minor league. The sale of the CBA, which Thomas and his long-time friend and confidant Brendan Suhr had vowed to turn into the "Harvard of basketball," was part of the conditions attached to his Pacers job. (Later in the season, the CBA would fold and Thomas would be under siege.)

As for the team he was joining, it was going through a transition. Under Larry Bird, they had reached the NBA Finals in June 2000, ending half a decade of knocking on that particular door but never getting in. Bird wanted out after three years of coaching, though, and with several of Indiana's younger players available for free agency, Pacers vice-president Donnie Walsh was forced to retool. Bruising power forward Dale Davis was traded to Portland. Canny point guard Mark Jackson signed with the Raptors. Centre Rik Smits retired, and aging forward Chris Mullin headed west to Golden State for his sunset years.

Walsh hired the former Indiana University star Thomas to replace Bird — one NBA legend for another, and Thomas had the allure of that Hoosiers connection. From a Toronto perspective, there was one very ill fitting piece in this new Indiana puzzle. On the bench, Thomas was flanked by lead assistant Brendan Malone. Thomas and Malone together again was surely the oddest of NBA couples, given their stormy history.

For the Raptors' first year, they had formed two-thirds of the early holy trinity — Thomas the GM and Malone his head coach. (Damon Stoudamire, Thomas's first and most triumphant draft success, was the third.) Thomas and Malone had been part of the Detroit Pistons' infamous Bad Boys era. With Thomas running the offence and Malone the lead assistant to head coach Chuck Daly, the Pistons won a pair of titles at the end of the 1980s with their brand of brutish, intimidating basketball. Transferred up Highway 401 to the toothless expansion Raptors, they were part of one big, dysfunctional family, but there was no doubt just who sat at the head of the table.

"If you understand where Isiah came from, you understand Isiah," Malone once said. "He's a street guy from the west side of Chicago. He's scratched and he's clawed and it's got him right to the top of the NBA. He was the best small guard ever to play. Now he's going to do that in an Armani suit instead. He's going to do whatever it takes to do that. He's his own man, and he wants to call his own shots, and if he plays a subservient role he's not going to be happy. He feels he knows more about the game than anyone in the organization, more than anyone in the entire NBA."

In some ways, Thomas was the perfect man to guide those baby Raptors. He was just out of the game and 34 years old. His name and his face were instantly recognizable to NBA fans in the United States, although when he walked down Toronto streets he'd likely be greeted by vague, don't-I-know-you-from-somewhere looks. (In trendy Toronto, scared more than anything of being regarded as minor league, that American cachet certainly helped.) Players who might otherwise regard Toronto as undesirable and unknown knew Isiah, or at least knew of him. While his counterpart Stu Jackson in Vancouver preached patience, Thomas exuded the opposite. He was always in a hurry, always scheming. He had undeniable smarts — NBA smarts, street smarts — but he yearned most of all to extend the boardroom smarts that had helped him form a couple of businesses of his own and a personal net worth upwards of $10 million.

"I think in a lot of ways he's too smart for his own good," Damon Stoudamire once said. "I tell him that all the time. I tell him that instead of talking, he should keep his mouth shut sometimes."

On the basketball court, Thomas had few peers, at six-foot-one a little sapling among the NBA's tall redwoods but with a well-honed hard edge sharpened by 13 years as the Detroit Pistons' heart-and-soul guard. He was recognized as inch-for-inch one of the game's greatest performers and perhaps its most fearless and fierce competitor. At the same time, he had an angel-faced smile that could light up a room and an easy, enveloping way of talking that made you believe you were his closest confidant.

No wonder that in his NBA playing days, he was known as the Smiling Assassin. In his management days, nothing really changed except the nickname: the Minister of Sinister. Isiah Thomas knew the angles and wasn't afraid to play them, making an ownership share in the first-year Raptors part of his price when John Bitove came calling, then trying unsuccessfully to take majority control on two occasions after Bitove was gone.

"He's like a duck on a pond" was one long-time intimate's astute assessment of Thomas. "He looks so serene and smooth above the surface, just gliding along. But underneath, his legs are churning furiously and he's going like hell."

Commissioner David Stern once commented: "If you want to shoot the three, you look at Larry [Bird]. If you want to slam dunk, you're like Mike. And if you want to be mean and ornery, you're Isiah."

Teammates loved Thomas for his steeliness and savvy in games. Feared him, too, for his steeliness and savvy at working other games. For many, it was no surprise that this fellow was the first to ever walk off the court and directly into a general manager's position.

"He has no in-between," said John Salley, a former Detroit teammate who clashed with Thomas that first Raptors season. "There's calm and there's hate, as Chuck Daly told me when I first got to Detroit. He can go from calm and loving to kill. Isiah, to me, has always been the GM."

At times, Thomas went off the wall. He would muse one day about scrapping the lay-up line before games, trying to dream up an alternative to keep his players "juiced and loose." And while most GMs are loath to go public about trade rumours, Thomas provided regular updates.

"He'd come right into the dressing room in front of everyone and point to you and say, 'You might be traded' or 'I'm working on a deal to get you out of here,'" Pinckney said. "No one had ever done that to me. Some guys hated it. But I liked it. I always wanted to know that kind of stuff."

None of this appears to have changed inside the Indiana locker room. "He talks congenial with you, but when he snaps he's like a thug with a slingblade," says Pacers veteran Sam Perkins. "He's snapped several times. You don't want to see it."

He was the lonely maverick to some, an egomaniacal know-it-all to others. He saw himself as a young Al Davis, at times revelling in that role. It was that way when he was a player with the Pistons, and it would be the same as a GM and owner, when he would sit in the stands in a disguise to go unnoticed as he scouted a player.

"You're lonely," he once said, explaining what it was like. "You might be together on the court, but when you get off they don't want to deal with you. It might be jealousy or fear that causes it, but that loneliness was hard at times."

To have an idea where the Raptors are today, you have to figure out where they were then, coming into the NBA just as Michael Jordan's second tour of duty was beginning, goosing that golden age one more time. The legacy of that era, of Bird and Magic and Jordan — and yes, even Isiah Thomas — was this bloated league of 29 teams. It had maxed itself out in the United States with a round of expansion that added four new franchises late in the 1980s at $32.5 million apiece, then looked north of the border.

The price tag for the Canadians was a daunting $125 million, as naked a money grab as any sports outfit had ever engineered. It could have been more, actually. Until Vancouver's Arthur Griffiths came along with a new arena and contacted the NBA, the figure being kicked around was $140 million for a Toronto solo entry. That it was Bitove heading up the successful group of the three that contended for the franchise was a huge surprise, too. Two weeks before the NBA welcomed his group into their club, Bitove met with rival Larry Tanenbaum to propose they combine forces. It was Tanenbaum who had started the whole expansion process in 1992, giving the NBA a $100,000 deposit as a demonstration of commitment. It was Tanenbaum who had put together a strong group, then nodded his assent when NBA commissioner David Stern told him other Toronto franchise groups would be allowed into the process, turning it into a bidding war.

Bitove figured that, between them, the price would end up at a more reasonable $100 million or so. Tanenbaum said he wasn't interested in combining forces. "I've got this thing locked up," one witness recalls him saying. Instead, he would go into shock when the NBA awarded the franchise to Bitove's group for a sobering $125 million.

It wasn't as if some sort of basketball groundswell had turned the game into a hot commodity in Toronto. It was actually baseball that had tweaked the NBA on to Canada. The Blue Jays were drawing 4 million fans into the brand-new SkyDome as the country climbed out of a recession in the early 1990s. The Jays won back-to-back World Series, the SkyDome was a continental success story, and for once, the NBA started looking at Toronto as Toronto looked to the NBA. Once he had the team in his grasp, Bitove handed the chore of running the basketball operations side over to Thomas, along with a promise of equity in the team. And thereby were the sparks for a conflagration.

Predictably, the Raptors would be the very definition of expansionitis, a late-twentieth-century illness suffered by pro sports leagues, the symptoms being marked by too much or too many (number of teams, ticket prices) and too little (talent, history, perspective). Add the element of naïveté and lack of knowledge from the media, the customer base, and even the office staff, and it made for some very strange moments.

"I'm here to create a framework where a basketball team can perform," Thomas told *Sports Illustrated*'s Mike Farber a year before the team began play. "But first it starts with educating your staff. I feel like a professor sometimes. NBA 101."

It did seem that way, education and razzmatazz staggering along in imperfect tandem as the 24-month startup gathered steam. When the Raptors had trouble selling season tickets behind the baskets, they put out a press release stressing the see-through, "smudge-free" backboards. They held splashy press conferences at the Royal Ontario Museum, with team employees decked out in safari suits and pith helmets wandering among the dinosaur exhibits. When the NBA insisted that the provinces of Ontario and British Columbia drop league games from their sports lotteries as a condition of entry, it was front-page cliff-hanger news for weeks.

Once the team began playing in the autumn of 1995, the learning curve was steep. This was definitely a new game for Canadians, uncharted territory for most. On opening night, ticket holders behind the basket waved those distracting balloons when *the Raptors* were at the free-throw line, a definite faux pas that drew giggles from visiting NBA officials. Newspapers printed primers on rules, which always got a laugh from visiting teams and writers, and even the Raptors themselves.

"[When] we were here, they had stuff in the papers like, What is a three-second violation? What is a jump shot?" recalled Carlos Rogers, one of the original Raptors. "Now they know when to cheer and when not to cheer. When I was here, they were cheering everything. There wasn't any home-court advantage. Anything that happened, they were, like, Yay, yay!"

Perhaps that was a good thing. Toronto and Vancouver fielded pretty awful teams. For their combined admission price of US$250 million, they entered the league with the usual expansion rosters of has-beens and never-wills, kooks and criminals, the lame and infirm, and plenty of salary dead weight.

Thomas took what he called a "clean slate" approach, forgiving a player for his past if he thought he could play. And so Alvin Robertson was a first-year Raptor, despite having been out of the league for two years with back problems — and a reputation as a dangerous hothead. Robertson had choked Detroit GM Billy McKinney during a Pistons practice and had been in trouble four times before for violent attacks on women.

How different the Raptors would be was clear on the day of their NBA debut. Robertson began his morning with a nine-o'clock court date at Toronto's Old City Hall, answering to a charge of assaulting his ex-girlfriend in a SkyDome Hotel room six nights before.

It wouldn't be the last time for Robertson, who scored the first basket in Raptors history and had a fine season — but only one season, his comeback limited by his worsening personal troubles. In Milwaukee later in the year, he sat at his locker stall, leafing through a sheaf of legal papers that had just been served on him. "I told Grunwald I could never go back to Wisconsin," he grumbled, just as Brendan Malone walked by.

"I expect you're popular like that in a number of states, Alvin," Malone noted wryly.

Robertson would resurface again, three years later, in the Raptors' dressing room in San Antonio, looking for a job with the team. With two more assaults and a felony burglary conviction, there was no hope.

Another guard, B.J. Tyler, was picked up from the 76ers in the expansion draft. He would suffer a career-ending injury before he had even played a game, falling asleep with an ice pack on his leg and suffering "nerve damage." Team insiders put the deep slumber down to too much marijuana, the drug of choice around the NBA through the late 1990s. Regardless, Tyler's $1-million-plus annual salary counted against the Raptors ledger until the 1999–2000 season was completed, making him the most overpaid Raptor in history.

Then there was Oliver Miller, the last player left standing in the expansion draft. The Raptors, with the final pick, in effect had to take him. Miller's reputation as an overweight jerk was well earned during stops in Phoenix and Detroit. The Pistons left him exposed in the draft after the 300-plus-pound Miller had been found to have doctored the locker-room scales to come in under weight.

Miller had a decent opening season in Toronto, hailed as his last chance, and Thomas regarded him as something of a pet project. Miller set the tone for his on-again, off-again performances by missing opening night because of a league suspension. His weight problems continued and, although it was a constant struggle keeping him trim, the troubles rarely came to light. Miller's contract contained a provision that he could not be listed in the program at more than 280 pounds. He was actually 50 pounds heavier, sometimes more. The wild fluctuations were publicly put down to his "metabolism," but the real reason was more mundane: Miller drank too much, favouring high-calorie rum and Coke. Before the Raptors' first season, his father had been found guilty of murder, and his marriage was on the rocks.

"If he had stayed at 280, he'd be an all-star," said Tracy Murray, perhaps Miller's closest friend on the team. "But he had a lot of problems. His life was a mess."

Team officials tried to turn him around, but to no avail. He was suspected of feigning injuries. Nasty and profane, he once told Chicago's Bill

Wennington that he was going to "beat his white ass" during a game, his comments broadcast to a national television audience.

Still, as erratic and volatile as he was, Miller was a fan favourite and the kind of player who could every now and then show just enough to keep his employers expecting and hoping for more. Sometimes it happened under the most unlikely of circumstances. One time, after badly spraining his ankle, he locked himself into his townhouse, not answering the door when the Raptors sent their gofer over to get him for treatment. Thomas phoned the house repeatedly, screaming at Miller, but still he stayed put, the gofer parked outside on the doorstep for three successive days. By game day, no one quite knew what to expect. Miller showed up in the dressing room, a little late and limping.

"What are you doing here?" someone asked.

"I'm here to play a game," Miller said.

"He plays, too," said Malone. "If he says he's okay, he's okay. We need him."

Miller's health was such a concern, though, that he had to sign a release absolving the team of any blame for damage he might cause to himself by playing. When he refused to get his ankles taped — "that's for pussies," he said — there were more releases to be signed. After all that, with Thomas and the rest of the front office holding their breath and expecting his ankle to fall off, Miller went out and scored 29 points.

Good or bad, Miller was dubbed "the Big O" by the Raptors' ear-splitting public-address announcer, Herbie Kuhn. But many shuddered at the handle, which had originally belonged to Hall of Famer Oscar Robertson. Personnel director Bob Zuffelato, with one eye on Miller's latest trip to the scales, regarded it as almost sacrilegious and took to calling him "the Biggest Oh."

Or perhaps that should have been the Biggest Owe. After the Raptors' first year, Miller tore up the rest of his NBA contract and became a free agent, incensing Thomas, who likened him to the scorpion in the old fable who kills the frog ferrying him across the river. "It's in his nature," Thomas said of Miller's move. It would be an incredibly stupid mistake. He found no takers on the free-agent market.

During a visit to Chicago and a meeting with Jerry Krause, the Bulls GM paused the videotape they were reviewing and asked Miller why he hadn't tried to rebound the ball on a particular play. Miller explained that the fellow who shot the ball hadn't passed to him the last trip up the floor. Krause thanked Miller for his time and ended the meeting. Instead of increasing the guaranteed $5.5 million he would have earned from his existing contract, Miller would play for the minimum salary the next two seasons — about half a million dollars in total.

For all that, Miller and the Raptors appeared inseparable. The following February, Miller returned to Toronto, walking into a press conference to announce the signing, chortling, "It's Martin Luther King Day, and I am free at last, free at last!" In November 1997, Grunwald's inaugural transaction, appropriately enough, was to pick up Miller for his third and last tour of duty as a Raptor. This time, he strode into the Raptors office and shouted, "Daddy's home!"

It wasn't just brains, professionalism and control that were in short supply with Thomas's first-year Raptors, though. Talent was also hard to find. Most of that came in the guise of Stoudamire, who actually wasn't Thomas's first choice — that would have been high schooler Kevin Garnett. But with Garnett gone fifth and expansion cousin Vancouver taking Bryant Reeves at no. 6, Thomas was next up and selected Stoudamire over his other preferred candidate, Michael Finley. (Finley would go much later, at no. 21, but became a top-drawer pro with Dallas.)

There is a certain neat symmetry to Stoudamire's short, explosive career as a Raptor. He was booed loudly when he arrived. He was booed just before he left. And he is booed now that he is gone.

The first set of boos came from a SkyDome draft-night crowd of 20,000 or so, most of whom would have had trouble picking Damon Stoudamire out of a police lineup. Stoudamire was not the one they wanted — he was regarded as too small at five-foot-nine, and too much of a scattershot. Ed O'Bannon, from the '95 NCAA champion UCLA Bruins, was the people's choice, if not the doctor's choice. O'Bannon's knees were so badly damaged that his NBA career would last just two seasons and 128 games.

"The boos don't bother me. They all know Ed from seeing him play on TV," said Stoudamire. "By the time I'm done here, they'll know who I am."

No one in the crowd would be complaining about Stoudamire for long. He was quickly dubbed Mighty Mouse, a tattoo of the cartoon hero on one bicep, and on most nights he was the only Raptor worth watching as he put together an NBA Rookie of the Year season. But it was Malone's use of the young star that created increasing friction between the coach and the GM. By March, Thomas was ready to order Stoudamire onto the injured list with tendinitis. The GM figured it was being brought on by the heavy 41-minutes-a-night workload Malone was putting on him. "Just because a player is willing to die for this organization doesn't mean you have to kill him," Thomas groused.

When Malone started tinkering with his lineup, putting out five shooting guards one night, ignoring them in another, Thomas fumed about being "embarrassed and humiliated in public."

In truth, Malone's job was hanging by the slimmest of threads for most of that first season, dating right back to training camp, when the coach preferred another guard, journeyman Chris Whitney, to back up Stoudamire. Instead, Thomas cut Whitney. In San Antonio at the all-star break, Thomas and Malone held a clear-the-air meeting in a hotel room. Thomas put Malone on notice, telling him he had to play more of the club's younger players for assessment purposes. A month later, as they hit the highest note of their season — beating Jordan and the Bulls in front of a juiced-up record SkyDome crowd of 36,131 — Malone's fate was already sealed. Still, the coach pointed triumphantly to the rafters as the buzzer sounded.

"I knew I was gone the day before that game," Malone said later. "I approached [Thomas] about whether or not I was going to be fired, and he sort of hemmed and hawed and said, 'Brendan, right now you're not patient enough to coach this team.' That's why I pointed up at the top of the SkyDome after we beat Michael. It was my way of saying thanks, and goodbye."

The final game of that first season fittingly matched two lame-duck coaches at the SkyDome. On the Philadelphia bench, John Lucas turned to reporters sitting courtside and joked, "We're going to turn the game back 150 years."

The Thomas–Malone marriage was dissolved officially two days later at a tawdry press conference. Thomas invited some Toronto players in to take potshots, none of them louder than those levelled by the permanently disgruntled Oliver Miller. Malone bit his tongue at his farewell press conference and was awarded a $325,000 buyout covering the second and final year of his contract.

"Plan? I wasn't aware of any plan," he said of Thomas's approach to team building.

The plain-speaking, Brooklyn-bred Malone had put up with a lot that one season. He'd had to endure Miller, enough to try anyone's patience.

He'd had to try to teach players who looked at his plain style and plainer wardrobe and called him Barney Rubble behind his back. His players clashed among themselves, Acie Earl and the poisonous Miller exchanging punches during a shootaround in San Antonio. Most of all, Malone clashed with Thomas, the two not speaking to each other during the final two months of the season.

"Brendan had the title, but we all knew [Thomas] was the real coach," said Willie Anderson, an original Raptor who was traded halfway through the first season. The older players, like Anderson and Ed Pinckney, recognized Malone's ability to coach, but the young players had trouble accepting him.

"Isiah would sit these young guys down — Jimmy King, Carlos Rogers and those guys — he'd put his arm around their shoulders and have these long, long talks with them about what it takes to be a professional and what was expected of them," recalled Pinckney, an original Raptor. "Then we'd get out on the floor and they'd forget everything. The things they would do, the mistakes they'd make, it drove Brendan crazy."

He would coax 21 wins out of them, and the first-year Raptors earned a reputation as a side that was always well prepared and rarely played soft or disinterested. This was the positive side of that early turbulence, the Raptors attracting in excess of 23,000 fans a night at the SkyDome and putting on a decent show more often than not. But at times, Malone had a hard time keeping his head up as the losses mounted — trouble for any coach, let alone one at the helm of a no-hope, first-year expansion team.

"The coach [of an expansion team] has to be a positive guy," Pat Williams, the wisecracking boss of the expansion Orlando Magic, once said. "When it seems like nothing is going right, he's got to say, 'Fellas, nice sweating out there tonight,' or 'You guys showered beautifully.'"

Instead, Malone fretted and worked overtime. He had trouble delegating to his assistants, so it was the coach himself who would stay up all night watching video, trying to come up with strategies to make this bunch of ragtags win games. But the tapes always ended up the same. Bill Fitch coached the debut season of the Cleveland Cavaliers, felt the same pain and expressed it succinctly: "War is hell. Expansion is worse."

In a way, it was just like Thomas to hire Malone in Toronto, seeking an old friend tested and trusted in combat during their Detroit days together, after others like Bulls assistant Jim Cleamons had turned him down. It also seemed perfectly reasonable that he would fire him. Thomas was mercurial and not particularly consistent. He had spoken during the Raptors' first pre-season about the importance of continuity — "I believe it is crucial to make it through the early turbulence with a coach intact," he said — but in fact couldn't stomach Malone's independence. Making a change, too, was part of Thomas's style. Athletes played the game, not positions. Coaches coached according to their set responsibilities. Like the athletes, they were interchangeable parts. All were replaceable — except him. On the floor, it was up and down — full-court pressure defence, up-tempo offence. Among his preferred list of candidates ahead of Malone was Arkansas college coach Nolan Richardson, whose "40 Minutes of Hell" method seemed perfectly suited. Richardson wanted no part of Thomas or the pros, though.

A week after he had fired Malone, Thomas sat down for lunch with him at a restaurant near their homes in suburban Detroit. He promised Malone he'd be back coaching the Raptors in three years. "I thought, what the heck, that's Isiah," Malone remembered with a shrug. "I guess he was sincere." Instead, Malone would go immediately to the Seattle Supersonics, helping them to the '96 NBA finals as a consultant, then catch on as the lead assistant for Jeff Van Gundy in his native New York.

Under Darrell Walker, Malone's successor, Thomas was assured of a more faithful supporter on the bench. But it was in his second draft that Thomas made his first and biggest mistake, taking brittle Marcus Camby ahead of Shareef Abdur-Rahim. It's not that Camby turned out to be such a bad pro. When he played, he was fine. But there were injuries, and even at his best he was no more than an energetic complementary player on a team that needed more. Camby had no jump shot and couldn't post up against the more solid bodies opposite him. With no defined position, he thrived playing run-and-gun basketball, crashing the offensive glass for rebounds or helping out with a block on defence. But his body was so frail he seemed to be constantly injured, and perhaps nothing bugged Thomas more than players who couldn't tolerate the pain of an injury. When Camby crashed to the floor and lay motionless during a pregame warm-up his rookie year, Thomas grabbed the arm of the trainer: "Don't move. He'll get up," he said. And he did get up. Meantime, Abdur-Rahim quickly slipped into the role of smooth scorer in Vancouver, the Grizzlies' lone star. Thomas's 1996 assessment of the two players turned out to be as wrong as it could have been: "Camby can step in and play 30 to 35 minutes, and he's got a big upside. Maybe four or five years from now, [Abdur-Rahim] will turn out to be something."

Sure, there were Thomas triumphs — drafting Stoudamire and McGrady, spotting a mouldering Doug Christie in New York and trading for him, reviving Tracy Murray's career and quickly turning over the dregs of that first-year roster — but there was plenty of friction too. Thomas claimed that after Bitove departed and Allan Slaight took over, the new owners blocked him from making deals that would have brought

Shawn Kemp or Jerry Stackhouse to Toronto. He would repeat that vague assertion in the hallway of the Air Canada Centre. It was the kind of talk Slaight deplored. According to a number of team officials, Slaight had approved the Stackhouse deal ("Isiah just couldn't pull the trigger," shrugged president Richard Peddie) and put together a financial package to cover the Kemp deal before it too fell through.

"Oh, he's a piece of work," was Slaight's assessment. "He could look at a glass of water on the table and tell you it was something completely different."

The rift between the two would eventually become a chasm, NBA officials fuming in silence as it played out very publicly in the media. In November 1997, three months after his second and final bid to acquire control fell $25 million short, Thomas resigned his post and began selling off his stake in the Raptors. He had financial concerns behind his move, Slaight having covered two $1-million cash calls as an eight-party arena syndication deal was reached and construction on the building sped up. But as far as Slaight was concerned, there was more: just as the GM job grew more demanding, just as the team graduated from a no-pressure novelty act to higher stakes, Thomas was bailing. Not surprisingly, Thomas saw it differently.

"I'm just a person. I'm not a corporation," he told a friend as he walked into his farewell press conference. "I don't have the deep, deep pockets you need to play in this game."

Later, he elaborated. "I only know one way, and that's to fight," he said, bristling at the suggestion that he quit the Raptors. "Basically, I didn't have a choice. It was either resign or get fired. Had I the financial means, I would have fought a lot harder."

More than any player, Thomas's most important legacy was the deputy he left behind. Glen Grunwald inherited his job and was charged with cleaning up the wreckage. There was plenty of it lying around, parked on the injured list or malingering through a 17-game losing streak. Without Thomas, there was no way most of the group left behind was interested in continuing. Walker was barely interested in coaching, leaving in February 1998 after Stoudamire had been traded and Grunwald's cleanup began in earnest.

"We had a strong foundation there with Isiah, and then the team split up," said Camby. "I always say you gotta have stability in the front office, which we didn't. It trickles down to the team, and we never bounced back from that."

Of course, there was another Thomas hire that would play a pivotal role in the team's fortunes: Butch Carter. "I made a big mistake," Thomas said. "So many people warned me. I brought him in because he was an old teammate [at Indiana]. I had no idea he would become the head coach. That was never an option."

After Thomas left the Raptors he spent three years as an analyst for NBC, the U.S. network that holds NBA broadcasting rights. He infuriated Butch Carter by claiming some credit for the Raptors' success whenever the subject came up. "You'd think he was the one who drafted Vince," Butch groused.

But there was a link in at least one sense. When Thomas was at the 1999 draft lottery in Secaucus, N.J., he got to talking with Carter, who was coming off his Rookie of the Year season and represented the Raptors on stage. It turned out Carter had moved into the waterfront condo Thomas had called home during his time in Toronto, a suite Carter would later buy.

The two crossed paths again when Thomas was a judge at the 2000 slam-dunk competition. Thomas was at his hammy best after Carter's show-stopping dunks, jumping over the table he and the rest of the panel sat at to give Carter one of those "we are not worthy" bows, then joining in a chorus of old-school pros who called the exhibition one of the finest they had ever seen.

Now, when they return to Toronto, Camby and Stoudamire are routinely booed, as if they are villains from a play the crowd would rather forget. When Camby played in the Air Canada Centre for the first time, a tape of a crying baby was played over the P.A. system. Stoudamire's first game back in Toronto was more venomous, bordering on hysterical. Homemade signs were everywhere — "Everybody Hates Damon," "Mighty Louse," "Money Mouse," "Hey Damon! Mouse Is Just Another Way of Saying Small Rat." One fan shone a red laser light into Stoudamire's Portland team huddle and at his teammate Brian Grant's eyes when he was at the foul line, causing arena security to go mad with concern as they searched in vain for the offender. As Stoudamire left the floor at the end of the game, a fan leaned over and took a swing at him. He missed, but the wild punch hit a security guard just below the eye. Of all the players to be treated this harshly, it seemed more than a little unfair that it was Stoudamire. More than any of those early Raptors, he would spill his guts every night no matter how hopeless the cause, retreating to the trainers' room after yet another loss and crying his eyes out more than once during his two and a half seasons here.

These days, Stoudamire is in Portland, a Trail Blazer. Miller is out of the NBA, getting bigger in Fort Worth. Camby is a Knick. Allan Slaight sold off his equity in the team and the arena to the Maple Leafs as a $503-million package, and there's Larry Tanenbaum, a Leafs minority owner and now the team's governor, sitting in Slaight's courtside seats. Malone and Lenny Wilkens meet at centre court. Charles Oakley wanders by, and

Malone gives him a playful punch in the shoulder, two former Knick teammates meeting in this strange new NBA world that is so different than the one they entered.

A few people call out Malone's name. And from the stands, John Bitove comes over to shake his hand. As far as they are concerned, this Thomas–Malone reunion is no big deal. Others close to them wonder how long before it flies apart again.

"We've always understood that what happened here was just part of the business of sports," says Thomas. "Even though you have personal relationships in sports, the business sometimes gets in the way. And for a while it was like that. But our families have always been close, we've lived in the same neighbourhood, we've stayed connected."

These Raptors, with the professorial Wilkens getting used to them, have had a fairly ordinary pre-season. Morris Peterson, the team's first-round draft choice, looks like a keeper, although like most incoming players his defensive proficiency borders on nonexistent. The closest to a real revelation is Alvin Williams, heading into a contract year but coming off two seasons as Butch Carter's personal yo-yo. During the Raptors' summer league entry in Utah, Williams and Wilkens have spent a lot of time together, the coach seeking to repair his young guard's damaged confidence.

Mark Jackson and Corliss Williamson, the new faces, have had some trouble fitting in. Yogi Stewart, the $24-million centre all but ignored by Butch Carter the year before, is the biggest disappointment. Stewart is slow to recover from knee surgery in August, rankling the team's front office. Stewart had the surgery at home in California, with his own doctor, and the operation went dreadfully wrong, a blood vessel bursting and internal bleeding delaying his recovery by two months.

The Raptors did not figure to be an improved team from the year previous. They are definitely older, perhaps wiser. They are also slower and less athletic, and as a team that had trouble playing solid defence the year before, they look to be worse this time around. The trade-off — Jackson and Williamson in, Christie and McGrady out — is not a good one. Jackson is giving them just what they thought they wanted, a steady hand at the tiller and unerring court vision. But just as much, he is the man they turned to after other avenues closed to them, no other free agent willing to sign with them. Williamson is an anchor, and as soon as October, Grunwald is wondering about the mix and trying to move him.

You'd never guess any of this uncertainty reading the Toronto papers or checking the pulse of the customers. In a TSN poll of viewers, 80 per cent predicted that the Raptors will improve on their 45-win total of the 1999–2000 season. The annual, and mostly worthless, prognostications of the media were on the same optimistic level. The salient point was that Vince Carter had raised the expectations level of the Raptors, had made them fashionable, and just about everyone was looking ahead to better things.

During the pregame formalities, when Isiah Thomas was introduced as the visiting head coach, there were lusty boos from the Air Canada Centre crowd. "If I ever get into coaching, just shoot me in the head," Thomas once said while he was with the Raptors. Maybe they remembered.

The Raptors hammer Thomas and Malone's Pacers. The customers roar with each basket. It's time for reality, time for the season.

CHAPTER 5

November 2000:

Selling Product

I t's the dinner hour on a snowy early-winter evening in midtown
Toronto, and tonight's serving is one very well done Vince Carter.

He can barely be seen, actually, breathing heavily under a suit of
electrodes and the heat of 29 key lights suspended from ceiling brackets
high above.

In the gym around him, a caterer dispenses plastic containers of beef
stew, while another offers a tray of tunafish and pâté on crackers. The
crew of nearly 40 dig in while they work. It's a mostly young and hip
crowd, lots of nose rings and goatees, and they take no more than curso-
ry notice of Carter kitted out under the glare of the spots.

They've gathered inside this recreation centre for a three-day shoot,
its basketball court transformed into a television studio. Two walls and the
hardwood floor are covered with a deep blue chroma-key screen. Exercise

equipment and technical gear is piled on the fringes. The bustle never stops, even if it's a hurry-up-and-wait kind of activity.

Carter wears a mesh singlet and purple Raptors shorts. Wires running off the white cups affixed to his torso disappear into a thin plastic tube that appears at his back like a tail and is plugged into a computer. A plastic headset holds a breathing tube in place in Carter's mouth. He is pouring sweat — at least it looks that way. It's actually water, the makeup artist coming by before each take to fuss and fret with the water bottle, spritzing him carefully and artfully here and there, occasionally playing with it on his skin like an Old Master manipulating his oils on a canvas.

The treadmill beneath his feet starts up slowly then picks up speed, and at the call of "action," Carter is going easily along from slow jog into steady trot. An attendant in a maroon suit stands alongside with a clipboard and marker in hand, watching him intently.

It appears to be a standard oxygen-uptake, or VO_2 test, the sort that Carter and any other serious athlete has taken before. But again, nothing here is as it seems. It is actually a television commercial for Gatorade, the sports drink that is one of Carter's biggest endorsements.

It was Gatorade, the Quaker Oats product, that made "Be Like Mike" something of a catchphrase in its long-running advertisements beginning in 1991, when Jordan was signed as the sports drink's first pitchman. It worked. Gatorade's share of the market was overwhelming. But Jordan retired. And now it is Carter's turn. He has something of a similar career track rolling along — North Carolina Tar Heel, slam-dunk champ, Olympic gold medallist — and as far as his off-the-court business life is concerned, it is the biggest day of his season.

On this one, he is not alone. Derek Jeter, the New York Yankees shortstop, has already been and gone, whisked to the airport in a stretch limousine after going through the same drill. Jeter and Carter filmed a small segment together, sitting at a table as they took an "exam," Carter stealing glances at Jeter's answers, the two breaking up between takes at some small joke. American soccer star Mia Hamm will be in the next day for her turn. And in another studio across the continent, basketballer Chamique Holdsclaw and football's Peyton Manning will get their camera time as well. Through the alchemy of digital technology and computers, all five will eventually show up together on the small screen, working out, interacting, fooling around and even jostling each other for elbow room in a Gatorade spot that's been dubbed "Lab Rats."

The 30-second ad carries a budget of US$700,000, making it just one of many buried in Gatorade's ad budget of over $100 million. A mere five-hour-day's work for Carter, it's nowhere near as strenuous as last year's shoot of his Gatorade debut, wherein the premise had him playing a basketball game against two digital dinosaurs. That one, shot at an east-end Toronto soundstage, took two eight-hour shifts to finish and had Carter dunking and drinking in take after take until he got it right. The final product had his sweat rolling off his face in blue and red and orange, just like Mike in his earlier shills for the product. First aired during the 2000 All-Star weekend, it was an immediate hit.

This sequel is another day's work for Carter. The night before, he scored 33 points in a Raptors victory over Indiana. The morning of, and it was a two-hour practice with his team. Then into the SUV and a drive uptown for this: a video session that puts him on a bike, at a table, doing voice-overs and finally on this treadmill — which is somehow an appropriate way to end it, given that tomorrow morning there will be a shootaround, and in the evening, the New York Knicks into the Air Canada Centre.

The trick for Vince Carter is the same one other pro athletes face in their short playing careers: perform at a high level and cash in on that outside the game without knocking oneself out. Carter's monthly schedule goes through a number of permutations, faxed from the Toronto office of his International Management Group agency, to the Florida home of his mother, and back up to his Toronto waterfront condo. It is Michelle Carter back home in Daytona who vets everything that IMG arranges for Carter, saying yes or no to the requests for appearances or endorsements while she works out of her home as the director of her son's Embassy of Hope, the charitable foundation established before he had played a single NBA game.

This is business, and it has proved to be far more thorny and nasty for Carter than any basketball game. Declaring himself for the NBA draft after his third year at North Carolina, Carter and his parents chose William (Tank) Black as his sports agent. It was a surprise choice. True, Black was one of the most powerful agents in the United States. But his rise had been sudden and full of questions. There was also the matter of NBA expertise. The clients using his South Carolina–based Professional Management Inc. operation were mostly football players, including five first-round picks in the 1999 NFL draft, enviable additions to an already well-stocked list for the 43-year-old Black. But Carter was Black's lone NBA client.

Originally, Michelle Carter wanted to represent her son. But Black made a strong pitch. Most of all, he charmed, telling the Carters his own Horatio Alger story, from a poor background in South Carolina to all-American college quarterback to the humble beginnings of his business a decade before, working out of his kitchen. There were the testimonials of former clients regarding Black's personal touch, and among the investments he suggested was a company that produced a trivia board game honouring the achievements of African Americans.

"I wanted someone who would be doing more than just looking at my son from the standpoint of money," said Michelle Carter. "That is why I've always felt it was important that I stay as involved. At the end of the day, he's always going to be my son and I'm always going to love him."

For a while, all went well, or at least seemed to go well. Carter was signed to a shoe deal with Puma. It wasn't huge money, not as much as the one his cousin Tracy McGrady had scored with Adidas the year before. But on the other hand, this was an era of shrinking returns and tighter budgets for the sneaker companies. And as Black kept saying, there was potential for more. Puma's deal was for 10 years, and loaded with incentives — only $150,000 guaranteed a year, but with bonuses that could push the total value up to $25 million.

Among Carter's smaller deals was Quaker, covering Canada only. But after his smashing Rookie of the Year season, it was expanded to cover North America, and out of it came the Jordanesque Gatorade commercials. Black talked like it was just the beginning, confidently telling Carter he expected he could earn $20 million in off-court income for the year 2000. "It all sounded very good," says Michelle Carter. "Little did we know of what was really going on."

Some of the problems were self-inflicted. Black had used his NFL background to hook Carter up with German company Puma, but the deal went sour pretty quickly. Carter, the first NBAer to go to the company in 25 years, stopped wearing the shoes in December 1999, complaining that they pinched his feet. A signature Carter shoe, to be dubbed the VI and available in seven colours at a modest $75 a pair, never got beyond the talking stage. Black talked of a clothing line as part of the deal, but it never materialized. Meantime, Carter was being teased. When the Lakers came to Toronto in December of '99, his old AAU teammate Kobe Bryant rode him all game long about his shoes, saying, "Vince, man, you've gotta get some new sneaks!"

It was Black, the engineer of it all, who would eventually tell him how bad the same deal was and how he had to get out of it, estimating he could escape before the end of the 1999–2000 season. Carter would be paid a grand total of $200,000 out of his Puma deal — and later give back much, much more.

While Carter continued to sizzle on the court and his performances were noticed in a wider and wider circle, Black was slowly being cornered. His predictions of riches to come were proving to be as empty as his repeated promises of more deals. The NFL Players Association completed its own internal probe of Black's operations in May of 1999 — as Carter was accepting his Rookie of the Year award — finding that Black had secretly paid football players at the University of Florida. The NFLPA stripped him of his right to operate as an agent, and Black's NFL clients began to flee.

With each day seeming to bring new allegations against Black, Carter and his mother stood by him through most of the winter of 2000, even signing a deal extending their relationship to 2011. While Carter's star kept rising and rising — following the slam-dunk competition, he dropped 51 points on the Phoenix Suns and an NBC national audience — the message from his camp regarding Black remained unwaveringly positive. "He's done what he has been expected to do for Vince, and that's my barometer," said Michelle Carter. "There have been no improprieties where Vince is concerned."

But the NFLPA probe was merely the tip of a very dirty iceberg. The Internal Revenue Service, the Securities and Exchange Commission and the FBI were all on to Black, investigators and former clients filing charges of money laundering, fraud, bribery and criminal conspiracy and lawsuits involving courts in three U.S. states. At Black's arraignment in Gainesville, Florida, Carter's stepfather, Harry Robinson, appeared alongside the agent as a show of support — but it would be the last such demonstration. All told, Black was accused of defrauding and mismanaging about US$15 million of his clients' money through bogus stock purchases in the board game and a pyramid scheme based in the Cayman Islands. Included was about $300,000 of Carter's money. There were allegations of drug money laundering and aiding a fugitive drug dealer in fleeing the country. It was a stunning and swift fall from grace for Black, but never did he admit anything was wrong to the Carters.

"He kept saying, 'Don't believe what you hear or read — they keep twisting the facts,'" Michelle Carter said. "But then it got to the point where Stevie Wonder could see what was happening."

Black ended up back at home in Columbia, South Carolina, wearing an electronic bracelet, with a 10 p.m. curfew, out on a $1-million bond and unable to leave the state without court approval after the fraud and money-laundering charges were brought against him. The Carters finally said good riddance to the man they had called Uncle Tank.

For Michelle Carter, it was a rude awakening into a world from which she thought she had shielded her son when she went to Black in the first place. Carter, who retired after 20 years as a high-school and middle-school teacher when her son turned professional, was in over her head at times.

"I honestly think that there comes a time when enough is enough," she said. "The Tank Black situation really convinced me of that. It became all about the pursuit of these deals and the accumulation of money. I always said it wouldn't be this way. But it had."

There were other problems, too, with the union with Black. "It wasn't just the money," said Michelle. "The schedule he was on was completely unrealistic at times. There was stuff there that could never be done, deals that were questionable in terms of time. It was impossible."

Never was this more evident than at the 2000 All-Star weekend. While he was winning the slam-dunk contest and starting for the eastern conference as the leading vote-getter in the league, he was being run ragged between Oakland and San Francisco.

For Vince Carter, the aftermath of the Black debacle would be long and drawn out — and ultimately, a financial and personal nightmare.

The shoe deal played out just as Black was. With Puma on the outs and the lawyers for both sides trying to come up with a solution, Carter declared his feet free agents. Suddenly, shoes began to arrive, along with clothing, handbags and just about anything else a lusting company could slap its logo on and courier to the Air Canada Centre addressed to one Vince Carter.

It became a standing joke around the Toronto dressing room to count the boxes of sneakers. All the major manufacturers comped him, and above his locker at the Air Canada Centre were stacked boxes of Adidas, Nikes, And-1s and Reeboks. After his win in the slam-dunk, more and more came in, some headed to a back room, others stacked up higher and higher and spilling over into the space above Tracy McGrady's cubicle. For McGrady, yearning to escape Vince Carter's space, it was difficult to take at times. Carter just shrugged, barely taking notice of the growing pile. Some of them he tried on for size. After taking them out for test runs in practices or games, they were discarded. Others never got out of the box. And-1, something of an upstart to this dance and the one with the most "street" image, was particularly ardent. The company whose first pitchman was Latrell Sprewell designed special T-shirts for Carter and his friend Joe Giddens and sent shoes and leather bags — and at least one of its company reps to infiltrate and take part in Carter's summer fantasy camp.

It was all part and parcel of this somewhat Quixotic search for the next Michael Jordan — the player and the icon, the marketing force and the brand name that came of age along with the NBA and turned over its traditional formula. The league and especially the TV networks had always promoted the NBA as a one-on-one affair — it wasn't the Celtics vs. the Warriors, but Russell vs. Chamberlain. Then Air Jordan came along, the nickname, significantly, coming from a Nike shoe that spawned a $200-million-a-year apparel and footwear line. For better and for worse, Jordan changed everything. Before Jordan, player agents were relatively minor characters, disliked by management but accepted by some enlightened club officials as a necessary and prudent part of doing business. Players got endorsements for a narrow range of products — shaving cream, razor blades and, in a bygone era, cigarettes — and were paid a pittance for their services.

After Jordan, though, agents could be power brokers. Along with commissioner David Stern, perhaps no one in a business suit was more responsible for the state of the NBA in the late 1990s than Jordan's long-time agent, David Falk. Falk parlayed his Jordan connection into a position as the league's top agent. He controlled a large block of players and wielded enormous influence — to some, like Stern, way too much influence. To many, Falk was just two horns and a pitchfork short of the devil himself.

With Falk running the business, timing also played a role: the confluence of cable television, marketing and basketball's global expansion produced

Michael Jordan, Inc. Besides the money spun off, a whole new range of casual fans suddenly were interested in the NBA — you've seen the commercial, now watch the player — a league that just a few years earlier was tottering on the brink of financial ruin and perceived as too black, too self-centred and too drug-infested. Long-time NBA officials love to tell stories of the days in 1980 when the deciding game of the championship final was shown on tape delay, beginning at midnight. A decade later, Bird, Magic and Jordan — and Stern and Falk — had revived what some thought was a corpse. It was a remarkable transformation. For everyone.

"I'm just a used car in the lot," said Charles Oakley, the grand old grump of the Raptors dressing room, and a man who broke into the league alongside a young Jordan in Chicago. "Back then you had some good cars on the lot, then there was Michael. Michael was a Bentley. He was a guy who made people stop and come into the showroom to look."

In 1985, the year Oakley entered the NBA and Jordan received his Rookie of the Year award, Nike launched its Air Jordan shoe. It became a $100-million seller almost overnight, and not only a star had been born. So too, was a new paradigm.

"With Michael, I've created a Frankenstein of sorts," David Falk told the *New York Times* magazine. "In 1984, Rod Thorn, the general manager of the Bulls, said: 'What are you trying to do? Make this guy into a tennis player?' And I said, 'Exactly.' He's not just another one of 12 homogenous guys. He's different. And now everybody wants to be like Mike."

Falk could never be accused of understatement when it came to Jordan or, for that matter, himself and his own role. But even a generation on, Jordan remained the yardstick. Even if it was impossible. Too much had changed, from the shifting marketing environment to the basketball arena itself, where kids were being discovered on playgrounds at age 12, breezing unencumbered through high school as coddled athletic prodigies, showered with shoes and money and favours, and coming into the NBA to make big money before they turned 20. The thirst and the maniacal competitiveness that drove Jordan simply didn't exist in this world of privilege and entitlement.

Michelle Carter had tried to keep both her sons away from that self-absorbed, basketball-only world for as long as she could. Vince was an all-state volleyballer, an accomplished little league pitcher and a star quarterback. He was also a drum major in high school, marching around at halftime of football games in front of the band directed by his stepfather. He wrote poetry and music. But still, the accolades mounted on the hardwood, where Carter was dubbed "UFO" and sellout crowds turned up at Daytona Mainland games to watch his high-flying act. Alongside Kobe Bryant and Tim Thomas on the AAU Tim Thomas Playaz team, he was part of the high-powered summertime circuit that has turned basketball into a year-round endeavour for kids still in school. At North Carolina, the Jordan comparison was pinned on him before he had even played a game. Once upon a time he had dreamed of that. Now, he was tired of it. Heck, no thanks to Black's bullshit patter, he had been burned by it. If this was business, it was ruthless and exhausting and riddled with peril. If this was business, someone else could handle it. And they usually did. But that, too, carried its own set of problems. Michelle Carter tells of how she found a $65,000 cheque for her son's share of NBA merchandising revenue among a pile of mail that was months old.

"He's not a mail person. He'll let it stack up for months and not look at it. Imagine if he was surrounded by the kind of people who could easily take that money away from him, and he wouldn't even realize it was gone.

"All he wants to do is play basketball," she says. "The business side of it is something that he's not very interested in. He's going to have to be some day, and I'm trying to get him more and more involved, but right now he's not really that way. I want to let him just think of basketball, to concentrate on that. And to me, at the end of the day when the basketball game is over, the most important thing is that I love him and I want the best for him."

Fresh and wary of it all, Carter was hit with another jolt in the summer of 2000 as he was readying for his Olympic trip. An arbitrator in Boston ruled that he had breached his contract with Puma and ordered that he pay $13,547,011 in damages. Included in the judgment was a clause prohibiting Carter from endorsing any other product for three years. Black's strategy regarding the Puma contract had been a complete failure. The claims against Puma that had been made so loudly a few months before were rejected as "meritless" by the arbitrator.

"We were stunned," said Merle Scott, Carter's new agent after Black was fired. "We just couldn't believe the number. It seemed so excessive. It wasn't as if he had made tons of money wearing the shoe, or made millions of commercials. That was devastating, because at that point, we didn't have another contract in place."

But this was Scott's job: to pick up the pieces in the wake of Black's mismanagement. It was hectic, but it was also the chance of a lifetime. He was 41 years old, a former draft pick of the New York Knicks who had never made the NBA but bounced around the game's minor leagues and Europe for seven years. Scott's first agent as an aspiring basketball pro was none other than David Falk, and after his playing days ended he worked as an aide to former Falk associate David Schwartzman. Scott coached in the minor-league USBL, but a couple of chances for an NBA assistant coaching job didn't pan out. Finally, he became a certified play-er agent himself, representing a small stable of baseball, basketball and football players out of an office in Philadelphia. He was feeling restless and uncertain about the future when he met Carter briefly at the 2000 All-Star game. The two chatted amicably, Carter taking an instant like to Scott's low-key, low-wattage persona, and although nothing came of it, a seed was planted in Scott's head. After Black and Carter split up, Scott approached the player through a mutual friend — Butch Carter — who set up a meeting.

Nearly a year after that meeting, the connection between Scott and former coach Butch Carter scares the heck out of the Raptors. But there is nothing they can do about it. When Scott was a counsellor at Five-Star Basketball Camp more than two decades ago, he met Carter's brothers John and Cris, and eventually their older brother, Butch, came into the picture. When Scott was drafted by the Knicks, it was Butch Carter who was there to give him advice. Now, Butch Carter retained some influence in the Vince Carter camp, being close to Scott and Michelle, and some in the Raptors camp were worried about how much influence.

Scott acknowledged the perception of a possible conflict and admitted that Vince Carter was upset by the firing of the coach, but as for any residual effects on the player's future in Toronto, he didn't see any. (Butch Carter declined a request for an interview.)

"I have my job here to do, and that's a relationship that's outside of this business," said Scott. "There's no conflict and no effect. But what is true is we have to be careful about how it is perceived."

Butch Carter's dismissal did affect Vince. Scott added, "They were close. But I think Vince understands what happened. It's kind of like breaking up with an old girlfriend. You have to be careful."

Scott's pitch to represent Vince Carter had a unique twist: He would be the point man and would bring in the International Management Group (IMG), the Cleveland-based agency that Mark McCormack began in the mid-1960s to handle golfer Arnold Palmer's business interests. IMG had since grown into an international colossus, with 62 offices in 21 countries servicing hundreds of top-drawer athletes, as well as managing events and brokering television deals, among them the Olympic Games.

"I think what appealed to them was the trust they had in me, and the reputation of IMG," said Scott. "They were very guarded because of what had happened with Tank. IMG's track record was important."

Mark Steinberg, the IMG lawyer who represents golfer Tiger Woods, now had Carter on his list, making him one of the most powerful behind-the-scenes figures in all of sports. The company hired Scott to come to Toronto and manage Carter's day-to-day business. Just like that, Carter had gone from the maverick Tank Black to a conglomerate, from the only NBA horse in one dirty and discredited stable to one star among many. And Scott had been elevated from no-name to big time.

IMG's first order of business was to clean up the shoe mess. Scrambling to get something done before the Olympics, Carter was left to practise and play exhibition games in Hawaii in shoes that had the logos covered over with tape — part of the court order out of the Puma case prevented him from showing any visible product tags on his uniform. In Hawaii, dazzling his teammates and the crowd, about the only thing anonymous about Carter were those shoes on his feet.

Make no mistake. There are other ways of making money, and for a player at Carter's level of popularity the possibilities are limitless. Among the rejected requests for consideration have been rubber bands, shoelaces and medical equipment. But it is the shoe business that is still big business, part of the $50-billion sporting goods business. Even McGrady's departure from Toronto was predicated to some extent on it, or at least on the notion that in Canada only so many endorsement opportunities exist and it is Carter whose star will shine brightest as long as he is here. With Carter around, McGrady's value to Adidas as one of their main faces was lessened. In Orlando, McGrady would be repackaged as one of the company's fresh young faces, with his own shoe and his own television commercial. Pitching shoes or soda or sports drinks has become part of the lifestyle, but also something more sinister. Shoe companies have their tentacles so deep in AAU basketball and some high-school and college programs that the entire balance of power at the game's grassroots has shifted. Such arrangements were expressed perhaps most aptly by Alonzo Mourning, with his infamous sign-of-the-times clarification after being taken second over-all by the Charlotte Hornets in the '92 draft: "I work for Nike."

Or there was the case of Chauncey Billups. When he was traded to Toronto in February of 1998, his agent, Eric Fleisher, immediately asked the Raptors to make up the amount he said Billups was losing out on with the move from Boston to Toronto — as much as $3 million, given his failure to hit a contractual target for appearances in major U.S. markets. Grunwald said no. The disagreement would have wider implications beyond Billups, who was traded before the following season began. Fleisher would clash again with Grunwald over the status of another of his clients, John Wallace, and Wallace eventually took less money than the Raptors were offering to sign with the New York Knicks in the summer of 1999.

The shoe business and the endorsement game is nowhere near the bonanza it once was for NBA players, however. Nike cut its budget in

1998, just as Carter was coming out of North Carolina. Its closest rival, Reebok, trimmed its roster of NBA endorsers at about the same time, including their cornerstone Shaquille O'Neal's $5-million annual deal. Players who once were promoted with gusto, with entire personas created for them — think of Larry Johnson's Grandmama character, Grant Hill as the anti-rebel and L'il Penny — were seeing no returns, or even losing their contracts by decade's end. The NBA was no longer a hot property.

"I'm hearing corporate sponsors don't want to have a relationship with the league because of the perception of what the league is or is getting to," said Hill, whose deal with Fila flopped, and so much for the "Change the Game" catchphrase that went with it. "The NBA does not have the pick of the litter any more, and people are backing out of their sponsorships."

Carter was trying to buck the trend, and he had a better chance than just about anyone in the league. The Nike shoe contract that followed the Puma breach amounted to nearly $30 million over six years, the product of feverish round-the-clock work that continued up until the day before Carter marched into Sydney's Olympic Stadium. He wouldn't get a chance to personally meet with Nike officials until a month into the NBA season, and that was a mere whirlwind three-hour visit to the company's Beaverton, Oregon, headquarters the day after the Raptors were in Portland to meet the Trail Blazers. True, more than half of the deal was used to pay off the judgment against him. But the $12 million or so left over amounted to large money in this shrunken economy. It was also large exposure. Shortly after Carter returned from Sydney, there were a couple of commercials to shoot in Toronto with his Olympic teammate Gary Payton. Nike was featuring Carter's live-wire act at the top of an $18-million ad campaign to promote its new Shox shoes, but the company wasn't taking any chances. Carter's role in the ads was limited to just being himself and reprising that signature dunk from the Games — vaulting over Payton to dunk.

So where was the attraction? In his second season, there was not just the slam-dunk title, the Raptors' first playoff berth and all that highlight-reel footage. There was the clean-cut image. If "Keeping It Real" meant tattoos and piercings and foul-mouthed hip-hop lyrics to the likes of Allen Iverson, it was quite another thing to Carter. Like Jordan with cable television, too, Carter was coming in at the top of the Internet wave. Within 24 hours of his slam-dunk championship, the league's NBA.com Web site registered one million downloads of his winning slam.

There were other tangible signs of public affection to indicate something extra was at work. An NBA.com poll had Carter edging Kobe Bryant as the people's choice as the player who will have the most impact on the league over the next decade. *ESPN* magazine picked him as their "Next" coverboy going into the year 2000, the cooing prose almost oozing off the page ("he's someone we just can't take our eyes off," wrote editor John Papanek). He was the league's leading vote-getter for the all-star game in just his second season. He outpolled O'Neal, Bryant, Grant Hill, Tim Duncan — all of them more established. Only Michael Jordan had received more votes in the annual fan balloting than Carter received in 1999–2000.

The 2000–01 season saw the same result: Carter was the leading vote-getter, Vinsanity showing only the slightest signs of cooling off. His no. 15 Raptors jersey started the season as the league's no. 1 seller, moving ahead of Bryant, Iverson, Jason Williams and Kevin Garnett in that parade after his slam-dunk win.

In Canada, Carter quickly emerged as the country's most popular pro sports import. In a poll of English Canadian males, he was second only to retired hockey icon Wayne Gretzky. Among the young, he was easily the no. 1 choice. And in Toronto, no one came close to him, Carter the first mention of 19 per cent of respondents, Gretzky at 8 per cent. He goosed Canadian television ratings 30 per cent, and again by the same amount in his second year. But alas, he was no miracle worker, and there remained room for improvement: On a prime-time Saturday night in February 2000, Carter's slam-dunk win pulled in some 800,000 viewers, a very good figure but still second to venerable *Hockey Night in Canada*.

It was upon the general health of the Raptors that Vinsanity would cast its most enchanting spell. In golf, marketers talk of the "Tiger effect," the estimated increase in TV audience (104 per cent, according to one estimate) when Tiger Woods is in contention. Carter did the same thing to Canadian TV ratings and Raptors attendance. In its debut year, the franchise had averaged a healthy 23,169 at the SkyDome. But then the season-ticket base dwindled alarmingly, from 17,000 to just over 5,000 the year Carter arrived in Toronto. That number had nearly doubled by his third season, and the Raptors were at no. 4 in the league attendance table at Christmas 2000, their average home count up nearly 4 per cent to buck a league-wide trend of slightly declining numbers, their season-ticket count just over 11,000. On the road, the Raptors were among the top five draws in the league.

As for TV, before Vince Carter's arrival Raptors numbers plumbed the depths, at a microscopic 17,000 per regional broadcast. For the first month of this season, Sportsnet had averaged six times that much — until Carter was hurt and had to sit out three games, knocking out one-third of the audience. Nationally, Carter had turned the NBA into a commodity that finally had some value, in stark contrast to the team's inaugural year, when cable sports network TSN terminated a 10-year relationship broadcasting games because the league insisted on a rights fee increase and control over sponsors.

It was Carter, and no one else, who had brought the Raptors their first sustained success, whether it was measured in T-shirts, at the box office or in TV ratings. This was a case of a player, a personality, carrying a business. Vince Carter had conquered Canada for the NBA.

"I don't know where we'd be without Vince Carter, and I'm sure glad we never went there," shuddered Glen Grunwald. "It would be different, very different."

But in this world, perhaps some things will always remain the same. More than two years removed from taking his last shot as an NBA player, Jordan the icon is still unassailable, and his flame is still being kept lit. When the *Chicago Tribune*'s Sam Smith came out with a scathing column comparing the two and (surprise) favouring the former Bull — "Raptors' Carter Lacks the Class to Carry NBA's Torch," read the headline — Carter shook his head.

"I know I'm not [Jordan]," he said. "I know I'm not even close to him. Regardless of what people say, I'm in my third year and playing in a different era. We played at North Carolina, but to me we play different games. It's tough, because sometimes people praise you as the next Michael Jordan, and the next day, people want to knock you down.

"I never said I was like him."

Others have. When the TNT cable network in the U.S. aired its promotional ads for the 2000 playoffs, the banner was right there in living colour, rolling by underneath the ubiquitous footage of another Carter dunk: "The Next Jordan."

The director stands in front of Carter now, a craggy-faced, under-nourished-looking fellow wearing a turtleneck sweater and carrying an aura of jaunty competence. "I want you to look like you've just run a million miles," he says, slumping his shoulders and exhaling as if gulping his last breath on earth.

Carter nods from under the apparatus. Of course he understands. There is just the hint of an ironic smile on his face, detectable even with the breathing tube. He seems to appreciate this man who doesn't fawn over him, who is all business, who knows so little about him that his first question when they met is not about Michael Jordan or last night's game but instead a simple and innocent "Do you live here in Toronto?" And a man who doesn't really know that, in his mind, Vince Carter has run miles — maybe not a million, but close to that and with more to come, carrying the weight of great expectations and overheated hype around with him every step of the way.

Carter looks up to the balcony overlooking the converted gym, a get-me-out-of-here look directed toward Merle Scott, who smiles back and holds up his wristwatch. It's almost over. Over the next five years, this sort of work will earn Carter $37 million. Leaving early is not part of the drill.

"I try not to be anyone other than myself," Carter says. "I don't think I'd be good at that. If I was giving a speech, say, and then had to watch it later, I'd hate to sit there and be thinking about how corny it is. I don't want to do that on the court or in person. I feel like I'm a decent guy. I think my family has taught me well. I don't think I've ever needed to pretend I'm someone I'm not, and I don't intend on starting now.

"My attitude about this stuff has changed since the whole Tank Black thing. It's just a better general awareness. I know a little bit more now about who to talk to, what questions have to be asked and what you talk about, and what an agent should do. But I still don't know much. And I still feel the potential is there — it could happen, but I so hope not.

Because that was terrible. Out of all the things that happened to me, that was maybe the toughest thing of all."

At the final take, the robotic track camera rolls in for its quick shot, and the attendant deftly passes a towel — a Gatorade towel, of course ("Great logo transfer!" one flack says) — to Carter, who is, yes, slumping and looking completely enervated, mopping himself like an athletic Olivier.

"Cut!"

The attendant reaches over and pulls the breathing tube out of his mouth. "Omigod," exhales Carter, hamming it up a little more, bearing it all patiently as the nest of wires is pulled off his torso.

It all raises the question of just who or what is driving this train that brings Carter into a Toronto rec centre under cover of daylight, needing everything but glasses and a beard to get in (the credentials hanging around everyone's neck say "Christmas Project 2000" to avoid tipping off the public to what's going on inside, but of course that's a group of shivering 12-year-olds huddled outside hoping for a glimpse of someone, anyone). Is Vince Carter a triumph of marketing over substance? Is Vince Carter more an NBA creation than the real deal? Is the hype a good thing, and is it still possible to expect marketing success as a by-product of success on the basketball court?

"I'm not saying he's not a great player, but that is what the NBA wants," sniffs Karl Malone, the Utah Jazz's elder statesman and a certain Hall of Famer when his time comes. "They've been looking for the next Michael Jordan for the last 10 years. Even when he was playing, they were looking for the next Michael. I see he's doing a Gatorade commercial right now, so I guess they found the next Michael."

Shaun Powell, writing in *Newsday*, put it even more bluntly after the Raptors were shuffled out of the 2000 playoffs: "Unless Carter actually wins something, he'll be just that: a desperate network and league's creation."

More than any of the other phantom reasons and suppositions and spec-ulations that have been tossed back and forth, the possibility of winning a title somewhere is why Carter could leave Toronto someday soon. It is Steinberg's Tiger Woods model applied to Vince Carter: until he wins a championship, the biggest paydays will elude him. If a championship is in the offing in Toronto, he will stay. And if not, if Carter deems them a big centre short of that goal, or not experienced enough, or not financially sound enough, he will leave.

"Does Nike care where he is when they sign him?" asks Scott. "Look what Gatorade did, expanding that deal to a global one. If you're at this level, they'll find you. Here in Canada, Vince has a unique opportunity to have a country as a market, not just a city."

Some already regard a move to an American-based club as a foregone conclusion, but that talk irritates Carter. Occasionally, these sentiments and business collide, as when he appeared at the opening of a Dave and Buster's arcade in Chicago, one of his half-dozen endorsements. When Carter walked in the door, the thousand or so fans on hand broke into a "Sign with the Bulls!" chant.

Until he wins a championship, there will always be something of the overrated and overblown and overhyped about Vince Carter, just as there was when Michael Jordan was learning his chops with the Chicago Bulls. It's just that, now, it all happens a lot faster.

"Jordan paid his dues one step at a time," says Carter's teammate Oakley. "He experienced a lot of things along the way, until the red car-pet was rolled out for him his fifth or sixth year. Now it's rolled out your first training camp."

Jordan himself says, "Today, the marketing of an athlete sometimes exceeds the potential of that athlete. Back then, the potential of the athlete built the marketing. Now it isn't as important."

None of this is new, nor is it news. Since Jordan blazed that trail and the NBA exploded a decade ago, the same Jordanesque model has been used and, mostly, found wanting. In the wake of Michael Jordan's retirement, NBA-licensed products declined 7 per cent. At the height of his popularity, sales of his Chicago Bulls merchandise amounted to 50 per cent of the entire league take. Since, TV ratings have gone into the dumps and paid attendance has flatlined.

Sports remains powerful at delivering an audience, but the television universe has splintered since Jordan left, and part of the reason for the attendance levelling off is all the new and bigger arenas that came online in the 1990s. But it's undoubtedly a world that desperately needs a showman, and everyone here at the rec centre seems to agree that the Carter kid might be it. No, he is not the next Jordan, doesn't want to be, but just plain Vince Carter might be able to make up for it.

"This is supposed to be natural, not something concocted or contrived," says Scott. "He's a nice guy who happens to be a good basketball player, and some of these guys he plays against are basketball players trying to be nice guys."

He jumps off the treadmill, freed of the wires now. Finally it's time to go home. Someone hands him another towel to dry himself, and soon he is going from person to person, shaking hands with everyone in the crew he can get to, thanking them for coming, thanking them for having him, making eye contact with each, laughing, smiling.

The commercial will be completed inside a computer, but Carter has not forgotten to finish the work here with a human touch. He is learning this salesman's role — slowly. It doesn't come naturally to him, even within the Raptors dressing room, where he is quiet and unassuming among his teammates.

He is working on polishing a persona away from that room, though, and learning a different kind of game. Sometimes a crowd of school-children make up the audience, gathered on the Air Canada Centre floor on any one of six postgame nights to hear Carter speak on education or growing up; or perhaps he's just reading to them, encouraging them. Sometimes it is a jock-sniffing politician or industrialist, making their way to his cubicle to shake his hand, take a picture, get an autograph — or sitting next to him at a fancy dinner, Carter asking as many questions back.

"I have so many things I'd like to do as far as business," Carter muses. "I haven't narrowed it down. I want to have a chain of businesses right next to each other and run them all.

"When it's time to move on from the game, I don't want to have to learn it then. I'm asking questions now. I'm paying attention. A restaurant, that's my next project. When I run across them, I let them know, hey, I want to do that, so keep your eyes open."

For most of this crowd schooled in television and advertising, Carter is as much product as pitchman. He has passed their test, and it has nothing to do with basketball.

"He's got that stud/rock star thing going," says one of the Gatorade crowd. "He looks like a cross between Mick Jagger and the Six-Million-Dollar Man."

Best of all, no one's comparing Carter to Jordan. No one even mentions him.

CHAPTER 6

December 2000:

Getting Younger

Kids. They don't make 'em like they used to. Precocious. Vain. Dazzling. Dim-witted. Promising. Forgettable. And, don't forget, completely irresistible.

With only a few shopping days left until Christmas, Glen Grunwald and nearly 50 others with NBA connections — from general managers and scouts on down the food chain to agents and, even lower, agents' runners — are sitting in an arena in St. Louis. This is part of their job, these nights out to watch and grade, only it's a little bit different this time. This is not a college game. It's high-school. And it's just *December,* for crying out loud. Some of the kids running up and down the floor have yet to decide whether to go to college or turn pro. Some of them may have just got over Santa Claus. And some of them have been scouted by the NBA since age 14, and by other adults since 12. And there, clustered together in a section behind the press table, are the men who will decide their future once they figure out their own, with their orange pebble-grain notebooks and their briefcases. All of this, at 18 years old.

Trying to make the leap from high school to the pros is no longer unusual. Given the success of players like Tracy McGrady and Kobe Bryant and (recently) Jermaine O'Neal, it's not even being regarded as perhaps that difficult any more. But of course it is. And even from these older gentlemen watching, there are misgivings. The GMs in attendance still murmur among themselves about just what they're doing here, at the Savvis Center, watching six-foot-eleven Eddie Curry of Illinois' Thornwood taking on Dominguez of California, defending U.S. high-school champions behind their stud, seven-foot Tyson Chandler. Both are considered surefire lottery picks for the June 2001 draft, and a third, DeSegana Diop, will come out of the evening with the same tag. As many as five high schoolers are being touted as NBA draft material in June of 2001.

Few if any of these GMs felt particularly good about it. They grew up in a different era, when a scholarship at a U.S. university meant four years out of your life, perhaps a college degree, and maybe then a shot (usually a long shot) at the NBA. Many of them, like Grunwald, were part of the same generation that produced Moses Malone and Bill Willoughby, two prodigies who entered the league straight out of high school a quarter of a century ago. They hardly started a trend, though, their moves dictated as much by the NBA's battle with the upstart ABA and the players' own dire financial straits — hence the term "hardship cases" that was applied to the likes of Malone and Willoughby. It was only in the 1990s, when NBA rookie contracts reached into the stratosphere while the talent pool was spread thinner, that the youngsters started looking at the league and the league started looking back. Kevin Garnett's entry in 1995 marked the first time a high schooler had come right in since Shawn Kemp, who in 1991 had been the first to make the jump since Darryl Dawkins in 1975. From that trickle has come a steady flow.

"I still think there's a feeling among us [GM's] that it's inappropriate," says Grunwald. "But given that the talent pool is getting younger and that some of these guys might be draftable players, this is the way the industry has gone. This is where we have to be."

The untold story revolves around the numbers you rarely hear about, the ones that seem to support the contention that even if these youngsters aren't quite ready, they will be, and soon. They have beat 50,000-to-1 odds that a high-school player will get to the NBA at all, let alone make that jump in one enormous swoop. They are bypassing a U.S. college system that delivers less than a 50 per cent graduation rate among basketball players. The NCAA's latest basketball television deal starting in 2003 cost CBS $6.2 billion to acquire, and none of that money is going back to the players — sorry, the student-athletes — who provide the show or sell the merchandise. Much as commissioner David Stern would like to institute an age limit of 20 years, the NBA can do nothing legally to stem the flow, but plans continue for a developmental league beginning in 2001.

Get to the first round and it means guaranteed money for five years. Eighteen of the 29 first-round choices in the June 2000 NBA draft were underclassmen or high schoolers, out of a record 56 early entrants. It is no longer a question of coming out or not coming out. It is simply a question of when.

"The big gamble usually backfires," says Atlanta Hawks general manager Pete Babcock. "For every Kobe Bryant and Kevin Garnett, there are many, many more who just aren't ready. That goes for the players who come out of college so early too. I think the more very young players declare, the more we're going to see them coming away from the draft disappointed."

But still, the dream is there, and it is a powerful one. The story of the last decade in the NBA has been one of expansion — from number of teams, to scouting, to global reach and money. And this trend toward youth comes as no surprise. With 29 team rosters to fill at 15 bodies per (including those three injury spots that are often nothing more than a place to stash an extra), that means 435 jobs, or nearly double the figure from two decades ago. No surprise, then, that the search for talent is exhaustive. The NBA has gone global, and it has also gone younger — much younger. In that same June 2000 draft, Darius Miles was the third player taken, the highest a high schooler had ever gone, and at the beginning of the 2000–01 season, 10 NBA players had come straight from the preps. According to this group in attendance at the Savvis Center, four more high schoolers may be NBA lottery picks in June.

The players they are watching exist merely as projections. Curry can dunk, but that 295-pound body is worrisome. Chandler is strong, but how strong — look at how slender he is. And where did this kid Diop come from? At the best of times, none of this is science. Throw in 18-year-olds, even 20-year-olds off two years of college, and it becomes a guessing game.

Meantime, as the NBA gets younger, these same scouts say that skills have eroded, that a generation weaned on highlight-reel dunks doesn't have the interest or the inclination to learn the right way to play the game. There is no doubt, watching the NBA, that the mid-range jump shot that the likes of Charles Oakley and Horace Grant and others have used so well is something of a lost art. Shooting has in general declined, but it hasn't happened overnight. Shooting percentages, both from the field and at the line, have declined steadily since the mid-1980s. Hand in hand has been a decrease in scoring — in the 1984–85 season, all 23 teams averaged more than 100 points. In 2000–01, only one of 29 teams is over 100 a night — and it has become a nearly annual exercise to debate rule changes to open up the game. Or to complain about the kids and the effect they have had on the pro game.

"These guys, some of them, have been coddled for so long," says Grunwald, who was a McDonald's High School all-star himself, but in his decade of the 1970s it was a far different, far less complicated era. "They play in so many all-star games, where it's just go out and do your thing. There's very little basketball involved. No wonder their fundamentals are bad."

But wait before you sound an alarm. Defences have become much more systematic and physical, and scouting reports are much more detailed nowadays (satellite television systems get just about every game, making it possible to see your opponent's every move and stratagem). Most of all, talent is spread so much thinner in this watered-down era. Still, the declines are often put at the feet of a league grown fat and — you guessed it — young. Too young.

And now, with the signs out there that the NBA is struggling, its attendance down, its star power lacking, it's enough to make some grown men cringe. On his thirty-seventh birthday, Charles Oakley sounds like some kind of Jeremiah of the hardwood. Oakley is an old-school kind of guy with an honour code that his rhetoric sometimes runs up against. But when he looks around the dressing rooms of the NBA, all he sees are nursery schools.

"The league is garbage ... To me, you've got two or three good guys on a team. After that, it's like high school. It's that bad. It's nothing but hype, and hype is like a kite. It goes up. It comes down."

This is standard Oakspeak, as his stream-of-consciousness rambles have come to be known. But he is one of the few still-active pros who can remember the leaner times, and while Grunwald is off scouting kids barely advanced from puberty but already dreaming of cars and women and that first contract, Oakley was not the only one sending out this blunt message. In Utah, Karl Malone was preaching the same sermon with slightly different words. Frankly, they sounded like nothing more than cranky old men. It sometimes seems as if this sort of curmudgeoning is part of the NBA landscape, having been around when Magic Johnson came to Los Angeles, when Julius Erving was departing the scene and in the mid-1990s when Jordan retired and the game looked like moshing. But their message was part of a growing debate. This December, it was not at all a difficult task finding examples of players who didn't seem to care or coaches who were having trouble getting their messages across.

In Denver, the Nuggets grew tired of head coach Dan Issel's ranting and raving. Led by second-year forward James Posey, they boycotted a practice Issel called for the morning after a late-night flight home following an overtime loss. "It was the first thing they've done together as a team all season long," snorted Issel, who reacted promptly. He loosened the reins and, wouldn't you know it, saw his team's fortunes improve.

Fresh off their first NBA championship together, Bryant and Shaquille O'Neal were feuding over who was more important in the Lakers' grand scheme. Never mind that the Lakers had won their title going through O'Neal, even if he couldn't make a free throw. Bryant wanted top billing now, and the story became the soap opera of the early season — and more fuel for the NBA-is-going-to-hell-in-a-handbasket crowd. In Toronto for the Lakers' annual game with the Raptors, O'Neal said he was getting tired of it and could see himself retiring in three years or so — this from a 28-year-old who had just signed an $87-million contract extension over the summer.

And no discussion of NBA dysfunction could be complete without the Washington Wizards, with whom Jordan now served as an executive and part owner. Tyrone Nesby cussed out his coach, Leonard Hamilton, then refused to leave for the dressing room when Hamilton tried to discipline him. Rod Strickland missed (another) practice and was pulled over and charged with (another) drunk-driving violation.

Then there were the owners, who tend to be forgotten when this kind of state-of-the-union hand-wringing and finger-pointing starts. Dallas's Mark Cuban's repeated outbursts about refereeing brought him a $250,000 fine from the league in early January. The Orlando Magic and the Charlotte Hornets were playing the old game of pushing their communities to build them a new arena while threatening to move out of town.

But no one was hurting worse than the Minnesota Timberwolves front office, hit with an unprecedented penalty from commissioner David Stern for evading the salary cap and signing Joe Smith to a secret deal. Stern fined the Wolves $3.5 million, stripped them of five future first-round draft picks and voided all of Smith's contracts with Minnesota. Owner Glenn Taylor was banned from watching his team for a year, and GM Kevin McHale took a year off.

The league sometimes failed these youngsters completely, too, as in the case of Leon Smith, drafted at 19 years old by the Dallas Mavericks — and abandoned by them after he attempted suicide. In Toronto, McGrady was virtually left to fend for himself his first year with the Raptors; that he would turn into a fine pro said more about him than any support system the team or the league had put in place.

It was as if the NBA's excesses had abscessed, and perhaps the most nauseating aspect were the denials and cover-ups and lame apologies that count for mea culpas in this upside-down world. Nesby, for instance, was said to have a "thumb injury" to explain away his departure from the bench area after going into his profane rant. The Nuggets went on their merry way after their boycott. The Knicks complained of harsh justice when Marcus Camby was given a five-game suspension for taking a run at opponent Danny Ferry, and the Raptors bitched when Oakley was given a three-game suspension for taking a punch at an opponent during a morning shootaround.

Malone and Oakley, two Jordan contemporaries, pointed the finger of blame at the youngsters. "It's all attitude," said Oakley. "Some guys just don't care. Some guys on this team don't care. The knowledge for the game just isn't there. Me and Karl, we're just two old warriors. You see a house burning, you call 911. We see the league burning, we're putting up a flag."

Malone, like Oakley a fellow who has sung this tune before, nevertheless sounded more disenchanted than ever in his bleak assessment. "Dr. [James] Naismith right now is probably turning over in his grave, seeing some of the stuff going on," Malone told Mike Wise of the *New York Times*. "And commissioner David Stern? It has to be a nightmare for him. Some of this could have been avoided, without any doubt. For the last eight, nine all-star games, it's been out with the old, in with the new. That's been the marketing theme. And I'm saying: 'Whoa, I'm still a big part of the Jazz.' But that's not what people want, I guess."

The irony was that for players like Oakley and Malone, sliding on the downside of their thirties, there was still a job for them if they wanted it, and the riches and glamour that went with it. "I'm still playing 35 minutes a night," said Oakley, who at $5.75 million is the Raptors' highest-paid player. "I'm 37 years old. Imagine that. The talent level is that bad."

Or look at Mario Elie. Elie won a championship in San Antonio in 1999, to go with two more earned while with the Houston Rockets in 1995 and '96. A modestly talented player, Elie has bounced around from the minor-league CBA to obscure basketball posts around the world (Argentina, Ireland, Portugal) before finally getting a full-time NBA job in 1991. A career nine-point-a-night player, he has held on tenaciously, landing in Phoenix this season. As the Raptors and the Suns were finishing up their encounter at the Air Canada Centre, that was Elie hooking Vince Carter with his right elbow and spinning the young superstar away from snaring a key late-game rebound.

"Veteran move," Elie explained to Carter as they lined up side by side waiting for a free throw.

Carter laughed. "I'll know next time."

Elie likes Carter. But he also shakes his head and admits, yes, of course, there is something of a generation gap in this NBA. "He's a great kid — a lot of these guys are coming into the league with an attitude, a chip on their shoulder, but he doesn't. Garnett is the same way. They seem to enjoy what they're doing.

"But now, you've got other guys who are so talented, but everything has been handed to them. There's no working on the fundamentals of the game any more. Every year I come in and I think it's going to be my last, but hey — that's why a lot of us veteran guys are still around. We know the fundamentals. Sometimes I think the fundamentals are a lost art."

On another night, the Raptors and the Jazz between them have seven players with more than a thousand games played. And the product stinks, at once putting the lie to Oakley's notion that the kids are to blame. The Jazz's flatfooted, going-through-the-motions approach is as aggravating for the customers to watch as it is for coach Jerry Sloan's stomach to endure.

Buried within it, though, is one of these fresh-out-of-school kids struggling to find his way. DeShawn Stevenson is 19. The year before he was averaging a triple double at Washington Union High School in Fresno, California. Now he's on the floor checking Vince Carter, giving away an inch and 15 pounds and five years of college and professional experience. He tries. Oh yes, he tries.

Carter jab-steps and spins, then hits a fallaway as Stevenson hasn't yet recovered from biting on the first move. Next time, it's another fallaway dropping over him. Then a spin move and Carter is going baseline. It's some education for Stevenson, who in a different era would be learning his chops as a freshman at some university. Instead he's here, ready or not. And apparently not.

"When he's on with that fallaway, what can you do?" says Stevenson. "It's like you're jumping as high as you can and he's jumping as high as he can, but he's got that separation.

"I thought I did a good job. I thought I played hard. Him and Stack [Jerry Stackhouse], they're the toughest guys I've ever checked. What else can I do but play hard? And never show fear. I can't show any fear. If I do, they'll just think — high-school kid. No fear."

In the opposite corner, Karl Malone barks. Stevenson looks up a touch nervously, then relaxes and smiles, even chuckles a little bit to himself. It is as if Malone is a lion in a cage — harmless, for now. "That's Karl. He's like that all the time." He smiles.

Malone is 37. Stevenson is 19. Managing the generation gap in the locker rooms of today's NBA is as difficult as managing egos.

Carter drives to the hoop during his junior year as a North Carolina Tar Heel, three months before he committed to the NBA draft. Carter's high-wire act inspired comparisons to Michael Jordan before he even arrived on campus. (AP: Alan Mothner)

Vinsanity in full flight, Carter finger-rolling artfully during a February 2000 game at the Air Canada Centre against the Chicago Bulls. (CP: Kevin Frayer)

Charles Oakley arrived in Toronto when Vince Carter did. He immediately assumed the same role of protector/enforcer he had over a decade earlier with Michael Jordan. Here, he steps in after a confrontation between Carter and Vancouver's Shareef Abdur-Rahim. (CP: Chuck Stoody)

Carter and Tracy McGrady share a laugh during the 2000 playoffs. After McGrady left Toronto for the Orlando Magic, the cousins' relationship soured. (CP: Kevin Frayer)

Two weeks after winning the 2000 slam-dunk competition, Carter feels the moment during an NBA season-high 51 points in front of a national network TV audience.
(CP: Kevin Frayer)

Carter had a strong relationship with Butch Carter. But it wasn't enough to save the head coach's job in the fall-out of the 1999–2000 season.
(AP: Kathy Willens)

The dunk heard round the world, as Carter vaults over 7-foot-3 France centre Frederic Weis at the 2000 Olympics in Sydney. Jason Kidd called it "probably the greatest play in basketball I've ever seen." (Reuters: Gary Cameron)

McGrady, with the Magic, is fouled by Carter during their first meeting as opponents, in Orlando. (AP: Tony Ranze)

Carter and Kobe Bryant were once AAU teammates, but by February of 2001 they played opposite each other at the NBA All-Star Game. (AP: Nick Wass)

Carter gets blanket coverage from a 76ers triple team of Jumaine Jones, Eric Snow and Dikembe Mutombo (upper right) during their 2001 playoff series. (AP: staff)

Latrell Sprewell has long been one of Carter's favourite players. In the spring of 2001 Carter's Raptors ousted Sprewell and the Knicks in a taut five-game series for their first playoff win. (Carlo Allegri, National Post)

Carter and his mother, Michelle, his closest confidante. Michelle's spirited defence of her son in the wake of Charles Oakley's challenge had Oakley shaking his head.
(Carlo Allegri, National Post)

Carter waves to his mother as he enters Kenan Stadium with former North Carolina teammate Max Owens before his graduation ceremony in Chapel Hill, the morning of Game 7 against the 76ers in Philadelphia. (AP: Grant Halverson)

Carter drives past Jumaine Jones during Game 7 of the eastern conference semi-finals. (AP: Rusty Kennedy)

Toronto Raptors GM Glen Grunwald (left) and coach Lenny Wilkens field questions at an end-of-season news conference in Toronto on May 22, 2001. (CP: Frank Gunn)

Perhaps some of this was going through Grunwald's head as he sat in St. Louis watching a high-school game. He had an old team. He had a team that had been swept out of the playoffs last season by a combined 12 points. Perhaps he had kidded himself that more maturity and veteran savvy could overcome that. So why did he feel so uneasy? It had started with the pre-season, and was only partly eased by the variety of excuses on offer: injuries to the likes of Dell Curry and Muggsy Bogues, and the inevitable (and lame) idea that it would take some time for this new group to get to know each other.

Grunwald always felt some nerves, but usually they were well disguised. For the most part, they would peak not on draft day in June, or during the fretful courtship of free agents in July and August. It was that run-up to opening night, and especially that whole first day itself, that got to him in the gut. "You put it all out there — and what if it goes terribly wrong?" he once asked. "I'm always asking myself that on opening day."

But this was different. This was not exactly fitting the way he wanted it to fit, or thought it would fit.

"I thought it would get better. I kept waiting for it to get better," he said. "It wasn't."

At the very soul of the NBA is a contradiction. It is a "player's league," more oriented to its performers than any other professional sports business. The nature of the game, with its individualism, its tight court, its teams of just five a side and the lack of equipment — wearing just singlet, shorts and shoes, basketball players are the most exposed of mercenaries, with just one ball to share — lends itself to that. The notion that one player can make or break a franchise reinforces that.

And here was the proof, two times over: Grunwald's 2000–01 Raptors, which had never recovered from the departures of Tracy McGrady and

Doug Christie. McGrady was let go for next to nothing. Grunwald had been burned, and he knew it. That was hard enough to take. Next to that, the Christie trade was given little attention, but it was nearly as important. Christie was perhaps the most underrated of Raptors and qualified as one of the team's genuine success stories, and one of the few that bridged the chasm between the Isiah Thomas tenure and Grunwald's time in charge.

Christie had been a quiet professional in the locker room, keeping mostly to himself. Before games, he would read at his cubicle — Deepak Chopra was one of his favourites. He would then retreat to the players' lounge or, if on the road, a quiet side room, where he'd bounce a basketball vigorously, dribbling it low between his legs and behind his back while listening to Kenny G on his portable CD player.

It was out of the locker room, and usually out of the season, that Christie could be a headache. He had asked to be traded two times before, but each time the Raptors managed to soothe him, his wife, Jackie, and whoever his agent of the day was. When Grunwald finally decided to take him up on it, though, it was about much more than just a trade request. "It was money, as usual," Grunwald says.

"It was the wife," grumbles Charles Oakley. "How can you trade a guy because of his wife?"

Jackie Christie had much input, her husband relying heavily on her for advice and support. But the roots of Christie's trade go way back to the time when Damon Stoudamire was dealt out of Toronto, the unofficial low-water mark of the franchise's post–Isiah Thomas period. Christie called a press conference at the SkyDome to announce he wanted to be next out of town. Then he called it off. Then it was on again, but almost as soon as the words came out of his mouth, team management shot him down. Not only would Christie not be traded but he was pilloried in the media for his stunt. He fired his long-time agent Brad Marshall, and Dwight Manley took over. Manley and Grunwald would spar, and in the summer of '99 Christie was all but ticketed for the Utah Jazz after another trade demand, until that club backed out of a deal. The way Grunwald tells it, he and Manley came to the understanding that Christie could stay or go when his contract called for it, no questions asked.

Grunwald explained, "The original plan with [Dwight Manley] was to let Doug make the call after the [2000–01] season when he had an out and presumably we'd be coming off a good season and his value would be higher with us being better."

With Marshall back in the picture replacing Manley by the summer of 2000, all bets were off. Christie was still fuming about Butch Carter, but once Lenny Wilkens had replaced Carter as head coach, it was still possible he would remain. For a price. Within a couple of days of McGrady announcing that summer that he was going to sign with Orlando, Marshall called Grunwald asking for McGrady's phone number.

"He said that it'd be a good idea that Doug could call Tracy and plead with him to come back to Toronto," Grunwald recalled. "I'm thinking, Does this guy think I'm born yesterday? I told him, 'Well, you know, Brad, I think Tracy's just said he's going to Orlando and I don't think he's coming back here.' But I gave him the number. What the heck."

A few days later, Marshall called Grunwald again.

Grunwald recalled the conversation with a bemused sort of bitterness. Marshall told him, "Well, Doug tried to talk to him, but I think Tracy's going to sign with Orlando."

"Yes, I knew that," said Grunwald.

Now came Marshall's pitch. With McGrady gone, it was time to reward Christie for his loyalty to the Raptors, he said. "You could take care of the guys who want to be in Toronto," Grunwald recalled Marshall saying. It was not an unreasonable request on the surface, because the Raptors did have money available now that McGrady was gone. But to Grunwald, it felt like a calculated shakedown.

"Well, I have to do what's best for the franchise, and look for the team's future, and we just lost a very important player for our future," Grunwald replied.

And from there, it all fell apart. "He didn't like that, and it just deteriorated from there to the point where we're swearing at each other on the phone. Next thing I know he's on the radio bad-mouthing us up and down."

Grunwald and the Sacramento Kings hooked up shortly thereafter. Corliss Williamson was available and would fit right in at the small forward position vacated by McGrady. It would also mean Vince Carter could play his natural shooting guard position. With McGrady gone, keeping Carter happy was now Grunwald's priority, and Carter did want to move back to that spot. Grunwald made the deal.

Christie departed with some bitterness. He claimed that the Raptors promised him the extension. It is the sort of he-said, he-said acrimony that is the norm for the NBA, a league of huge egos and salaries and equally large senses of entitlement and grievance that transcend money. "It was time to pay," Christie said. "When money becomes involved, people show their true colours. There were promises made, and they were supposed to pay up. They didn't.

"It's a young organization that makes young mistakes. That's understandable, that is the same for any organization in the same position. It looks to me like they're still in that mode, of trying to find an identity."

In Toronto, Williamson was supposed to give the Raptors a post-up presence, but he craved an up-tempo pace. In the Raptors scheme, all he did was clog up the offence. The coaches were disappointed at his work ethic. Antonio Davis played a similar role in the post, but Davis could provide something extra, rebounding and blocking shots and playing centre, not his natural position. Davis worked hard as well. Williamson had no outside shot and didn't rebound much. He was the classic undersized back-to-the-basket forward. Defensively, Williamson was half a step slow, which aggravated the Raptors' poor team defence. The Big Nasty, as he was known, was more like a Little Gently most nights.

Christie, meantime, had gone to the Kings and given them the kind of perimeter defence the Raptors were so sorely missing. Sacramento, formerly a scoring machine but among the league's weakest defensive sides, were suddenly making stops and leading the league. Doug Christie for Corliss Williamson was being called the biggest mismatch of the off-season, and Grunwald was on the short end of that equation.

"I was glad to get out of there," said Christie. "Glad to get away from Butch — more than anything, the things he did to divide and conquer the team [bothered me]. He would tell lies, pit one guy against the other. I talked to Lenny in the off-season after he took over. Then he didn't call again."

Like everything else that summer, it had flowed out of the McGrady debacle. Like everything else that summer, nothing seemed to work.

Grunwald had wined and dined Maurice Taylor, a scoring forward with the L.A. Clippers, even getting Taylor to verbally agree to come to Toronto with a three-year, $18-million package. But then Taylor was saying no deal, and around the league, GMs nodded their heads and said two words: David Falk. The superagent hadn't been so super lately and needed to get Taylor something more than that in terms of money to prop up his reputation. Soon, Taylor was a Houston Rocket — for one year, at $2.25 million. Strange world, this NBA.

Cuttino Mobley, Carter's good buddy and an eight-ball enthusiast, was another tough woo. The Raptors offered him $30 million over five years. They even went out and had a snazzy billiard cue custom made as the deal-clinching token for the player. Instead, Mobley was signing back with Houston for $1 million more than the Raptors offered. The pool cue? It was shopped around the Raptors office, a souvenir of the one that got away.

"It came down to one day of decision, and that was a long day for me," Mobley said. "The opportunity to play with Vince was very serious. It was something I thought a lot about. It was close, about as close as it could be, but I was comfortable in Houston with Steve Francis."

They struck out on Rashard Lewis, who took less money to stay in Seattle. They came up short with Austin Croshere, who took the Pacers' seven-year offer over the Raptors' six-year, Toronto offering a little more in the total package.

Instead, there was 35-year-old Mark Jackson and 26-year-old Williamson. Jackson was a canny floor leader with wonderful court vision. He provided a strong hand and strong leadership. But without a strong defensive cast around him — and especially a big centre to fill the lane against quick, penetrating guards that had blown by Jackson — he could be woefully exposed.

Old? Yes, the Raptors were that. But as far as Grunwald was concerned it was a case of guilty as charged with mitigating circumstances. He had tried. Now he was going with plan B in Jackson and Williamson. And holding his breath. The team he put out on the floor to start the 2000–01 season was hardly the running and gunning outfit it had been capable of being a year earlier. Losing McGrady and Christie, and replacing them with Williamson and Jackson, was like pouring quicksand on a racetrack.

As December turned into January, just getting to the playoffs looked problematic, and that had been something that was regarded as a certainty in the weaker eastern conference. Lenny Wilkens was asking Grunwald for help. Vince Carter was getting the Jordan treatment from opponents — constant double-teaming and banging that was forcing the ball out of his hands and wearing him down physically. Some nights Carter got the calls; other nights he didn't. Whichever way it was breaking, he let the officials know with grimaces and glares whenever he felt he was fouled. By late December, Wilkens had seen enough. He got angry, figuring the histrionics and the ref-baiting were too much. "You're wasting energy doing that stuff," he told his players. It was Wilkens's way to get on the team en masse about such matters. Rarely, if ever, did he ride players individually. Rarely did he raise his voice.

Less than a month into the season, Carter missed five games with a sore knee. It was the first time in his life he had ever sat out and missed playing time. Wilkens worried that his star wouldn't have much left to finish the season, that the rigours of his Olympic summer were catching up to him.

When he did play, Carter forced himself at times, trying to barge through the double teams and putting up ill-advised shots. It bothered his teammates, but in his defence it wasn't as if they were making shots or trying to find open space away from the ball. This was a pretty poor-shooting group overall, unable to find a consistent second scoring banana. With Dell Curry a non-factor, still recovering from an injury, there was no one to stretch opposing defences with long-range shots. Thankfully for Wilkens, Antonio Davis and Oakley were rebounding well to get the team second chances. Oakley in particular was having a superb season, on some nights seeming to pick up the entire team by the scruff of its neck and carry them through rough patches. Davis was moody, moping when he didn't get the touches of the ball he wanted, but he was giving them a solid effort rebounding and defending.

Defensively, Carter blew mostly cold. He could match up against his favourite opponent, Latrell Sprewell, and shut him down with superb coverage. But the motivation was fleeting, and it drove the coaches crazy. Good as he could play one night, he would watch disinterestedly the next as Dirk Nowitzki dribbled by him for a lay-up, or loaf getting back on defence when the calls didn't go his way. Still, Carter could dazzle offensively, relying more and more on an outside shot that was getting to be automatic and demanded respect. He beat Denver on a last-second bomb, rescuing the Raptors from another sub-par night.

Most of the time, though, he was working alone, a brilliant soloist surrounded by a group that might as well have been playing kazoos. The Raptors had one of the most exciting young players in the game, and certainly the most popular, and they were — boring. They were supposed to be more mature. They were supposed to be wiser. Instead, they played dumb.

The morning of December 1 underscored all that, saying more about these Raptors and the direction they were headed than could be said in any game. Carter was in the middle of his injury hiatus, the Raptors had lost two games in a row without him, and there was Oakley, punching the Clippers' Jeff McInnis in the head. At a morning shootaround. Over an argument involving a woman the two knew back in Charlotte.

Wilkens, as was his custom, said nothing publicly. But in Oakley's first game back following a three-game NBA suspension for the sucker punch, Wilkens took him out of the starting lineup.

The truth was, Wilkens was losing patience. For some time he had been contemplating putting rookie Morris Peterson into the lineup, and removing the lead-footed Williamson. Grunwald had long since put Williamson's name in the trade pipeline, but nothing came back the other way. By early January, he was sent to the oblivion of the bench, and Peterson's young and lively legs went into the starting lineup.

At the same time, Grunwald was talking seriously — again — with the Denver Nuggets. The two teams had kicked around scenarios for three months, with ex-Raptor Tracy Murray and Williamson prominent in their discussions. What finally transpired, though, had its roots in that Denver player revolt of December: the Nuggets had improved so much from there that they were a legitimate playoff contender in the tough western conference. But they were a young team that would need an old hand to help them. They weren't interested in Williamson. What they did want was veteran backup centre Kevin Willis to come in and help their youthful front-court pair of Antonio McDyess and Raef LaFrentz.

Grunwald was looking in the opposite direction. He wanted Murray for his outside shooting, but the most intriguing prize was 25-year-old Keon Clark, a skinny six-foot-eleven shot-blocker who wasn't getting along with Dan Issel. Clark had already been traded once in his career, the Orlando Magic dealing him to the Nuggets before he had played an NBA game. The knock on Clark going back to college days was a lackadaisical attitude and a reputation for smoking pot — he had been limited to just 10 games in his senior year at Nevada–Las Vegas in part because of a suspension for marijuana use, the overwhelming drug of choice among NBAers. For a team based in Canada, with about 30 border crossings a season, a history like Clark's was always a worry. Grunwald thought Clark worth the risk, though, and with Denver also talking about throwing in another young seven-footer in Mamadou N'Diaye, there appeared to be some upside potential.

The one sticking point was Stan Kroenke. The Nuggets owner didn't want to part with two young big men like Clark and N'Diaye. But Kroenke had more pressing concerns. With a moribund Pepsi Center arena to fill, the prospect of a playoff run and the heightened box office that went with it was too enticing to ignore. If Willis might help that now more than Clark or N'Diaye could, the deal was there. And finally, that's what Kroenke okayed — Tracy Murray, Clark and N'Diaye to Toronto in exchange for Willis and two young Raptors suspects, Alek Radojevic and Garth Joseph.

Willis had predated Oakley by a few days in the makeover of these Raptors from the chumps of the fractured 1997–98 season to a team coming off its first playoff appearance and looking to return there. He had short arms — "lobster arms," in the cruel vernacular of one scout, and Oakley would kid him constantly about having arms too short to reach into his pocket and spend money — but he was a valuable backup centre who could spot start. He had lasted 16 NBA seasons by taking care of his body and doing one move particularly well. The Raptors would miss that little jump hook of his from the left block, but they wouldn't miss its predictability. They'd miss his work ethic. They'd miss his suits. No one would miss his blown assignments on defence, Willis not being the most dependable of help defenders, or his aversion to passing out of the post.

Radojevic had been a complete bust after being taken twelfth in the 1998 draft. During the 2000 Summer League, the annual festival of scrubs in sneakers, he had distinguished himself by not winning a single jump ball. It was an almost subsonic mark, given that he was seven-foot-three. In a season and a half, he had played three minutes in a Raptors uniform. Joseph, a surprise to make the club coming out of training camp, had managed nothing but garbage time himself. He was released by the Nuggets within days of arriving.

It was a trade that Grunwald hoped would address two gaping holes in the Raptors lineup. They lacked a shot-blocker, and Clark would audition to fill that position, even if he had yet to make a sustained impression in two and a half seasons in Denver. But it wasn't as if the Raptors didn't know what he was made of. Clark had a strong workout in Toronto during his pre-draft rounds in the spring of '98. They saw something and filed it away for later.

As for Tracy Murray, he was no stranger. In Toronto's first-ever season, he had been one of Isiah Thomas's finer reclamation projects. A former UCLA star, his work ethic was questioned in the pros, along with his defensive attention. Then there was scandal, after he and a couple of Portland teammates were found with underage girls in a Salt Lake City hotel in 1994. Murray had rejuvenated his career in Toronto, the Raptors ignoring the obvious defensive deficiencies and welcoming his outside shooting. He averaged 16.6 points, showing the biggest scoring improvement of any player in the league — and in effect priced himself beyond the Raptors' ability to pay under the rules. Toronto was unable to match a $19-million offer from Washington and Murray had left, literally in tears. In the intervening years, he would drop by the Raptors offices on road trips into Toronto and wasn't shy in voicing his desire to return.

"I've never been accepted anywhere else like here," he said. "My first three years were heartbreak for me. I never thought I was going to get the opportunity. This was different for me, after being drop-kicked out of two other places."

Now he was back. Whether his shot was what it once was, was another question entirely. Still, around the NBA, the deal was regarded as a winner for Toronto, for the simple reason that young big men were hard to find, and here the Raptors were picking up two of them.

It hadn't exactly turned out as planned, but Grunwald had finally got what he so desperately wanted: a shot of youthful brio. And he didn't have to go to a high-school game to find it.

CHAPTER 7

January 2001:

Escape to Florida

Charles Oakley sauntered below the empty stands of Orlando's TD Waterhouse Arena, noting with a slight shake of his head and a wry smile the small knot of media hanging on Vince Carter's every word.

"Y'all tryin' to do this up into Ali–Frazier IV!" he hollered.

Later that night, Oakley was looking up at the same stands, just about every seat filled now — a rare ray of sunshine for the Magic's owners, given a season where heightened expectations had been offset by declining attendance. They were enthralled, this crowd of 16,131, watching the Raptors against the hometown Orlando Magic.

At least, that's what it said on the tickets. As far as nearly everyone in the house was concerned, it was effectively Vince Carter against Tracy McGrady. And yes, at times it did look like Ali vs. Frazier — an elbow to the kidney here, a slap to the chops there, and plenty of obligatory woofing and yakking — when it didn't look like Laurel and Hardy, that is, given the errant shots and trying-too-hard-for-effect moves that sometimes took over. Their fairy-tale days together were over. In a building named for an international counting house, the cousins (the Dissin' Cousins, as just about every newspaper headline writer called them) matched each other nearly shot for shot and drive for drive, brick for brick and turnover for turnover.

It was enthralling stuff, all building to this climax. Nearly two and a half hours removed from tip-off, while Orlando's downtown sidewalks were being rolled up for the night, Oakley gazed up at the crowd on its feet, the noise they created hitting the hardwood floor like a steady rain, flags waving to the beat — Canadian flags, fancy that, with more than a few northern tourists in the house.

Only 30.1 seconds left on the clock.

Tie game.

And who do you think is going to get the ball?

As far back as he could remember in basketball, it had been like this for Vince Carter here in Florida. As far back as Tracy McGrady could remember, it had rarely been like this. If they had stayed together in Toronto, one of them would be taking a backseat for this kind of moment. And there's no doubt who that would have been. There's only one basketball to go around, as the saying goes, and only one pair of hands will end up shooting it. In Toronto, those hands belong to Carter. And right then, right here, McGrady's departure had a reason that made sense, if not perfect sense.

"It was just a matter of looking toward the future and seeing what I could become here, as opposed to there" was how McGrady would describe it. "In Toronto, I don't think I could have become all I was going to become."

What does that mean? You want the ball, that last touch, the chance to be the hero, or the goat? "Yes," he says instantly. So it is about being the Man, the one in charge, the one who *has* to have the last word? No, no, he says, his brow furrowing and a sour look spreading across his face. "I'm not about that," he says quietly. "I'm about getting everyone involved, doing all the things you have to do. That's my game. That's what I couldn't do before."

In Toronto, McGrady had to defer. To wait for a chance instead of make one. It was not what he had dreamed about during those long days in the condo waiting out the winter. Back home in Florida, in just four months of playing the game he had become something. It's not always easy to back up what you say. But McGrady had done everything he promised he could do, and Oakley, not one to toss around compliments, was calling him the NBA's most complete player. Shaquille O'Neal, the former Magic centre, deemed him the model of the unselfish star. McGrady had come home again. So much for what Thomas Wolfe said about that one.

He had never gone to university but here he was graduating with a degree in livin' the largest of large. Included in the new package was an address in Orlando's exclusive jock-on-every-block Isleworth community, in a mansion on five acres, with a lake, previously owned by the late golfer Payne Stewart. Tiger Woods, Dee Brown, Andre Reed and even former teammate Michael Stewart were among his neighbours. With his brother Chance and long-time friend Bradley Rogers living in the house with him, a personal chef and the same personal trainer he's had since his Mount Zion days, all of Auburndale now calls him their own. McGrady can barely stop smiling, showing off the teeth now free of the silver braces he wore for most of his time in Canada.

"I'm so excited at this opportunity," he cracked. "Here, you don't have to put the heat on in the car driving to the game."

Nothing to say about the way it went down? No explanation as to why Toronto didn't merit any sort of goodbye? "I have no regrets. I made the best decision. I made the right decision for myself. It all boils down to whether I am happy or not. Oh, I'm happy."

Warm. Happy. Home. McGrady was the very picture of contentment in a number of other ways as well. Across the board, his production increased dramatically. In Toronto, he had picked up his scoring slowly as his playing time increased, from 7 points as a rookie, to 9.3, to 15.4. And then there was this growth spurt, to 26 points a night, and suddenly he was within a point or two of Vince Carter in the league's scoring race.

The NBA, eager as ever to throw a new name up onto its marquee, featured him on the cover of *Inside Stuff,* its house organ aimed at teenagers. When *Sports Illustrated* handed out its mid-season report card, McGrady was ranked higher than Carter, among the top 10 players in the league. His Adidas connection suddenly rose to the fore, too, as the company announced a brand-new shoe and an ad campaign built around him. Within days of this first reunion meeting with Carter, he would be voted onto the eastern conference all-star team — to start alongside his old Toronto teammate.

A year ago, McGrady went to the all-star weekend to do little more than tee up the balls for Carter in the dunk contest. But now he had stepped out from under Carter's shadow and was projecting a pretty formidable aura of his own. There were those in Toronto who wondered how high McGrady could take himself. Butch Carter, among others, thought that he might one day be a better basketball player than Carter. McGrady felt the same way.

"I could have done all of the things I'm doing now last year," he told *Slam* magazine. "But that was Vince's team, it was Vince's time to do all of that and he deserved that. That's why I'm not trippin' — I knew my time was going to come. I knew."

And now the Magic, which had mixed results from their summer free-agent campaign, were building him up as their new foundation stone. And it surprised even them.

"We didn't think he'd be this good this fast," said GM John Gabriel. "And tough? For a while there he had this injury, it was like a hole in his hand, and he still played and played well, with this oven mitt kind of apparatus covering his hand."

Gabriel is a 44-year-old Philadelphian who spent half his life in NBA front offices. He had staked his reputation and Magic owner Rich DeVos's money on a risky strategy, the results of which were inconclusive. The 1999–2000 Magic had been a bunch of ragtags, an unheralded group who broke all the standard rules about NBA team building. There were no stars, no single "go-to" player, no egos to coddle, a head coach in Doc Rivers with no previous experience as an assistant or head coach — under normal circumstances, it was a recipe for sub-mediocrity. And yet the Magic had stayed in the eastern conference playoff hunt until the final week of the season. They fell a three-point shot short of making the playoffs, winning 41 games and losing 41. They had overachieved, and it didn't go unnoticed. Rivers won Coach of the Year honours, while Gabriel was named the league's Executive of the Year.

But as quickly as their season ended, so too did that story. Gabriel was going after far bigger game. The Magic roster had been gutted, with an astounding 55 transactions involving 51 players, a 17-month revolving door that cleared out all but a few players with long-term contracts to leave the team with enough money to be a big-time player in the summer of 2000's free-agent chase.

This is the game that NBA general managers play each summer. There was a time, long ago, when teams were built through trades and the annual draft of incoming college players (including, increasingly over the past decade and a half, players from overseas). But the age of the reserve clause, when players belonged to their teams as long as their teams wanted them, had ended in pro basketball with Oscar Robertson's challenge more than 30 years ago. Free agency had gone through numerous mutations, but since then it had been a given. And in theory, at least, each team operates under a salary cap, set at US$37 million in the 2000–01 season.

The draft was still important, but most players coming in through that portal required time to develop. Trades have become harder to make under the constraints of the salary cap — with most teams over the cap number, players A and B cannot be traded for player C on another team unless the salaries on each side of the deal are roughly a match. To go after free agents, cap room has to be cleared, with the only large loophole remaining being one that allowed teams to sign their own free agents without regard to the cap.

Free agency had become the most important element of team building as the NBA entered the twenty-first century. Sign a decent free agent, a proven player, and it was a major success story and a great leap forward. Lose a major piece, like a McGrady, and it was seen as an indictment against your entire organization.

The Magic had three blue-chip players in their sights: San Antonio's multiskilled young big man Tim Duncan was the prize, with McGrady and smooth wing man Grant Hill of Detroit only slightly less coveted. The way Gabriel had positioned them, it was possible to sign all three without breaking any rules. Accomplish that, and the Magic would be a serious outfit, moving immediately to the front of the NBA's class.

Gabriel's general manager brethren were watching this experiment with interest — and equal parts alarm and admiration. The Miami Heat had tried a similar tack in 1997, filling their roster with bodies to be jettisoned at season's end when their contracts ran out. But Juwan Howard's $105-million contract with Miami was disallowed by commissioner David Stern for circumvention of the salary-cap rules. Now the Magic were going down a similar road, but their way was novel in terms of scale and scope, guts and patience — and at this last hurdle, Barnumesque promotion. This last quality irritated many around the league, including Glen Grunwald.

"It's become like college recruiting," Grunwald grumbled. Indeed, pay scales and cost certainty won during the lockout of '99 were supposed to level the playing field between NBA markets of varying sizes. Instead, it seemed to have made the perks — the size of the team plane, the ardour of the pep rallies, Tiger Woods enlisted to greet Duncan and Hill during a golf/brunch outing put on by the Magic — as important a part of the free-agency landscape as the money.

The Orlando approach was precise and player friendly. Former employee Alex Martens was hired to coordinate the on-the-ground strategy, his tenure beginning on May 1, a full two months before the July 1 beginning of the free-agency period. Martens's job involved everything from hiring caterers to drawing up schedules, with no detail left to chance. Hill and Carter arrived in Orlando on that opening day, having been flown first class by the Magic. Actually, the team bought the entire first-class section for them and their representatives and family.

As for McGrady, the Magic's first contact was supposed to happen earlier — as early as it possibly could, given the league's rules. Doc

Rivers called McGrady's house at 12:01 a.m., just as June turned into July. Brainy and personable, Rivers knew McGrady well. During his tumultuous rookie season, he was the in-studio analyst for CTV on the network's national broadcasts of Raptors and Grizzlies games. He had survived 13 years in the NBA as one of the league's smartest point guards. He kept his sense of humour even during his stint in a Toronto TV studio, commenting once a week on perhaps the most horrible post-expansion basketball ever — the Raptors staggering through their 16-win season, the Grizzlies a little better (hey, it's all relative) at 19 W's.

As the Raptors reeled through that horror film, I wrote a column describing Rivers as perhaps the best young untapped basketball brain available and suggested the team hire him to take over their basketball operations. The next time I saw him, he chuckled and wagged his finger in warning. "Now don't you go planting any ideas," he warned with a grin. As he jested, Rivers was deadly serious. He had no interest in a reclamation project like the Raptors.

It turned out he could afford to wait: he had ended up in Orlando, a key piece in Gabriel's grand plan. Rivers was 37 when he got the coach's job, and perhaps his finest quality was his ability to understand today's generation of younger players and the way they played the game today. Like McGrady. It would be Rivers's job to schmooze him, and he had planned this moment meticulously, reserving a table at one of McGrady's favourite restaurants and arranging to have it remain open past the 2 a.m. closing time.

So there was candlelight and wine, and knowing the Magic, probably a strolling violinist or two. There was everything, it seemed, but McGrady himself. Rivers called his home number twice and all he got was the answering machine. Reluctantly, he dialled one more number, cancelling the reservation. In some ways, it was typical McGrady, the type of guy who could sleep through a hurricane. He was away in the Bahamas on holiday with friends and returned home a couple of days later. The Magic might've been ready for free agency, but for McGrady, it could wait and it did wait.

The waiting turned into a roller-coaster. The NBA's free-agent period has erased the old notion of an off-season. It is a different season, but the pressures and anxieties are intense. For general managers and player agents, it is the critical time, and the Magic had so far been batting .500. They struck out on Duncan, landed Hill, and now the McGrady pursuit intensified. During a tour of the team's practice facility, a banner hung from the ceiling: a gigantic blow-up of McGrady in a Magic uniform, with "Imagine" printed beneath it. Magic employees wore T-shirts bearing the same image. But even with the home-court advantage they enjoyed with the local kid, and even with the verbal commitment they received from him a few days into July, the Magic were taking nothing for granted. Indeed, they were getting confused. "It was almost like we wanted to put him in quarantine," Gabriel shuddered.

The Chicago Bulls had taken their best shot at McGrady, greeting him at the airport with a brass band and taking him to Wrigley Field to meet Sammy Sosa and take infield practice. There was a message from Oprah Winfrey, and the Bulls had also taken their best shot at the Magic, presenting to McGrady a flow chart they had put together of Orlando's future — and how bleak it would be with all the first-round draft picks they had stockpiled clogging up the works. McGrady certainly seemed to be interested. He called Bulls GM Jerry Krause "a great man" and talked of Chicago as a serious option for him to consider. In Orlando, they were getting nervous as McGrady seemed to be treating the process like the recruiting dance he only peripherally went through before. One *Orlando Sentinel* columnist dubbed him McWaffle for his flip-flopping.

But the Magic's most serious competitor took a more undercover approach. The Miami Heat and their Machiavellian coach Pat Riley were literally lurking in the shadows. Riley had designs on McGrady, even making a clandestine flight into Orlando airport late one night aboard the Heat's team jet. Riley summoned McGrady to a late supper aboard the plane, where he presented him with a 256-page Heat playbook with the player's name engraved on the cover, and launched into the hard sell.

This was a little bit more brazen than anyone could imagine. The Magic's team plane was in the hangar when McGrady got his tour. As far as Orlando management was concerned, it was as if the Prince of Darkness had swooped in, hungry for fresh blood.

"I couldn't believe it," Gabriel said of Riley's visit. "I called the league about it. Isn't there some rule about professional stalking?"

Just when they thought they had him, the Magic watched in dismay as McGrady appeared ready to elope. Egged on by his advisors, the Heat and the Raptors cooked up a couple of sign-and-trade scenarios that looked promising. Alonzo Mourning took over the courtship duties from Riley, inviting McGrady down to south Florida for his annual summer charity game and clambake.

Then suddenly, McGrady was back talking to the Magic. Rivers's persuasiveness (two visits to the player's house and two impassioned pleas) and a Toronto sign-and-trade deal that earned him the maximum $92.4 million, seven-year contract available would finally rule the day. McGrady told the Magic he would definitely be signing. Until the day that was made official, no one in Orlando was ready to truly believe it. And when it was made official, just into August, McGrady was wearing an

Orlando uniform with the number 1 — his idol Penny Hardaway's old number (a fellow Magic fans had booed out of town two years before). Back in Florida where he felt he belonged, he called his apprenticeship in Toronto nothing less than "hell."

"My first three years, it was a learning process for me," he said later. "I was playing other roles. I had a young coach. I just needed to be somewhere where I could play free, man. Somewhere where I could play the way I wanted to without looking over my shoulder. To be free ... and Doc had a lot to do with it. I don't know if I'd want to play for any other coach than Doc Rivers."

Freedom is something Vince Carter has always had in Toronto, almost from the day he arrived to work out for the team's coaches and officials back in June of 1998. While McGrady developed slowly out of high school, the more seasoned Carter showed up in full form.

For the Raptors, it was love at first sight. Around their team office, Carter's private workout is remembered as an almost holy experience for those who were in attendance (on a Sunday morning, appropriately). His workout in Denver the day before had been a good one, surprising Nuggets GM/coach Dan Issel with his shooting prowess. "It was not only how well he shot the basketball but how fundamentally sound he was shooting it," said Issel. "If you were going to make a film to teach youngsters how to shoot the basketball, you'd use him as an example before anyone else who had been in for us."

As good as Carter had performed, though, he limped out of Denver. Part of the Nuggets' workout regimen was weightlifting. Carter strained a quadriceps muscle doing squats. By the time he arrived in Toronto hungry and tired after a four-hour delay getting out of Denver, it was after midnight and his left leg was tight and sore. To make matters worse, his luggage had been lost and his hotel reservation cancelled. When he finally got into another downtown hotel, the room service he ordered never arrived.

This was all unfolding according to a pattern, or so Grunwald thought during his bluer moments. The general manager had been dismayed as, one after another, players said no to working out for the Raptors. Still getting over the Isiah Thomas debacle, the Raptors were a 16-win team, located in Canada — and in the average NBA player's mind, that meant high taxes, high costs, low recognition and cold temperatures. Most of all, it meant bad teams. Carter's teammate Antawn Jamison had told the Raptors he wouldn't even bother coming up. Mike Bibby, who would eventually be selected by Vancouver, also wasn't interested. Oh well, thought Grunwald, that can cut both ways. Carter had already told the Grizzlies he wasn't interested in playing for them.

Carter's schedule and his travel delays meant that the Raptors' usual approach was cut short. Grunwald was not one for flash and dash. He put much stock in one-on-one contact, replacing slick patter and recruiting-style pitches with a handshake and his word. That meant a quiet dinner the night before the workout, the GM and the prospective player joined by the head coach or team president Richard Peddie and perhaps one of the assistants or another team official. The next morning there would be a short presentation on Canada. "It could be taxes, or climate, culture, location — anything to clear up the misconceptions out there," Grunwald explained.

In Carter's case, though, none of the usual ice breaking had been possible. As Grunwald made his way to the University of Toronto gym for the workout — the Air Canada Centre, with its in-house practice facility, was still months away from completion — he wasn't sure what to expect.

It was the Raptors' last workout of the pre-draft period, and so far no one had been all that impressive. And Carter was not a given in the Toronto front office, with some of the scouting staff liking his package and others looking elsewhere. Heck, with the foul-ups and the sore leg, Carter wasn't even going to get a full two-hour workout, Grunwald figuring he'd go easy on him.

"I kept thinking, what a disaster," he recalled. "We were having all that trouble getting guys to even come visit us, and now this. I figured he'd be in a bad mood, all pissed off. But he was in great spirits. It was just the opposite. That made a good impression right away."

Carter proceeded to put on a show. "He showed unbelievable athleticism," said Grunwald. "For the sprints and testing, he was off the charts on all of them, the best scores we'd ever seen. But it was more his personality on top of it all. He had a great attitude. He wanted to do everything. And he seemed to have everything. Not only athleticism and skills but attitude and personality."

Athletic trainer Chuck Mooney administered the fitness tests, as he has done for nearly every one of the aspiring pros during their Toronto workouts. As Carter cleared each of Mooney's hurdles, it became obvious that this fellow was unlike any other player who had come through. A 37-inch vertical leaper, he stunned the small audience by leaving a palm-print on the glass six inches *above* the box marked on the backboard above the rim. "By far, he was the best jumper we've ever had," said Mooney. "And he was pretty quick too — not the best sprinter, but right up there in the top three or four."

Carter breezed through the five-spot shooting drill. About the only hole in his game appeared to be ball handling with his left hand. At the usual finale, the beep test, running foul line to foul line according to an electronic beep that gets faster and faster, Carter lasted an exhausting 11 minutes. "He was a stud," Mooney assessed. Carter seemed to be able to do it all — including going the whole two hours after all, telling them he felt fine and would like to continue when they tried to cut it short.

"It was a tremendous performance," said Grunwald. "It was the best thing I'd ever seen. I found I couldn't sit down as it went along. I was too excited. I was pacing around the gym. I couldn't believe what I was seeing."

Grunwald wasn't alone. Assistant coach Brian James found himself shaking. "In six or seven years of working out players in the NBA, *this* was sending chills up my spine," he said.

The Raptors of that era were a scrawny, skinny outfit — Butch Carter's first change after taking over as interim coach was to put them on a systematic weightlifting program — and bigger players than Carter were available. Trouble was, their no. 4 draft position wasn't going to get them what they wanted. "I wish we'd gotten the second pick, to be honest with you," Grunwald said a month before the draft and two weeks before Carter showed up for his workout. "There are some big players and obviously we have to address that need. I think we need help with our rebounding and defence. We need some size and strength."

It's hard to believe now, but Carter had his doubters, and Butch Carter was one of them, favouring centre Michael Olowokandi or widebody forward Robert Traylor as more suited to the Raptors' needs.

At six-foot-seven, Vince Carter was regarded as a slasher with otherworldly hops, but there were questions about his shooting and his defence, his in-game concentration and even his work ethic. All of that, the good and the bad, stemmed from the North Carolina pedigree.

There had been talk of Carter bypassing college, of going to the pros straight from Daytona's Mainland High School, where he had led the team to the state title and become a household name in central Florida. But his family, in particular his mother, Michelle, was having none of it. That was Dean Smith (North Carolina head coach) making three visits in person to schmooze at Carter's house. That was Lon Kruger (Florida head coach) tripping over himself to show up four times on the Carter doorstep, the NCAA maximum. And that was Carter drawing one of the biggest ovations at the University of Florida's Midnight Madness season-opening practice — all for just sitting there and watching. But Michelle Carter wanted one thing clear: Vince would go to a top-drawer basketball school and come back with a college degree. Instead of Florida, Duke or Kentucky, though, he chose North Carolina, arriving in the autumn of 1995 as one of the fabled program's most heralded freshmen, the Tar Heels having won another intense recruiting battle for one of the country's top basketballers.

It would progress anything but smoothly. Carter, fresh off playing for the United States junior team at the world championship, felt the backlash from the recruiting wars, the ones that have to do with high expectations, the ones that can leave scars, or worse. It wasn't just him feeling the pressure. As Carter was finishing a rocky first year at Chapel Hill, Kruger was canned at Florida. His fate was sealed when he failed to land enough big-name recruits, and none were bigger among the ones that got away than Carter, recipient of Florida's Mr. Basketball award.

For a time, it seemed as if North Carolina wouldn't work out. Carter averaged just 7.5 points his first year, and there were rumours he might transfer. Smith parked him on the bench for long stretches. He had come in with those Jordan comparisons shadowing him, but the Chapel Hill faithful were unconvinced. "Everything he did was under a microscope," said Carter's close friend Cori Brown, a manager with the Tar Heels. "When he came in, he had to score 20 a night and slam on people."

Carter wasn't quite sure what was happening. At the Deandome, fans would boo the legendary coach when he took Carter out of the game. Then Smith would get on him for not playing defence. As ever, it was his mother who would run interference for him. She could be as tough and demanding as she was supportive, and here was that approach all at once. "Dean Smith is City Hall, and you don't fight City Hall," she told him, even as she herself travelled to Chapel Hill three times that season to sit down with Smith and find out what was going on with her son's playing time.

"At times I almost said it was political," she said of what she saw as a disparity between the treatment afforded Carter and Antawn Jamison. As big an advance buzz as Carter had generated, Jamison had equalled it as the local state hero from Charlotte. And while Jamison thrived as a freshman, Carter had struggled.

The experience would stay with him. He was in a new environment, being forced to adapt and increasingly out of the safety zone his mother had built around him. "He grew up a lot," Michelle Carter said. "He realized that everybody's not with you all the time. There's going to be wolves in sheep's clothing. Vince was very idealistic in his thinking. He never thought anybody would think of doing him harm."

Sometimes, it seemed to Vince Carter as if it was him and his mother against the world. Michelle Carter has been called "smothering" in no less than the *New York Times,* and her fitness and even her motives have been questioned in other publications. A *Sports Illustrated* profile of Carter cast light on his brother Chris, growing up in Vince's shadow, and his father, Vince Sr., who was estranged from his sons after the divorce.

But Michelle Carter is the closest confidante Carter has in the world. Smothering? A too-sheltered life for her son? She shrugs her shoulders:

guilty as charged. "I know I should leave him alone, that he's 24 years old. But I'll probably still be like this when he's 48," she says. They are close, mother and son, with Michelle Carter serving as his sounding board, his business advisor, the person he talks to every night for encouragement or a kick in the pants. On this trip, after the Raptors arrive late on a Sunday evening after an overtime win in Philadelphia, Carter and Morris Peterson drive over to Michelle's house 90 minutes from Orlando, waking her up with the surprise visit past midnight.

"These are the trips I look forward to the most," says Vince Carter. "Any time I'm coming back to Florida, it's going to be a little special."

This is home for the Carters. A Miami native who grew up in the city's Liberty City neighbourhood, her mother a teacher and her father a banker, Michelle moved north to attend Bethune-Cookman College in Daytona Beach. She met her first husband, Vince Sr., there, and the couple had two kids, Vince and Chris, before it all went sour and ended in a divorce. Vince Jr. was seven years old and Chris was four when Michelle took them back to Miami. But she realized quickly that was a mistake. "It wasn't like the place I remembered," she said. "I didn't even let Vince and Chris outside the house to play. I was afraid of a drive-by shooting."

Michelle would move back up to Daytona Beach, complete her master's degree and begin a 20-year career as a teacher. She would remarry; her second husband was Daytona bandmaster Harry Robinson, who raised young Vince and Chris with her. Vince Sr. would show up later on, when Vince was in high school, but the two would never get any closer. The two boys, meanwhile, were encouraged to try anything, and they did, playing soccer and tennis as well as basketball and football. Vince began playing the saxophone in the fifth grade, a year before he first dunked a basketball, and he was Daytona Mainland's drum major, good enough to lead them to top honours among the state's marching bands and a music scholarship offer from Bethune-Cookman. "If I wasn't involved so much with basketball, I'd have some kind of career in music going, be it producing or recording or whatever," Carter says now.

Vince Carter had no problem standing out or looking good. Until that first year at North Carolina, that is, when he found himself sitting down.

It would get better for Carter from there, but that sort of treatment was precisely what the Carolina program was known for under the long and successful tenure of Smith. Starting at Chapel Hill in 1961, he won more Division I games than any other coach. He also produced a legion of coaching acolytes by preaching and teaching team play — and, not so coincidentally, doing it with the best players in the land, however submerged their talents were during their time there. The old joke about Smith was well founded: he truly did seem to be the only man on the planet capable of holding Michael Jordan under 20 points. That's because at Carolina, you *learned the game*. Players weren't "featured," and highlight films were frowned upon unless they involved cutting down nets after a championship. Dunks weren't celebrated — "Act like you've done it before" was Smith's long-time order. Even if it made scouting a little more difficult, such tutelage was most appreciated by NBA general managers, especially in the late 1990s. Smith would groom nearly 60 future NBA pros in a 36-year career at Chapel Hill, the last two being Jamison and Carter.

"You know they know how to play," says Miami coach Pat Riley. "When they come to the pros, they're refined. They're ready to step right in."

"UNC is a plus-four school," says the Magic's GM, Gabriel. "That means that if I rate a player as the tenth-best in the NBA draft, being a Tar Heel automatically jumps him to no. 6."

Carter would go on from his freshman-year uncertainty to put together a superb college career, but it wasn't as if he was universally regarded as a lock for NBA stardom when he decided to come out for the draft after his junior year. It isn't just the heavier hand of coaching that makes college ball so different from the NBA. With its zone defences and motion offences, it doesn't include the kind of one-on-one isolation play that's so much a part of the NBA. It's rare to see a Tar Heel player shoot more than 10 or 15 times a game.

In Carter's case, he was the third option in the offence. Jamison got the lion's share of the ball up front. Shammond Williams shot three-pointers. At times, it seemed like all Carter was doing was backdoor cutting to the basket to finish a Williams lob with a thunderous dunk that was the stuff of a young man's dreaming.

Craig Neal, who had been a big McGrady booster, had seen Carter play perhaps 30 times. Along with Raptors consultant Jack McCloskey, an Isiah Thomas hire who was the architect of the 1988–90 Pistons' back-to-back championship years, Neal was a big believer in Carter's pro potential. But the Raptors front office was divided as May turned into June. Until the workout, that is.

"He came in and totally surprised us with his shooting," said scouting director Bob Zuffelato. "We didn't think we'd see that [shooting] so quickly. He was just a great athlete who could shoot the ball. We already knew he was unselfish, he could pass and rebound. I just shook my head. We kept looking at each other, as if to make sure we were all seeing the same thing."

With more than 30 years in college and pro basketball to draw on, Zuffelato rated Carter as among the top three or four he'd ever seen in the harsh environment of the private workout. It was high praise. In two hours, Vince Carter had done something far beyond just impress a tough audience. He'd also changed their plan. Butch Carter was still convinced the Raptors should draft a big player like Robert (Tractor) Traylor, but Grunwald shifted gears and wanted Vince Carter. Eventually, after the Raptors had managed to arrange a couple of trades for veteran big men Kevin Willis and Charles Oakley, Butch Carter would come around. Vince Carter was the choice. But the Raptors' toughest task was still ahead of them: they had to draft the guy.

Perhaps the most underrated factor was Don Nelson. The Dallas Mavericks coach and GM is unpredictable, eccentric, daring and out there — no one can ever quite tell what Nellie is up to when it comes to the NBA draft. At the '98 draft, Nelson had the no. 6 pick and thirsted for young German club pro Dirk Nowitzki. One problem, though. The Mavs were worried that Golden State, at no. 5, was going to take Nowitzki ahead of them.

"We wanted to find out if Golden State was serious about Dirk," said Nelson's chief assistant coach and son Donnie Nelson. "We had conversations with Toronto to smokescreen a little bit. We found out it was Jamison the Warriors were interested in most. Toronto picked up on that."

The Raptors began calling the Mavericks back, again and again, as a smokescreen of their own, talking about their interest in Jamison. Looking for insurance, the Warriors made the deal for the player they wanted — Jamison. The Mavericks did fine, picking Traylor with their no. 6 slot and dealing down to Milwaukee at no. 9 to pick up — surprise! — Nowitzki in return.

The machinations with the Warriors, the double smokescreens — it was pure Nellie, and the Raptors took full advantage. And when the smoke cleared, the deal saved the Raptors $1.025 million, the difference between the contracts of Jamison at no. 4 and Carter at no. 5. Vince Carter was not just a steal. He was a bargain.

Three years later, in January 2001, and here they were in Orlando — the Raptors' one-time foundation pair, the Dissin' Cousins, now on opposite sides with a game on the line.

"We were too tight in Toronto," McGrady says of his time with Carter. "The relationship, we were like brothers. Still are."

The preamble to this meeting, the first since their parting, showed once again the differences between them. At times, Carter seems irritated by stardom, barely tolerating the attention and the variations and permutations of the one question everyone wants answered: his future. He would insist that this reunion with McGrady was no big deal to him, but of course it was. He was stung by McGrady's offhandedness over the summer, even if McGrady now put that down to simply not minding what he said.

McGrady, getting his first real turn now under the glare of the spotlight, found he didn't mind it at all. Of course, he said he had circled this game a long time ago. He admitted his eagerness with a smile, a young man clearly having a good time — who wouldn't like this kind of night? He has grown up a long way from the kid who was berated by Darrell Walker in Toronto, the kid who stayed in from the cold.

"You can't shy away from it," McGrady said of the attention. "It's not going to kill me. I'm definitely enjoying that part of it."

With Grant Hill a huge disappointment for the Magic — a badly fractured ankle and surgery limited him to but four games of play and made his future career dicey — McGrady represented a gamble that had paid off beyond anyone's wildest dreams. In the stands, his mother and grandmother watched from their usual seats. Obbe and Bradley and Chance were there, McGrady's closest friends and family. Michelle Carter had led a small contingent over from Daytona, including Joe Giddens. Vince Sr. was supposed to be somewhere in the arena.

They all knew what was going to happen. After the timeout, McGrady nailed a short turnaround jumper over Carter. Carter isolated against McGrady, blew by him with a crossover toward the baseline that drew help defender Bo Outlaw over — then he stopped and hit a pogo-stick jumper. Last possession, and that was Carter overplaying McGrady, darting in to tip the ball away, forcing a wild no-hope heave. Buzzer. Overtime.

They would play a couple of extra periods, and it was more of the same, the Magic finally winning, McGrady embracing Carter at the end and shouting something in his ear above the din.

Oh sure, they would do this again. Vince vs. Tracy was just one round old, but it was already shaping up as an epic. Predictably, Carter would keep as tight a lid on his emotions as he could, but afterward he was talking to a friend in the corridor outside the locker room. Already, he was looking ahead. "Wait until they come into our place," he said. He caught up with McGrady down the hall, their misunderstanding from the previous summer just history as they chatted and went over the evening. A couple of weeks later, McGrady called him, asked him about the April 1 rematch in Toronto.

"Do you think they'll boo me?" he asked.

Carter chuckled to himself, not quite sure if he was serious.

"Yeah, they'll probably boo you," he said.

CHAPTER 8

February 2001:

Making a Point

V ince Carter looked forward to the NBA's 2001 All-Star weekend as a time to get away from it all. That pretty much sums up the kind of year it had become for him. There was a knee injury that kept everyone guessing almost right up to the time to go, the one that everyone wanted to ask him about, the one that he didn't want to talk about. There was the slam-dunk competition, the same one he'd won the year before with such style, the same one he had no intention of entering this time around. He was tired, the long summer catching up to him. He was cranky, snappy with the media and his representatives. He was banged up and limping around. He was wondering about the Raptors' future, and his own, given the team's halting first half to the season. He was telling friends that he was not only going to skip the dunk show but perhaps blow off the game as well. Just contemplating that was a surprise since for

Vince Carter, appearing in the all-star game alongside his peers was per-haps the only item on the agenda that made the weekend worthwhile.

There were powerful reasons behind his reluctance. Carter yearned for some kind of Lourdes effect. For most players, that's exactly what the all-star break is — a restorative four days to go home and rest, or go south and lie on a beach. Muggsy Bogues was on his way to Puerto Rico, and Alvin Williams was headed to Philadelphia to visit his parents. Other Raptors were headed to D.C. and peripheral roles in the league's biggest schmooze. Mark Jackson was taking his family to Washington to watch the all-stars as a fan; and until the night before, when he was named to replace injured Theo Ratliff, Antonio Davis was going to take part in NBA players' association meetings. Morris Peterson was part of the rookie game, and Charles Oakley was heading down to hang out with his Virginia Union buddies. Unless there was some solid reason otherwise, rest was at the top of everybody's agenda.

But Carter couldn't get any rest. In January, the morning after the showdown with the Magic and McGrady, he awoke to the realization that his knee troubles of December had promptly reappeared. He missed a game for the Raptors, after being limited to just three minutes of play his previous time out. The absence from the lineup, Carter's second of the season due to the soreness and a condition known as jumper's knee, fuelled a brushfire of opinion and speculation in the Toronto media. Carter should play. Carter shouldn't play. Carter should sit down. Carter should shut up. When his mother asked him if it might be a good idea to take some time off, he flared up at her: "What are you, crazy?" The mag-netic resonance imaging test that Carter received immediately after his injury's recurrence sparked a mini-controversy in itself, considering the lengthy waiting list for such procedures in Ontario hospitals. During one game against Boston, he rode a stationary bike when not on the floor, in order to avoid cooling down the knee and perhaps causing further injury.

Maybe he went to Lourdes after all. Hard on the heels of all this, he was playing some of his finest, most energetic basketball of the season. Opponents were still treating him with the Carter Rules — quick and automatic double-teaming to get the ball out of his hands and force other Raptors to carry more of the offensive load, and as much bumping as the referees were allowing — but he was showing a new dimension. His passing out of those double teams was getting better. He was finding those teammates and getting them shots. It seemed the treatment and the little time off in February were enough to get him what he needed and thought he would never get: a break.

"I can't remember the last time I had a real, real break," he said later. "Maybe the closest thing to it this season was when I missed those five or six games. It took some time for my body to catch up. I was always going, going, going. All of a sudden I could rest. I knew I wasn't going to have to practice. I knew I was going to have treatment. No games. My body wasn't on 'go' all the time. Mentally it was difficult, at least at first. It took three or four days to really accept it. Then I could say, well, it's not going to be so bad. It's doing something."

To no one's surprise, Carter still scratched himself from the dunk competition. But given that encouraging week leading up to the all-star break, he decided to play in the game, vowing that otherwise his weekend would be low-key, with appearances kept to a minimum.

Of course it was impossible. His was not exactly going to be a Garbo act, but even trying on some simplicity for size was impossible at basketball's most opulent and over-the-top gathering. Every limousine available within a 75-mile radius was called into duty to ferry the beautiful people around D.C. through a non-stop round of parties, concerts and get-togethers. The limos, the Navigators, the Cadillacs and the odd Hummer crawled through gridlock that extended into the early morning, with many of the top nightspots closed to the public. There were private parties, some more private than others, and plenty of them. Rasheed Wallace's and Jerry Stackhouse's. Shaquille O'Neal's and Michael Jordan's. Iverson-Webber-Bryant. TNT. Playboy.com. Jay-Z. Some of them attracted as many as 5,000 people. Finery was everywhere, and perhaps no one looked louder than Quentin Richardson and Darius Miles, a pair of Los Angeles Clippers playing in the rookie game, walking around in matching diamond and rhinestone necklaces.

Up the street at another hotel, NBA general managers were meeting to discuss that seemingly annual topic of What's Wrong with the Game, and how they could fix it. But as far as the crowds at the MCI Center and in the hotel lobby were concerned, there was nothing wrong with the game. As far as city officials were concerned, looking at the 100,000 or so visitors on hand for the all-star events, there was absolutely nothing wrong with the game.

"I've never been to the Super Bowl, but the all-star game is pretty big," said Ray Allen of the Milwaukee Bucks, one of Carter's closest friends in the league. "Off the court, everybody wants to be on the court. And on the court, everybody wants to be off the court. Everyone wants to see each other, and everyone wants to trade places."

What the all-star weekend is, is a bonanza. Carter was a top-of-the-bill headliner, and this was the Black Thanksgiving, in the pithy appraisal of *Washington Post* columnist Michael Wilbon. Playing it low-key would be like trying to sleep through a hurricane.

Actually, all he wanted to do was scale back his schedule from the exhausting grind of the previous year in Oakland and San Francisco, when it seemed the entire world wanted a piece of Vince, a minute here or there, and nobody thought to ask whether it was all right with him. Carter had been hauled around like a prize pony, from the time he landed at San Francisco airport and was immediately whisked to a late-night photo shoot for *Sports Illustrated,* to the last seconds of the all-star game itself. It would be Tank Black's last stand, the final act before the curtain came down on his head, and he was at home in an ankle bracelet. Black and 13 others had travelled to California to be part of Team Carter through a demanding three-day schedule of appearances, leaving barely enough time for the slam-dunk competition and the game.

With Team Carter staying with the rest of the NBAers in San Francisco and the game in Oakland, the wakeup call came at 5:30 a.m., heralding a seemingly endless commute from one function to another. "I got to know the Bay Bridge real well," Carter later grunted of perhaps the most glamorous, high-profile weekend of his life.

By midday of the Saturday afternoon, before any kind of basketball was required, Carter was on the verge of mutiny. He hadn't eaten anything during four hours of morning appearances in Oakland, then returned to San Francisco for a last round of interviews. Eager for lunch and an hour of sleep before going back to Oakland for the slam-dunk contest, he passed up on the league transportation and stayed late at the hotel. When it came time to leave, Carter and five others in his group, including McGrady, couldn't find a ride. They finally piled into an ordinary sedan. "There we were, wedged up against each other and all over each other," he chuckled. "We couldn't move. We must've looked like clowns getting out of one of those tiny circus cars at the other end."

After that unlikely warm-up and with all the pressure of being the favourite, Carter delivered three otherworldly and imaginative jams that had observers slapping their foreheads. But while they wanted more, he was looking in another direction: winning the slam-dunk title and the $75,000 in prize money and bonuses that went with it was something of a hair shirt. "This doesn't help me," he sighed with an air of resignation, as ever ready to downplay the kind of high-flying plays that had made him so popular.

This time, Carter looked for quiet time. The entourage was much smaller: Michelle Carter and Joe Giddens, Merle Scott and Dave Haggith of IMG, and that was it. There would be opportunity for a leisurely dinner. With but a couple of promotional appearances on Friday night, he and Giddens popped into Stackhouse's party.

For many, the female groupies and the corporate groupies alike, the parties were the most attractive and glamorous feature of the weekend, going through the night and into the predawn gloaming. U.S. sports writer Norman Chad put it best: Anne Rice would have a great time covering the NBA. For Carter, though, this was a quick appearance. One hour and they were gone, back to the hotel.

"It was pretty packed," said Giddens. "It can get crazy at times with the autographs and people chasing you. Everybody's after you at those things. He handles it pretty well. That night, and for the whole weekend, Vince was more interested in just hanging out at the hotel."

If that sounds like vacuous entertainment, there was some thought behind it. Leading up to the weekend, flyers had been circulated around Washington advertising "Vince Carter's Party." News outlets began calling Scott and Haggith about it, anxious to get on the guest list, and fans gathered in the lobby of the official hotel grilled anyone with a Toronto connection about getting a ticket or entree. There was only one problem: it didn't exist.

Getting away from that kind of scene was another reason for Carter's low-profile approach. It continued Saturday night. Instead of sitting courtside with other players who weren't participating in the slam-dunk contest or three-point shooting or two-ball, he sat in an anonymous private box at the MCI Center with Giddens, refusing to even show his face for the cameras or journey down to floor level to say hello to the competitors on the floor. It was a desultory show without him, and as it wound down, Carter left the building. This was his new face to the world: no face at all.

But even trying to be bland and to blend into the night, he was going to stick out. Even in anonymity, Vince Carter was going to make some kind of noise. In Hawaii, it had been his preternatural hops that spoke louder than any words could. In this case, at least for one moment, it was another kind of noise, and even rarer for Carter than a missed jam: he talked about his future. Or at least, it sounded that way.

Carter was talking about the Raptors, and it all came out wrong, a quick answer to a long-winded question, just 10 words that would make many back in Toronto wonder. It happened at the Friday media availability, which is what passes for media access at these kinds of events — a one-hour session in a Hyatt Hotel ballroom, each player occupying a table with his name on it, and as many of the more than 2,000 accredited media as could get in asking questions.

At Carter's table, it is never quiet. He draws a huge crowd, full of the usual suspects from around the world asking him about any of a number of topics. They might ask him to say hello to the Dominican Republic, or whether his travel plans next summer will include Iceland, or what he thinks of the debate on rules that dominated this year's serious business. Last year in Oakland, a reporter from Argentina fished a toy pink saxophone out of the bag he was carrying, handed it to Carter and then took out a little toy trumpet for himself. With the entire table of reporters spellbound, he asked Carter if he would join him in playing. Carter looked at him for a long time, shook his head. "Man, is he serious? I think he is serious," he later admitted to thinking.

It's those moments of madness that make the media availability session something of a pain in the ass process for the players, many of whom will arrive late, barely concealing their disdain for the whole business. Some will not bother coming at all, risking a $10,000 fine from the NBA that goes to any no-shows without a note from the doctor. Meantime, the reporters are divided into different camps. There are the regulars who cover the league intensively and come in well versed on the issues that should be covered. Then there are the more casual, like the Argentine toy musician (who, it should be noted, came well armed and showed commendable initiative. Also in his bag was a container of green spinach dip for Gary Payton to sample, a palm-sized piano for Grant Hill to play, and a sailor's cap for David Robinson). With nearly 40 television crews from around the world on hand to broadcast the game to 206 countries, it is something of a United Nations by design, the NBA anxious to make its message global and even paying the way for some of the overseas contingent.

One of the key figures of the weekend this year was Chris Webber, formerly a headliner with the Washington Wizards, now an all-star playing in Sacramento — and a free agent in just five months. In the hotel lobby upstairs, where hundreds of early fans have staked out the prime star-gazing positions, balancing a drink in one hand and a cellphone in the other, Webber was greeted like the second coming as he waded through the throng. "There's C-Webb," they would say, nudging each other, pointing, some zig-zagging through the crowd to get up close to the six-foot-ten Webber. "You coming back here, C?" one asked. "You're not staying away out there, are you, Chris?" said another. "Better soul food here, dog."

The week before, Webber told Ric Bucher of *ESPN* magazine he was "bored to death" in Sacramento, complaining that he can't get anything to eat after 9 p.m., that the nearest soul food joint was hours away. Webber was going through the annual dance of impending free agency, and these interviews are parsed and interpreted like some kind of unholy writ. Put a star player into the last year of his contract and all of a sudden the rules change. It's open season, and everyone wants to ask the same questions, about what you'll do, who you like, why you're leaving or whether you're leaving at all. Tracy McGrady went through it a year ago. The Raptors' Antonio Davis is bumping along through it this season. And although it has already started, it is what Vince Carter will face in earnest next season — if he lets it go that way. And no, he doesn't want it to go that way.

"I surely hope we get it straightened away this summer," says Michelle Carter, speaking as much as her son's business advisor as his mother. "I'd rather we take care of it sooner rather than later. I look at what happened to Tracy, and how he handled it and the people around him handled it, and we don't want that sort of thing happening. It would get ridiculous. It would mean no peace."

But downstairs in Washington, the prelude to that no-peace is already happening. Someone in this crowd of mostly unfamiliar, jostling faces is asking Vince Carter about Webber. Sacramento management is deathly afraid of losing their stud player to a town that has better barbecue, or a jazzier nightlife, or a better team plane, or any of the many things on a free agent's checklist. There is a banner on the Kings' Arco Arena — "C Webb's

House," it proclaims — and on the freeway that Webber takes to the arena, a billboard has the Kings owner promising to cut Webber's grass if he will sign a new contract when it comes time. And someone from somewhere wants to know if Carter will receive that kind of love from the Raptors when it's his turn for free agency leading up to the summer of 2002.

Carter shakes his head. A slight smile that looks like a grimace crosses his face. "They don't care about me, man," he says. "Naw, nothing like that."

As soon as the remark leaves Carter's mouth, he is on to another subject. No one seems to take much notice, but in those 10 words he has lit a fuse. The Raptors not caring about Carter? Carter dissing the Raptors? The general consensus in this room, anyway, is that Carter will indeed be leaving the Raptors when his time is up. His cousin and old running mate McGrady, like him an eastern all-star, is saying that very thing (not for the first time) at almost the same time, halfway across the crowded hotel ballroom. And here is an inkling, it seems, right from Carter's very lips.

Of the Toronto press contingent, only Bill Harris of the Toronto *Sun* was at Carter's table when the remark was dropped. Harris wasn't quite sure what he heard and after reviewing his audiotape, spoke to Carter that evening for clarification. "I was joking," Carter told Harris. "Really, I've felt nothing but love from the Toronto fans in all the time I've played there."

This was damage control. If there was one rule Vince Carter lived by in his dealings with the media, he knew he had just violated it. When Latrell Sprewell had openly talked at the start of the season of Webber coming to New York to play with the Knicks, commissioner David Stern reprimanded him. For Carter, it was an example and a lesson. "Of course I notice that kind of stuff. That's why I never say anything," he said.

"You never know who is listening, and how they're going to take it. You can't say anything."

It was a sad admission. Here was one of the NBA's brightest young stars, basically saying he practised a sort of self-censorship. And it was another indication of how removed the NBA's elite players were from the fans paying the freight. The very fact that he had refused to clarify his status with the Raptors was taken by some as an admission that he wasn't coming back.

As far as those closest to him were concerned, Carter was just being himself. The remark wasn't serious. It was just the media misinterpreting what he had said, and not for the first time. "The same thing happened in Sydney at the Olympics," said Michelle Carter. "He missed a couple of dunks, and in the dressing room he was joking with [a Nike representative], saying, 'It must have been the shoes.' A reporter from the L.A. *Times* overheard the remark and wrote it as if he was blaming the shoes. There was a lot of fixing that had to be done on that one."

So, too, did this one require "fixing." The party line went this way: Carter loved Toronto. Free agency was a decision for another day. Nothing was certain. What it would boil down to was whether or not the Raptors could win enough, and show enough promise for the future, to justify his hanging around.

Left unspoken was the fact that there are 29 teams in the NBA and only one of them can have Vince Carter. If Carter decided to leave, he would basically have his pick of destinations. Salary-cap considerations would not enter into the equation — they hadn't in the case of McGrady, remember. Whomever he wanted, and whoever wanted him the most, would be where he would go. But yes, said agent Merle Scott, that included the Raptors.

"He's dealt with the city, and it's fine," said Scott. "He's dealt with the cold weather. He's dealt with the 24-hour dining issue. All that stuff is fine with him, and it's out of the way. It's okay. It's not a factor. What it is going to boil down to is a basketball decision, whether the Raptors are capable of winning a championship."

And that was where the business and the basketball collided. Vince Carter was already a great basketball player. But an ultimate winner at the highest level he was not. As of February 2001, he had yet to win an NBA playoff game. He had been handed the mantle of one who would change the game, anointed as one of the post-Jordan era's standard-bearers. He was also something of a missionary, taking the game to a new level in a new land. It was heady stuff for just one basketball player. But this other side of the story was a sobering reminder of where he was and just how difficult a job it was. There had been no Carter-led rise in the NBA's key American television ratings. Canada was still an NBA outpost. As far as America was concerned, Carter played *out there* — which is mostly regarded as the other side of the moon.

It was an attitude that was fuelled by almost willful ignorance on the part of Carter's peers, almost all of them American. The players hate having to go through customs 30 to 40 times a year. "It's not anything really, really major," said Vancouver's Tony Massenburg during the Grizzlies' visit to Toronto, "but it's just something that other teams don't have to go through. I stood in line for half an hour yesterday at customs carrying my heavy bag, These issues should have been addressed from the start." The cultural touchstones of American life were missing, or transmuted. There was no ESPN to watch, with its familiar highlight shows — and with its placement of the NBA high in the sporting firmament. Instead, players unlucky enough not to have a grey-market satellite dish capable of pulling in the U.S. sports network (Carter had one at his place, but Alvin Williams and Charles Oakley did not) made do with local carriers and their diet of hockey, curling and figure skating.

George Lynch, a former Grizzlie, opined that one of the problems players encountered in Vancouver was the lack of proper grocery stores. Haircuts were another tough order on Canada's west coast, with former Vancouver GM Stu Jackson sending anyone who asked (including visiting black reporters) to his barber. As journeyman forward Anthony Avent was driven into Vancouver from the airport after being traded from Orlando, he noticed the lack of black faces on the streets. "Where do the brothers hang?" he asked.

"Oh, the Grizzlies dressing room," the official replied brightly.

The winters were cold, and so was the interest in the NBA, at least relative to their homeland. The taxes were high, and so were the prices. "I can't believe it," Patrick Ewing moaned to his Knicks teammates during a stop in Toronto in the Raptors' early days. "These batteries cost me $5.99." Ewing was making US$18 million at the time.

The tax issue was what bothered players the most. In B.C. the top rate for residents is 49 per cent; in Ontario, 46.5. That's much higher than the highest U.S. rate of 39.6 per cent. But there were ways around it. Nonresidents get a knockdown to 43.5 per cent in Ontario, and a further reduction by declaring the number of days spent in Canada so that a proportionate share of income is taxed at the Canadian rate. Grunwald would combat what he called the "misconceptions and myths" surrounding the issue with a mailing to NBA agents and media in the summer of 2000. According to Grunwald's numbers, and in the opinion of a Toronto tax lawyer experienced in dealing with American athletes and actors, the issue was overstated. Some in the Toronto dressing room agreed.

"There are tax strategies now that didn't exist in the first year I was here," said Tracy Murray. "But still there's an attitude about it."

For a player like Charles Oakley, though, at $5.76 million the team's highest-paid player, the cost of playing in Canada amounted to a couple hundred thousand dollars — without any kind of strategies in place, such as deferring some income or negotiating a signing bonus. For others moving from teams in Texas and Florida, where there is no state tax, the difference is marked. One former NBA executive estimated at most a 20 per cent difference in the amount of taxes paid while playing for a U.S.-based team versus a Canadian-based team. "It's just about equal if you're playing in New York or L.A., but if a guy comes in from Texas or Florida, there is some sticker shock," he said.

There were other reasons, too. Just having to file a second return, in a foreign country, was a pain to American-born players. The idea of a foreign country compiling personal information was another concern. "It's irrational, but it is a very real concern," said the tax lawyer.

To others, like Croatian Zan Tabak, an original Raptor who spent two-plus seasons in Toronto, it was at its most basic a case of whining ignorance.

"Most of the Americans in this league don't know what they're talking about," said Tabak with a shrug. "They don't seem to understand that the quality of life is higher in Canada. When I played here, I felt it just as soon as I crossed the border. Yes, the television stations are different, and the newspapers are different, but they're all reporting the same news."

The Raptors had overcome some of the stigma by adding players like Charles Oakley and Mark Jackson, although their overall record of attracting free agents still indicated an uphill struggle. Vancouver, with its constant losing, was another story entirely. "Players don't want to go there," said

Vancouver's Erick Strickland. "They think it's like the desert."

"It's ignorance," said Steve Nash of the attitude. Nash is Canada's most celebrated basketballer, a Victoria, B.C., native who plays for the Dallas Mavericks and starred for Canada at the 2000 Olympics. "They go to Toronto and they don't seem to mind it there. Winning is always going to be the constant."

And now, in Washington at this all-star weekend, Canada's other NBA team, the one that could only seem to lose, was on the skids and preparing to leave the country. Grizzlies owner Michael Heisley had bought the team in August of 2000, pledging to keep it in Vancouver as long as possible. A scant few months later, he was telling a different story, claiming losses of US$46 million and talking about relocation. He had found an ally in Stern.

It was quite a turnaround for the commissioner, and for the NBA. Once upon a time, Stern had crowed about this expansion. Call it a beach-head to further international exposure, and he didn't disagree. Call it a move into the largest untapped market outside of the United States, and he nodded enthusiastic assent. The Grizzlies actually made a little profit their first two years, until their payroll started rising while the Canadian dollar continued to erode.

In six years they had gone from expansion newcomer to an unquali-fied failure. So much for Stern's golden touch. He had taken special pride in the fact that no NBA franchise had relocated in 17 years, going all the way back to his first year as commissioner. Just 18 months before, Stern had blocked St. Louis businessman Bill Laurie from buying the Grizzlies because Laurie made no bones about wanting to move the team out of Vancouver. Since then, the numbers had only grown worse. A difficult task to begin with, selling the Grizzlies in Vancouver had become impossible.

The reasons were simple. The Grizzlies and the Raptors had started off at the same time, but from there the paths diverged wildly. If the Raptors were a rocket in their early days under Isiah Thomas — going up in a blaze of colour, then coming down as shards of flaming wreckage — then the Grizzlies were never anything but earthbound. While Thomas was drafting the dynamic Stoudamire as his foundation stone, his Vancouver counterpart, Stu Jackson, was building a team around lumbering Bryant Reeves, more stone than foundation. Vancouver's first coach, Brian Winters, was a Lenny Wilkens protégé and shared his mentor's lukewarm demeanour; Toronto would get the real thing in Wilkens five years later. Perhaps most important, the Raptors' most significant ownership changeover did not result in an absentee, American-based owner taking over. Vancouver's Arthur Griffiths, though, had become quickly overextended and sold out to Seattle billionaire John McCaw, who was followed by Heisley.

The Grizzlies had a star in Shareef Abdur-Rahim, but Jackson failed to build around him. The Grizzlies never got off the expansion treadmill. With Jackson running the basketball operation, they finished with the worst record in the league three times in five seasons, winning 78 games and losing 300, a stupendously unsuccessful mark.

There were factors working against them other than bad management. Because of the NBA's expansion agreement, they (and the Raptors) were precluded from getting the top pick in the annual draft until 1999, one of several conditions that hamstrung their chances. Throw in a Canadian dollar that had shrunk in value from 75 cents U.S. when the Raptors were granted a franchise, to below 64 cents in 2001, and the odds of success were further reduced. With no local broadcast revenues to speak of, both the Raptors and the Grizzlies rely more heavily on gate receipts — in Toronto's case, over 50 per cent, well above the league aver-age of 43 per cent. All of those ticket dollars come in Canadian loonies, of course. Jackson once estimated that it took the Grizzlies three or four game nights to generate the same kind of revenue the Knicks would in one evening of basketball at Madison Square Garden, a staggering difference.

Even with all the ineptitude and uncertainty in the front office, though, the Grizzlies drew respectable crowds at their GM Place home. But they weren't the right kind of fans, according to the NBA head office. In Washington, D.C., an uncharacteristically crabby Stern blasted Vancouver for not supporting the Grizzlies. In his view, it was specifical-ly the Vancouver corporate community who were to blame, failing to step up and provide the money in sponsorships and promotions and ticket and suite sales that would have meant a turnaround. It was hardly surprising, though. The size of that community had always been limited. And while Ontario was enjoying prosperity in the late 1990s, B.C. was going through much tougher times.

The Grizzlies' impending departure was regarded as just another of many disappearing acts in Canadian pro sports in this big-ticket age, more fuel for those American-born players who played in Canada but fled the country the day after the season ended. Would Vince Carter follow them? Take Carter out of Toronto, and many felt the Raptors would disappear into the ether, but keep him and …

"Even if they re-sign Vince Carter, they won't be able to afford it," predicted Grizzlies vice-president Dick Versace, adding that in 2002 the Raptors would be in the same precarious position as Vancouver was.

Versace, one of the loosest of NBA cannons, was Heisley's basketball brain. That he would offer an unsolicited opinion on the Raptors' future drove Toronto management wild with rage, and club president Richard

Peddie was on the line to the league office pushing for disciplinary action immediately. Versace was dutifully fined $10,000, and went to his public-relations staff and demanded that they pay the fine themselves for letting him say it. (Not surprisingly, they told him to take a hike.) The Raptors still seethed, wondering why players like McGrady, with their regular pronouncements on Carter's future, weren't disciplined as well.

While Versace's words dripped with overstatement and envy — Tank Black had advised the Grizzlies not to bother drafting Carter in 1998, saying he had no interest in playing in Vancouver — the notion that the Raptors were heavily dependent on Carter for their credibility inside and outside their community was not. And skepticism that the Raptors would be able to afford not just Carter but the requisite cast around him was hardly surprising. Yes, that was his teammate Antonio Davis who wanted the maximum, or close to it, to stay beyond this season.

While Vince Carter tried to shrug it all off, the fact was that for many south of the border, he *is* the Raptors. Nowhere was that more evident than at this all-star game, where popularity means everything — and Carter, if his jersey sales are the measuring stick, is the most popular player in the league today. After his victory in the slam-dunk contest the year before, Carter's no. 15 in Toronto's purple colours passed Kevin Garnett, Kobe Bryant and Allen Iverson as the top-selling uniform in the league.

Those Carter jerseys were out in full force this all-star weekend long, including Saturday morning, time for the league's annual Team Up celebration. It is a place of strange, mixed messages, where corporate interests meet motherhood issues on a basketball floor set up at a Washington hall. McGrady and Carter are part of the "celebration," their 30-second appearance a hit with the audience of schoolchildren. Shaquille O'Neal walks out to centre court with a microphone in hand and earnestly tells the primary-school kids four rules to live by: obey your parents; go to school; be true to yourself; and lastly, "eat plenty of Nestlé Crunch bars."

The NBA used to call this its Stay in School celebration, but dropped that tag when even the league couldn't avoid the irony of its youngest players skipping university to become instant professional millionaires. Now it is known as Team Up, pitched at the same young audience. It preaches the importance of teamwork and community spirit with the likes of Carter and McGrady up on the stage — once together, now flying solo as the undisputed stars of their teams. Until the next free-agency period, anyway. Team Up, indeed.

And if you came looking for the spirit of competition? The slam-dunk event was turning into a non-event. McGrady, Carter, Steve Francis and Kobe Bryant had ruled themselves out for one reason or another. Together, the quartet were arguably the NBA's best in the air — the order of finish in 2000 was Carter-Francis-McGrady, and Bryant had won the '98 title — but their excuses included injuries, boredom and the fear of finishing second-best. "I'll never do it again," McGrady said. "I don't think I'm a very good dunker. I'm okay, but not good enough to win. Not with Vince around."

Bryant wondered about his chances, too, after a sore ankle nearly caused him to skip the whole weekend. "I'm too old right now," he said of the dunk contest. "Maybe down the road I'll be able to compete in some of those events, and do the things I did when I was 17." Bryant is all of 22 years old.

The primary aim of the slam-dunk contest is to delight the fans, but that seemed far from the minds of these pros. In a way, it's understandable. Aesthetically, the contest walks a fine line. Carter in 2000 had delivered a "masterpiece" in the estimation of no less than Julius Erving, reviving an event that had grown stale. Now he was bowing out, because of that sore knee. And everyone followed his lead. For the others, the only thing worse than losing to Carter in a dunk-off would be to win it with him on the sideline.

No wonder the slam-dunk in Washington turned into such a dud. Baron Davis turned into the poster boy for the whole sorry spectacle, the pre-show favourite who went in for his final dunk with his headband pulled over his eyes. He launched and missed the rim completely. Instead of appreciation, there was derisive laughter from the MCI Center crowd and an early move to the exits. Even if the all-star weekend was no longer just about basketball — the best 10,000 seats in the 20,374 sellout house go to the NBA for their sponsors and preferred customers, pushing the local season ticket holders to the rafters or out of the building — it was a singularly uninspiring day, from Team Up to Tune Out.

When Sunday rolled around and the showcase event of the all-star game beckoned, Bryant and McGrady and Carter answered the call. And the contest, at least by its own standards, turned out to be a decent enough exhibition.

It was certainly different, and Carter had much to do with that from the first moment he and Bryant found themselves matched against one another. Here, amid these brightest of lights, came the biggest matchup around in this post-Jordan era: the two players who had been judged to be closest to His Airness in terms of high-flying derring-do, if not in achievement.

Whenever Carter and Bryant meet, there is a heightened sense of anticipation in the arena. No thanks to expansion and a bloated 29-team league, Bryant's Lakers and Carter's Raptors play just twice a season. It isn't much time to get acquainted. But they know each other well, going back to their AAU days, and this all-star stage is another opportunity. Because it is Carter vs. Bryant, just like that game in Orlando was Carter vs. McGrady. Purists abhor the focus, but the NBA long ago tied its ratings to the hype created by the likes of the Lakers' budding young superstar and his eastern reflection. On the television networks, their meetings will be sold in that now rather tired NBA fashion: on a first-name basis. Vince vs. Kobe (ouch, go the purists). Big enough to sell tickets at the mere mention. Big enough to make their coaches flinch at the complete sublimation of the team ethos.

And big enough to eclipse the rather large figure of O'Neal. When the Raptors and the Lakers met for the first time in December, the seven-foot-one centre of L.A.'s defending champion team was for long stretches little more than an enormous bystander, picking up two quick fouls that sent him to the bench and in effect yielded the stage to the two protagonists. They made the most of it. When Phil Jackson got verbal on referee Eddie F. Rush, Carter breezed by the Lakers bench and told him, "Stop whining!" It was a strange admonishment — like most young NBA players, including Bryant, Carter acts as if every whistle against him is a cruel injustice.

In the game's final minutes, Carter roused himself and the Raptors, bringing them back from 15 points down. He even played some spirited defence, rising to block Bryant's shot just before the buzzer sounded, forcing overtime in a game that was tied 91–91. Bryant played defence and returned the favour, rejecting Carter's shot in the extra period. Like Carter vs. McGrady, it is hard to take your eyes off them when they meet, and this was no exception. The Lakers won the game, just like they would win again in Los Angeles three months later, and Bryant would joke about killing two birds with one stone: the game, and his matchup with Carter.

So much for their mutual denials that these games don't matter any more than others. As the two Jordanesques, they will be yoked together for some time yet, subject to the inevitable comparisons. It was Jordan himself who made the observation in the spring of 2000 that Bryant was the better all-round player. And just about any NBA player or observer concurs. Bryant does play much better, more consistent perimeter defence, and he showed it in that matchup with the Raptors in December. A first-team all-defence selection in voting by the league's coaches, Bryant three times funnelled Mark Jackson into the sideline, trapping him there helplessly, forcing turnovers, making him look completely befuddled.

Carter bristles at such categorical judgments, pointing out that there is no presence like O'Neal on his side, no intimidating big man behind him to allow him to freelance with just a little more swagger and daring.

"I sure could use a big centre," he said during the Olympics, when news of Patrick Ewing's trade to Seattle made its way to the antipodes. "You get to relax. You can gamble. I can do that here [at the Olympics] with the guys behind me, and I'm really enjoying it. It's different."

For now, this Ginger-vs.-Marianne debate for the millennium percolates, at least among the NBA's younger set of customers and in the media. "Vince Is the Prince, But Kobe Is King," read a *San Francisco Chronicle* headline during the spring of 2000, when Carter was crashing out of the playoffs and Bryant was on his way to a title, his first, with the Lakers.

In the wildest imaginings of *Sports Illustrated* and presumably David Stern's marketing department, it would grow into the kind of bicoastal game-within-the-game that the league cashed in on when Bird and Magic went at it a generation ago. That pair began their rivalry in the NCAA title game of 1979 matching Magic's Michigan State with Bird's Indiana State. From there, it seemed not a year went by when the Lakers and

Johnson, and the Celtics and Bird, were not in the thick of it when it counted the most. For the first decade they were in the league, one of them would play in the finals. Three times, the Lakers and the Celtics faced one another with a championship the prize, L.A. winning two of those encounters. It was a lot of time to build respect and an edge.

Banking on another, similar contest between Bryant and Carter is futile, at least for now, like searching for the next Michael Jordan. For one thing, college basketball has changed drastically from Bird and Magic's era, when the usual practice had players staying through their senior years, building up a television following and recognition — and a foundation as a basketball player — that served them up ready-made and cheaply for the pros. For another, who knows where they'll end up when the current contracts run their course? The NBA of this era is a movable players' feast.

At least their backgrounds have been similar. Both of them grew up in basketball hothouses, albeit in vastly different environments. While Carter went to North Carolina, Bryant, the son of a former pro, went straight from high school into the NBA, his handlers engineering a trade to the glamorous Lakers before he had even played a game.

Now, after one championship year in Los Angeles, he was showing signs of rampant egomania in his feud with O'Neal. If there was an NBA soap opera that had legs in this winter of 2001, O'Neal and Bryant was it. Bryant started it in the preseason, saying that O'Neal had come into training camp overweight. When Bryant pined for more of the ball and the limelight, O'Neal shot back a reminder that the Lakers had won a championship running the offence through him. The Lakers had become a case study in NBA dysfunction, their "Who's the Man?" debate overshadowing their season. Lakers head coach Phil Jackson shook his head and blamed Bryant.

"Someone told me that in high school, Kobe used to sabotage his own game," Jackson told Rick Telander of the *Chicago Sun-Times*. "So the game could be close. So he could dominate at the end. To sabotage the team process, to be so self-centered in your own process … it's almost stupefying."

Carter was free of such self-absorption. While Bryant's first trip to the NBA playoffs four years earlier had ended in him putting up a welter of brainless, long-range airballs, Carter's most telling moment in his postseason debut in the spring of 2000 had him first shooting 3-of-20 in a Game 1 loss, then passing up a potential game-winning shot next time out. The knock on Carter wasn't so much about selfish play, although at times he was guilty of that. It concerned his desire for the game, and for sporting greatness itself.

The parallels to Bird and Magic are tenuous, if not nonexistent. That Carter-Bryant had been suggested at all tells you (again) about the NBA at the dawn of a new millennium: tired, overhyped and trying desperately to go back to the same formula that worked so well for so long but that doesn't fit the times. Carter and Bryant are in a unique situation: they have conquered a league that is showing all the signs of being conquered in the battle for public affection. However it plays out, wherever they're playing, as long as they're playing, Kobe vs. Vince is going to top the marquee. The only question is how big that marquee is going to be within the universe of pro sports and whose uniform they will be wearing at the time.

At this all-star game, their matchup began innocently and spectacularly enough. Carter showed the ball on the left wing, facing Bryant, who with that sore ankle looked to have all the mobility of a tired dog. Carter switched his dribble from right to left hand, his first step as lethal as ever, but nothing of the sort that Bryant couldn't match under normal circumstances. But not this time. Bryant yielded the baseline to Carter like he was the doorman at a swanky hotel, and Carter lifted off, rotated 360 degrees and finished with a nasty flourish. So far, it was so good: just another all-star moment, the sort everyone in the moneyed sellout crowd was here to see, and the most expressive among them was O'Neal, contorting into a hilarious, rubberfaced sneer for the TV camera.

Down at the other end, it was Bryant's turn to isolate Carter on the left wing. Except Carter came right up on Bryant's flank. His chest bumped Bryant, pushing him off his spot, keeping him from finding a comfort level from which to begin his drive. Crowding him. Bugging him.

As far as Bryant was concerned, Vince Carter had picked a hell of a time to play tight defence. All-star games are to classic, two-way basketball as a hot dog is to well-marbled sirloin, and the players know it. The west's Vlade Divac, when asked what youngsters could learn from watching the all-star game, looked at his interrogator disbelievingly: "I don't know if they can pick up anything," he said. "It's better for them to just work with their coaches on the basic things. This is very far from them."

But Carter had a point to prove, and he would take whatever opportunity he could get, not with some fancy display of dunking but with this show of feistiness, however misplaced it seemed to some. It was especially fitting given that Jordan, now a Wizards part owner and vice-president and general manager, was sitting up there in his private box watching, the spotlight shining on him during a timeout, the crowd as ever calling out his name.

In NBA circles, it was something of an open secret that Vince Carter, should he make himself available, would be the most desirable, most sought-after player on the free-agent market in the summer of 2002, his first chance to go that way. It was also plain that Jordan and the Wizards were making every possible move they could to clear up their under-achieving roster with a view to having major free agent money ready at that same time.

It was Jordan who had once criticized Carter for his lack of interest in playing defence. And it was now Jordan who was rumoured to be making a comeback. He dropped hints here and there: he would love to have matched himself against the likes of Carter, he said; he began working out harder, but claimed it was just to take off some excess pounds.

Fact was, Jordan had tried on two occasions without success to con-tact Carter's mother in the hopes, perhaps, of explaining his comments and rebuilding a bridge that had been damaged. A prospective photo opportunity of the pair in Washington before a Raptors–Wizards game had failed to come off.

They had once been at least as close as any superstar would be with his purported protégé. They had played in the usual sort of summertime scrimmages that are part of the Chapel Hill scene. Carter had worked for two years at Jordan's summer basketball camp and at that of Jordan's friend Fred Whitfield. Before Carter was drafted, Jordan had given him a good-luck pep talk. And when Carter went to the Raptors, Jordan called his old buddy Charles Oakley and told him to watch Carter's back.

And now it was Jordan who was criticizing Carter. Given Carter's reluctance to rock the boat in the public, it was Michelle who would be the most vocal, suggesting that Jordan was jealous of Carter's fame and success. "I question the sanity of someone who comes out and says something like that, just from the standpoint of how it might come back to haunt him," she said. "I think there is some jealousy there.

"It really hurt Vince. It wasn't so much what he said, but it was the fact that here was a fellow Tar Heel making the comments. It's drilled into you there that you are part of a family that stands up for each other. But not in that case."

Given all that, Michelle Carter was surprised at the response when she asked her son whether he would ever go to Washington and play for Jordan.

"He thought about it for a long time and then he said, 'Yeah,'" she related. "Part of me didn't really expect that, and didn't really want to hear that. But Vince explained it this way: he said Michael Jordan is a guy he still really respects."

And right here in front of Jordan and the rest of the MCI Center crowd, Carter and the eastern conference were supposed to lose a game against the more powerful west. Even if it is a game that is usually forgotten the next morning. Trailing by 19 points as the third quarter drew to a close, Carter discarded the NBC microphone he had been wearing. He went out and never stopped D-ing up Bryant. And when it was down to the last stroke, a one-point game, he made the play — defending on a screen and roll, the staple of the NBA offensive diet, and the one that he tends to sleepwalk through most nights. Carter jumped out to get just a piece of his hand, perhaps a knuckle and a half, on Tim Duncan's last-gasp shot from the baseline, and the eastern conference wins 111–110.

After beaming through his interviews on the floor, Carter looks up just for a moment at Jordan's private box. It's just a quick glance, but telling. He trots off with a satisfied look, intent on getting Lil' Bow Wow's autograph along with the rest of his teammates' scribbles on his all-star jersey. The locker room is unbelievably crowded. Just another all-star weekend party, the last one, and Carter never stops smiling.

No, it's not a real game. At times like these, it looks like a lot more.

CHAPTER 9

March 2001:

Bland Is Beautiful

I t is twelve noon on trade deadline day. High noon, in the NBA date-book, a scant few hours before the cutoff to make changes that might do any number of things to the average NBA general manager: make your season, break it (along with your reputation) or just get the owner or the media or the customers in the stands off your back for a day.

For this group, it is big-balls time. Earlier in the season, with the games stretching off into the distance like telephone poles on the Prairies, there are conversations between them that swing between joking and jabbing, and most of the time mean very little. Throughout any season, there is nothing in the world easier to find than an NBA trade rumour. Then the deadline arrives, and the inevitable moment when you show me yours and I'll show you mine.

Being an NBA general manager is a high-wire act at the best of times, but the trade deadline is something else entirely. It's not at all the vortex of activity of popular imagining — more like an uncomfortable wait at the edge of a high cliff. Make the wrong call, and it could mean the end of your job. Stumble just a little, and there are serious consequences. Show any signs of distress, and everyone notices. "The truth is, this is a piranha tank," Portland's Bob Whitsitt said as he acquired Damon Stoudamire from the Raptors in 1998.

So here is Glen Grunwald, Whitsitt's partner in that deal three years ago, just hours away from making two trades that will change the face of his playoff-bound team. Another grey February day is passing over the railway lands below his corner office window, and he is simply lounging. Hell, he is almost lolling. Grunwald has always been among the most unassuming and unprepossessing of GMs, and he certainly can look it. He sits nearly horizontal on the sofa in his office, one long leg propped up on a cluttered coffee table, the other splayed off at a 45-degree angle to the floor. The television is on — one of those 24-hour sports highlights shows, and every 10 minutes or so the same reel of goals and baskets and fights is repeated. He idly flips his tie as he talks. It is not disrespect, or boredom, or wanting to be somewhere else. Grunwald is a shy man. He acts as if he can't understand why anyone would be interested in anything he has to say.

"So," he says. "You still want to hang around here all day?"

There is no time to answer the question, because (finally, it seems) the phone is ringing. On the television's sports ticker, the news that prized centre Dikembe Mutombo has been traded from Atlanta to Philadelphia, the eastern conference leader, signals that this trade-deadline day is officially open for business. Grunwald excuses himself and takes the call in an adjoining room. He is out a few minutes later, and his two-fingered typing hunts and pecks away on the laptop. "Just checking some numbers," he explains.

For the rest of the day he will have his head down, working the phones like a boiler-room pro, bouncing from rival GMs to player agents to club president Richard Peddie and the public-relations staff and, finally, whenever possible, to the players themselves.

Just after the 6 p.m. deadline, he will sign off and step in front of the cameras almost apologetically to announce a couple of occurrences that in this cozy world qualify as earth-shaking. First, the underused and ill-suited Corliss Williamson, the consolation prize when Grunwald and the Raptors lost Doug Christie once and for all, has been traded to Detroit. Williamson had been "on the block," as they say in the newspapers, for the entire season. Jerome Williams is the man coming the other way, a fifth-year forward of boundless enthusiasm who immediately packs his 4 x 4 and drives through the night, arriving in Toronto at 4:30 a.m. (Williams is the self-declared "Junk Yard Dog." When he is introduced to Raptors governor Larry Tanenbaum the next night, he is at his typical enthusiastic, bordering on manic: "JYD," he says, pumping Tanenbaum's hand. "Pleased to meetcha.")

There is little surprise here. It is a swap that had been bandied about between the two teams for the past couple of months. Indeed, Grunwald has been following Williams for the past three years. When the Stoudamire watch was down to its final few hours in February of 1998, the Pistons backed out of a possible deal that would have made Williams a Raptor. Instead, Grunwald's first trade as GM was to send Stoudamire to Portland.

It's the other half of Grunwald's communiqué that shocks. Mark Jackson is gone to the Knicks, his old team in his hometown of New York.

Jackson was another consolation prize, the free agent Grunwald had signed when no one else seemed to want to come to Toronto. Just four nights before this trade deadline, he had moved past Isiah Thomas into no. 4 on the NBA's all-time assists list. The Air Canada Centre crowd had stood and cheered respectfully, like one would cheer a dignitary — they would never have the time or the chance to gather him any closer. Jackson was a smart, cerebral point man who was purported to be another calming influence in the Raptors dressing room, post–Butch Carter. Now he was being sent away along with Muggsy Bogues for Chris Childs, a prickly backup point guard.

Grunwald has always been known as a nice guy, the quiet fellow in the background. But in this picture, with these moves, it is almost as if he is thumbing his nose, partly at himself. Jackson and Williamson were being written off as mistakes — his mistakes. But as well, they were moves made at least partly in response to the Butch Carter hangover.

Until now, this was how it had been for Grunwald. When he inherited the job from Isiah Thomas, he had to accommodate Stoudamire's trade demand and work from that starting point. Later, he worked in tandem with Butch Carter, bringing in veteran players who would mean credibility and victories to try to recapture a fan base that had been dwindling; he wasn't about to accept the same old thing of building around youth and waiting patiently. More importantly, he realized that the paying customers weren't going to accept it, either.

Even the Jackson signing had an air of face-saving about it, a public-relations gesture after a summer of getting his butt kicked in the free-agent wars. Williamson had been a huge flop, and it was Kings GM Geoff Petrie who was being hailed as Executive of the Year material for getting Christie.

And now Grunwald was reversing ground. Big balls? It certainly looked that way.

The Jackson trade had implications. No longer did it matter to Grunwald that Jackson's buddy Antonio Davis would be pissed off — and by extension, perhaps, Davis's agent, Bill Duffy. Davis was already telling his teammates he was going to opt out of his contract in the summer and test free agency. As far back as the Sydney Olympics, Duffy had begun turning the screws on the Raptors: "If Antonio goes, Vince isn't going to want to stay either," Duffy warned. It was an agent's rhetoric, sure.

Davis would henceforth send out the kind of signals that indicated he had no interest in coming back to Toronto. Soon after his all-star game appearance, his body language turned tortured. He marked his sneakers with Jackson's initials, an NBA cliché that proclaims a malcontent as it commemorates the departed. (After Thomas left the Raptors, Stoudamire printed "Who killed J.R.?" on his sneakers, the initials his shorthand for his GM buddy Isiah.) Jackson talked about how nice it was to play with his friend Davis for four months, then slammed Grunwald for "unprofessional" conduct in not informing him first of a deal that he gleefully celebrated by sending to his teammates the pager message "I'm a Knick again."

The one person Grunwald couldn't afford to upset was Vince Carter, who was indeed the only Raptor Grunwald informed before the deals were made. Publicly, Carter offered little in the way of an opinion one way or another. And although he was not going to rock the boat in private, it was clear he wasn't entirely pleased. Like just about everyone else in the Toronto dressing room, Carter wasn't really clear on why the changes were made.

"It was difficult to see those guys go," he said. "Jax and I were just getting to know each other. We would go out and eat dinner together on the road, and spend time on the bus, just talking. That was tough for me. To lose a friend like Muggsy, too, well that's rough. The hardest thing was trying to just move on like nothing really happened. I was disappointed."

To Grunwald, it was as much a case of who was staying as who was going. The look of the Raptors had changed dramatically. With Jackson's departure, Alvin Williams, free of Butch Carter's leash and enjoying his best season, was promoted from backup to starter. Williams qualifies as Wilkens's major triumph, a reclamation project Grunwald had given up on a year previous. Now, Grunwald was setting the stage to re-sign Williams, who would be another free agent come summer; he was banking on more long-term progress with him than with the aging, defensively challenged and expensive Jackson. Indeed, in practice, Williams had been destroying Jackson in their one-on-one matchup.

This was different, for sure, with a yappy, tenacious perimeter defender in Childs, not as big as Christie or as much of a scorer, but the sort of player they felt they needed. Only five players — Carter, Davis, Charles Oakley, Alvin Williams and Dell Curry — remained from the 12-man playoff roster of the previous year, an enormous turnover with the 2001 playoff season less than two months away. "I think we're better," Grunwald mused. "I wonder if the players believe that."

The popular notion of Grunwald and Wilkens is of a pair of low-key, almost pulseless personalities — the bland leading the bland. By extension, the Raptors' cool demeanour, their listless mediocrity through the first half of the season, their lack of urgency, it all seemed in perfect harmony with the image. Part of it was calculated. After the tumult of the final days of Butch Carter, Grunwald could feel some relief with Wilkens at the helm. "This is great," he said during one of December's quiet days. "I haven't looked twice at a headline."

But Grunwald's actions during the trade surely belied the image. He had brought about a wholesale makeover in the very midst of a season that could take more definitive shape — or not. That was Grunwald's gamble to make, and in truth, it was a huge gamble, with Wilkens in the background, nodding his assent.

For both, looks are deceiving. Underneath the GM's bookish exterior is the competitive flame of an elite athlete whose immensely promising career ended before it had a chance to take off. Then there is Wilkens, who has managed to keep his head for 40 years in the rough-and-tumble world of pro basketball, a man who still feels he has much to prove, despite having proven so much.

In the sideline huddles during timeouts, he pulls up his chair and spends the first 20 seconds or so staring down intently at the markerboard, as if the scrawl and the numbers in front of him were some code to be cracked. If someone has something to say, he yields the floor. If it is criticism of a blown assignment, he will listen and turn to the transgressor — "Did you get that? Did you hear what he was saying?" he told Carter and Morris Peterson after Childs had dressed them down for failing to go over an opponent's screens. When it is Wilkens's turn, he suddenly snaps to attention: You go here. You cut there. You set the screen here, and on and on. At halftime, there is no videotape to hastily cue up from the first 24 minutes. Wilkens goes straight to the blackboard, pulling the patterns out of his head, a head that started soaking up the game before the Sputnik satellite was sent up, when the Dodgers were his heroes in his hometown of Brooklyn and yes, that was Jackie Robinson he delivered groceries to.

Comparing the NBA that Wilkens came into in 1960 to this era's version is like putting the Sputnik up against the space shuttle. There are fundamental similarities, but so much has changed. Wilkens has not. The suits may be different, and the hair may have turned a distinguished, muted grey, but he is still the same: dependable, low-key, easy to remember. And perhaps, given the criticisms that he is too nice, or too laid-back (he cringes at the term), or too old-fashioned, he is even easier to forget. Wilkens has been around so long, he has been taken for granted at times.

"The thing with Lenny has always been his patience, his willingness to work with players," says Steve Jones, whose last pro season coincided with Wilkens's first as head coach, in 1975–76 at Portland. "It was easier for him then, I think, because players had more incentives. Today, the players have huge guarantees. They don't understand how to play, but they do understand the money they're being paid."

As a player, Wilkens was the model point guard: a silky driver who could find his mates with the perfect pass, making everyone around him better. He could also score, with a running flip hook and a one-handed set shot from another era. "A skinny little man with no jump shot and a hair-style by Dagwood Bumstead," wrote one early *Sports Illustrated* chronicler. "He plays guard with one hand — his left — better than all but a few pros do with two."

He was "Sweety Cakes" to Elgin Baylor, "the Little Fella" to his teammates in Cleveland. Wilkens was made player coach in 1969 with Seattle, and his low-key, nice-guy style was a good fit from the start. It became his trademark.

"Lenny likes to do most things with a quiet dignity," says Jones. "As a player he was a feisty guy, and very competitive. That doesn't translate when you see him on the sidelines. When you think of competitive people, it's always supposed to be about ranting and raving. Lenny's not that way at all. When you're looking at him, he's not yelling and screaming. He's not going to make the players look bad. For a lot of coaches, noise gets mistaken for doing the job. It goes back to his background, how he was brought up and how he was treated as a pro."

For Wilkens, the players were their own policemen. He wasn't going to play that role, so it was Oakley, one of two co-captains, who ran the dressing room. The Oakley rules regarding game days were absolute: no cellphones, no music, no food, no television other than game tapes. When Morris Peterson showed up late for a flight out of Toronto, it was Oakley who chewed him out. Wilkens was content to stay in the background and let his players work it out. In Cleveland, he kept a couple pairs of boxing gloves in his office. When two players got at one another, he'd point to them and invite them to settle it right there.

"I'm not an emotional person," Wilkens says. "Or let's say, I don't show emotion. I don't feel I have to broadcast what I say or do. If people want to take time to know me, fine. I'm quiet, but don't mistake quietness for weakness."

It is more than a little amazing that with this kind of low profile and patrician bearing, Wilkens has endured. Coaching is the ultimate in high-risk, high-reward sports jobs. Fashions change quickly, and burnout is as common as self-promotion. In this first season of the new century, some oldtimers at the top of the profession were looking vulnerable. In Los Angeles, Phil Jackson's halo has been knocked askew as Bryant and O'Neal bickered, Jackson openly siding with O'Neal. He is putting on weight, looking less Zen-like with each headline. And Pat Riley, the very model of the *GQ* coach, is beginning to look more and more like a Mount Rushmore figure. In March, the Raptors visited Miami on the night that Alonzo Mourning returned to action for the first time since the Olympics. Riley worried about Mourning's health, and the Heat promptly fell into a tailspin, their chemistry upset. They would eventually be swept out of the playoffs.

This is an era of young coaches, of ex-players who jump directly into the head coach's chair with minimal or no experience coming up the ladder. The success of Indiana's Larry Bird, like Wilkens a sideline minimalist ("nobody calls him laid-back," grumbles Wilkens), or of Doc Rivers in Orlando, has led to a search for coaches with "people skills." Relating to these sometimes unreachable young pros is more important than X's and O's. And so McGrady gushes about how much he admires Rivers. Scott Skiles in Phoenix and Byron Scott in New Jersey arrived the same way.

Wilkens has been around long enough to see the wheel turn 360 degrees. When he began coaching, the same prevailing wind was blowing, and it brought him into Seattle with the Sonics. It has changed direction often since. For a time it was fresh-faced, fast-talking college coaches who were flavour of the day, or ex-assistants of a certain type — the Five-Star Basketball Camp products, for instance.

Mostly, though, it has been about hiring white guys. The NBA's player base is more than 80 per cent black. But only eight head coaches and four general managers were African-American at the outset of the 2000–01 season. The NBA has tended to give black head coaches more chances to fail than flourish. There are few second chances, too. Charlotte's Paul Silas, who wound up his playing career under Wilkens in Seattle, had to wait more than fifteen years after being fired by the Clippers for the opportunity with the Hornets. The daunting numbers and fickle winds make Wilkens's longevity all the more remarkable. "Our league is kind of funny at times," Wilkens says acidly. "We're kind of trendy. It's not always consistent. I've always felt if you can coach, you can coach."

This time of year, all 29 of them in the sideline fraternity share the same video tan and terminal crabbiness. So much can go wrong so quickly, as Riley and Jackson can tell you. Wilkens made a deal with his wife, Marilyn, a long time ago. He wouldn't let the game eat him up. He would build breaks into his routine. And there would be routine, with the family settling in Seattle in the 1970s and staying there through Wilkens's various moves. The kids had their own friends that way, and a support system, and roots.

This season, despite all its frustrations and underachievement leading to these dizzying changes, is no different. When the Raptors blow a game before Christmas, Wilkens comes into practice the next day staring daggers, then gathers everyone around and organizes a lighthearted two hours of shooting games. On the bus to the airport, where as usual game tapes are the coach's preferred viewing pleasure, he substitutes a sitcom. As for himself, when the spirit moves him, he will go to mass at St. Michael's Cathedral on a weekday morning to augment his usual Sunday worship. The night of a gut-pounding win over Seattle, he goes home to his west-end condo and watches a movie instead of dissecting more games on video.

"Sometimes I'll read a book or watch a football game, just so long as I get away," he says. "You've got to relax, and so do the players. There's such a thing as overload."

Once upon a time, Lenny Wilkens wouldn't have deigned to look in the Raptors' direction. After the disastrous 1997–98 season, when Grunwald was pondering whether or not to keep Butch Carter, the GM's decision was made considerably easier by the fact that no candidate of any quality was interested.

Two years later, though, and Wilkens was jumping at the chance. Work had always been a constant for him. And there was this one element to his long career that had been missing: the opportunity to coach a budding superstar instead of being gored by one.

For seven years in Cleveland, Wilkens had the misfortune of being in the same division at the same time as the ascension of Michael Jordan from the best one-man band in the league to the best player to ever play the game. The Cavaliers of the late 1980s were very good, winning 50 games three times. But the Bulls and Jordan were always lying in wait. Four times they met in the playoffs, and all four times the Bulls advanced. Included was "the Shot," Jordan's levitating jumper that won their 1989 series, the Bulls' victory over Cleveland in the eastern final of 1992, and Chicago's 4–0 sweep of Cleveland in '93 that brought an end to the Wilkens era.

"Forget Jordan for a minute," Wilkens demurs. "What about Magic? What about Larry Bird? What about Julius?

"I've finally got the kind of player that can take the big shot, make the big play, when there's six seconds left and the game is on the line. And I'm loving every minute of it."

Wilkens has coached great players with otherworldly athleticism, of course. David Thompson played for him in Portland, and Dominique Wilkins in Atlanta. The difference is that those two were winding down their careers.

"With Vince, I would rank him up there with all the great players who've played the game, and he's still maturing," Wilkens says. "He has great athleticism, but he also has a great feel for the game. I tell him the sky should be the limit. That should be your goal — the sky. It's a good goal to have, because even if you don't touch the sky, you can make the stars or the moon, and that's pretty good too."

Wilkens has spent 41 years, two-thirds of his life, in the NBA. He has had more than 100 teammates and coached 174 more, while participating in nearly 4,000 games. Even with this breadth of experience, though, there were still moments watching Carter that made his head shake. During the Raptors' first exhibition game against Minnesota, Carter was in the right corner yo-yoing the ball when Wally Szczerbiak gave him just the tiniest sliver of an opening on the baseline.

"I'm watching and thinking there's no way he's going to get there. And he does. Reverse lay-up, and so easily," Wilkens says.

It is living proof of the old adage that something good, maybe even the One, may be just around the corner, no matter how bleak it seems at the time. And the 1999–2000 season was just that kind of time for Wilkens. He had gone to Atlanta from Cleveland, and the Hawks under Wilkens were solid regular-season performers for six years but could never advance beyond the second round of the playoffs. Then Atlanta GM Pete Babcock signed Isaiah Rider, a player of considerable talent but even bigger headaches off the floor, with failed drug tests, marijuana and assault convictions, missed practices, flagrant fouls, spitting on fans and even a cellphone-cloning charge on his lengthy rapsheet.

Rider's troubles continued in Atlanta. He was late for training camp. He would be late for practices, or miss them altogether. For a while, Wilkens covered up for him. Then came the incident after which everything went off the rails, when Rider was caught by teammates in an Orlando hotel room smoking pot. It placed him at odds with some of his teammates, splitting the locker room, and in trouble with the league. Rider would eventually be released before the season was out. Wilkens was not long to follow him, after the Hawks limped to a 28–54 record and missed the playoffs.

He has been around the NBA long enough to understand that keeping an even keel is what gets one through the long seasons with sanity intact. But Wilkens's patience wasn't the only thing tested by Rider. The experience made him question what he was doing as well. By contrast, Toronto offered more than just Vince Carter: there was emotional sustenance, and a chance, once again, to prove himself.

"It was total disenchantment," Wilkens said of the final season in Atlanta. "It was different than anything I'd ever experienced. There were days when you didn't even want to go to the arena. It's been such a quick turnaround coming here. But that part doesn't surprise me. I'm an optimist. I don't dwell on what's gone by."

For an optimist, though, he can be touchy. The bristles come out with the popular notion that he is a hands-off, uninvolved coach, or that he doesn't like to play younger players. In this Raptors season, Alvin Williams and Morris Peterson emerged as exhibits A and B for his defence.

While Wilkens was dragging through his closing days with the Hawks, the Raptors were giving up on Williams. He was a good perimeter defender and an excellent ball handler in transition, but he had been deemed a flop as the Raptors' starting point guard under Butch Carter after just a nine-game trial to start the 1999–2000 season. There were problems with Williams's game. He was not a particularly good distributor in the team's halfcourt schemes, and his shooting was streaky — when he came to Toronto from Portland in the Damon Stoudamire deal, his shot had a large hitch in it that would take a couple of seasons to be corrected.

But such technicalities were overshadowed by his loss of self-confidence under Butch Carter, who would bury him on the bench for long stretches. Over the final two months of that 1999–2000 season, the two barely looked at one another, let alone spoke. The last time they communicated with each other, in fact, was in a one-sided, 10-minute tirade that Williams levelled at Carter during a late-season team meeting that turned into a three-hour group therapy session. Williams's rant took his team-mates by surprise. "Boogie can be so quiet," said one Raptor, using Williams's locker-room nickname. "But that day he just about peeled the paint off the walls. We were all, like, way to go, Alvin!"

Williams showed up dressed in combat fatigues for the Raptors' final playoff game, as much personal statement as fashion statement. He felt he was under siege, and this was the only way he could show it to the world. After all, he had never been a complainer at any level of his basketball career. It was not the way he was raised. But he was certainly smarting as the summer of 2000 beckoned.

"That was the low point for me," said Williams. "Not playing, then playing, then not playing — then hearing the talk that we needed a point guard, when I knew I was a point guard. I had to be strong. At times, it was hard to do that."

With Wilkens, it was as if Williams finally had a coach who empathized rather than antagonized, and who understood the demanding nature of the position he was in. Wilkens, a former all-star point guard, still sees the game from that central, all-encompassing perspective. "You are a camera," his first pro coach, Paul Seymour, told him. He recognized the unique pressures and pitfalls that go with being the one person responsible.

It almost always has been that way for Leonard Wilkens Jr. He was the product of a mixed marriage, his white mother, Henrietta, a devout Irish Catholic, his black father, Leonard, a chauffeur who died too young, thrusting Wilkens into the role of man of the house at five years old. He was an altar boy who ran with a gang, even if the gang went by the unlike-ly moniker of the Aristocrats and was more interested in sports than turf wars. One day, Wilkens and his gang mates were stopped by police, who found only rosary beads in his pocket. He had a job delivering groceries at age seven, and three younger siblings to guide. He would learn to depend on no one but himself. He would get used to being the strong and silent type, the one who kept his emotions firmly in check.

"At CYO [Catholic Youth Organization] games and high-school games, I'd see the other kids with their fathers, and I missed my father," he says. "It was the same when we won the championship in Seattle [in 1979], the same when I passed Red Auerbach in wins and lit up a cigar. He was in his early forties when he died, and for a while I thought I might die young. I suppose that idea has always driven me, at least partly."

His mentor at the family's Bedford-Stuyvesant parish, Father Thomas Mannion, will perform the nuptials at his youngest daughter's wedding this summer, just as he did for Wilkens's eldest daughter, and just as he did for Wilkens and Marilyn. His son Randy works for the Raptors. Marilyn has spent this season back in Seattle, overseeing the finish of construction on their 8,000-square-foot dream house — just a few cracks the outcome of an earthquake in January that had Wilkens frantically calling home to make sure she was all right. She was. As for Henrietta, she lives in New York and still sees her son as many times as the NBA schedule permits.

For Wilkens, it had been a sometimes lonely winter. But as always, there was the game to cling to. As the Raptors passed the halfway point, there were signs of progress from the two youngsters. Williams had been splendid most of the way. Peterson was not nearly as consistent. He was erratic and aimless and out of control at times, driving veterans like Oakley crazy with his unpredictability. With almost no plays called for him, he tended to disappear in Wilkens's halfcourt schemes, employed merely as a cutter or an offensive rebounder. At the other end, he was a nearly automatic target for opposing attackers to pick on. Peterson struggled most nights. But if the Raptors managed to get a running game going, he could hit shots and finish the break. He was, in the broadest sense, the typical rookie finding his way and deferring to others.

Wilkens's rotation was a mystery to many, and in the postgame talk shows or the media reports it was a subject of much discussion, most of it negative. But going deep into his bench and mixing up how he used players was not a surprise. Wilkens had gone 10 men deep in the past if he felt he had the talent to justify it, believing the competition for minutes made players work harder. He also believed in matching to the opposition. It led to some quiet bitching in the Toronto dressing room about the roles from the likes of Tracy Murray and Davis. For Davis, it was a matter of not getting as many touches of the ball as he was used to. Murray could go from a 20-minute night to being ignored the next time around. Players often describe minutes as oxygen, and the same could almost be said for touches. And these two were suffering from a lack of it.

"This is a completely different situation than the one I was in the first time I was here," Murray said in March. "I'm used to either playing or sitting, but not this in and out. [Wilkens] said it's a matter of getting the new guys acclimated. I understand that. We're winning, too, so I can't say anything. But I don't like it. It's not what I thought, coming back here. I go home at night wondering, thinking — the other night, I couldn't sleep about it."

It was all a byproduct of the change Grunwald had wrought. But Wilkens and his staff were still waiting for a change in the group's overall character. They were still a mediocre defensive club — better than before, definitely, with opponents nowhere near as prone to stroll through the heart of their coverage.

While some things had improved, NBA scouts rated the Raptors poorly in some areas: lackadaisical; no sense of urgency or desperation; no interest in playing defence; not particularly smart; will go through droughts but are athletic and explosive and must be respected for that; let them run on you and you will be destroyed. "Not a very aggressive team — they do not like to get hit," said one. As for Vince Carter, there was this memorable line from one report: "Double-team him on the first bounce, flood his side of the floor, and hope for no illegal defence calls."

It was Carter who was taking more of a leader's role in practices, as Wilkens and the coaches struggled to get their message across. Behind the scenes, Carter had become much more vocal and demonstrative. From the start of the season, when he was named the club's other co-captain, he was much more prone to get in a younger player's ear, with Morris Peterson and little-used Michael Stewart hearing the most from him. He was being pushed, too.

"I've been riding him pretty hard this year," said Oakley. "I didn't do too much of that last year, but there's so much more he could do with the talent he has. I just don't see that hunger for the game in him. I don't see him playing in the league for 10 years without that hunger."

Oakley's criticisms of Carter were pointed. Carter and Peterson, he said, were just not interested in learning the game, and it showed in the Raptors' weak team defence. For Oakley, there could be no bigger sin than their lack of commitment to playing defence. And when they messed up offensively, forgetting plays, it rankled him further. "They just haven't picked it up. It's not that hard," he said.

To ease the transition the club was going through, Carter was taking more responsibility. He played all five positions in practice. He was the point guard for a while, to help Childs get used to Wilkens's schemes.

Carter loved the variety, but he was still a long way away from coming close to fulfilling Oakley's idea of a co-captain. Carter's quiet demeanour was another issue. With Wilkens's cool attitude, there was no one in the Toronto dressing room, at least at this juncture in the season, willing or able to take charge. It was one aspect in which Wilkens's easygoing manner was a bad fit for this group: there was no voice to speak up and take the initiative among the players to whom he had delegated some authority. Oakley was more likely to sit in the corner and brood; his critique, though, was typically unsparing.

"It's an uptight dressing room," Oakley said. "Vince doesn't say anything. Nobody says anything, actually. It's not good. You know the old saying: a closed mouth can't eat."

Grunwald was just looking for the players to believe, thinking it half the battle. And it seemed they were coming around, despite their grumbles. As March drew to a close, the Raptors were playing better. They had more versatility, Wilkens able to go quick and up-tempo, or more defensive-oriented on the perimeter. Childs's ability to pressure ball handlers and defend the pick-and-roll, perhaps the most foolproof of all NBA offensive plays when it is run well, made him a new and most welcome addition.

"I like what we've done," said Carter, the most important judge of it all in the long term. "There were times there when it wasn't a lot of fun for me, with the injury. Then after these new guys came in, I had to step up as a captain and help them. They've been great. It took a while to see it all, but it seems we're better."

It was all very gratifying, even if the last two people to stand up and get credit were the ones charged with setting it all up in the first place. That went for Grunwald, as much as for Wilkens.

But while Wilkens's life in basketball had been an unbroken line from Brooklyn to Providence University to the NBA, Grunwald had taken U-turn after U-turn. That he was even here at all had an accidental element. He was a high-school prodigy in basketball before a series of knee injuries literally grounded him. He was part of an NCAA championship team at Indiana under the mercurial Bobby Knight, with whom he still relies upon for advice, but it was in the schoolroom that he most distinguished himself. He stumbled into and out of the NBA, then came back in with the Raptors.

And now he was this: a brand-new Canadian citizen. Two weeks before changing the face of the Raptors for their late-season push, Grunwald was in a citizenship court in Toronto with a hundred others pledging allegiance to the Queen of England and singing "O Canada."

"I mangled the French part," he said.

It was a telling moment. American NBAers have enough trouble dealing with customs and weather and taxes and television and all the other things they bitch about. Here was one of them doing something completely different: he embraced the country.

"This is home now," Wilkens explained. "My kids are up here. I'm not going to be general manager of the Raptors forever, but I still want to live here and work here. To me, Toronto is a lot like my hometown of Chicago, a big city but similar in terms of the people who live here, the weather, the way it's set up with a strong downtown where there's a lot going on."

The players paid little attention, and Grunwald didn't make a big deal of it, which fit a pattern. Ever since he was a teenager, Grunwald had done his best work out of the limelight. "I wish I could be an anonymous person," he was quoted as saying at age 17, in a magazine article about him. Anonymity wasn't possible, not then anyway. To those who saw him play high-school basketball, he was the Truth. Growing to six-foot-eight, he was a first-team all-American. He remains the only player to be named Illinois all-state four times — in effect, an all-star from the time he entered high school playing against older players, to the time he left.

It was a much simpler era: the game didn't allow dunking, and the three-point line was no more than an aberration used only in the upstart ABA pro league. There were no feeder leagues ushering kids from grade school to high school; no shoe-company lampreys scouring schools and playgrounds and telling the kids how wonderful they were and promising them the world; no cable television showing their all-star games. Grunwald grew up and grew to love the game unfettered and unflattered, the son of the custodian at the high school he attended right across the road from the house he grew up in, hard by Chicago's O'Hare Airport.

"Oh, he could play. He had a pump-fake drive before anyone had ever heard of that," said Norm Goodman, his coach at East Leyden High — and in his retirement, a part-time scout now with the Raptors, Grunwald's way of saying thanks. "And he was smart. A straight-A student. Never had to tell him anything more than once. I don't think I ever raised my voice at him, ever. He wasn't that kind of kid."

College recruiters deluged Grunwald with scholarship offers. With Goodman's advice, he chose Indiana. But just a few months before he headed to Bloomington, everything changed. He was playing in a summer league game against a team of older players, including future NBA player Dave Corzine. Running by himself, he went up for a dunk and came down awkwardly on his left knee.

"No one was near him, but he turned kind of funny and I watched him fall and I thought, well, that's odd," recalls Tom Dore, an East Leyden teammate who is now a broadcaster with the Chicago Bulls.

"It's gone!" Grunwald cried out. "My knee! I know it. It's gone."

Grunwald possessed the athlete's intimate awareness of his own physical well-being. His instant diagnosis was accurate. He would have surgery for the injury: a torn anterior cruciate ligament, in those days a virtual death sentence. He would still go to Indiana and play basketball — and tear up the same knee again, after his sophomore year. As far as having an impact as a player, those days were over.

"He was never the same player," Dore said. "Anyone who saw him then had no doubt he would play in the NBA someday."

Not surprisingly, Grunwald isn't as sure. "I never thought about playing in the pros. That kind of thinking was not really prevalent then." But what about now? "The older you get, the better you were," he says with a smile.

He was actually never anything more than a spare with the Hoosiers. Teammates were impressed by his knowledge and preparation, and still recall the impassioned locker-room speech he made at mid-season in 1981, after the Hoosiers lost a string of games. They would go on to celebrate the title, a victory over North Carolina (that Vince Carter still gets ribbed about), then Grunwald graduated with honours. He followed that up with a law degree at Northwestern, then an MBA back at Indiana. It was Knight, he figures, who was primarily responsible for his future ability to make it through tough times.

"He didn't bullshit me. He said when he recruited me that he'd be tough, he'd yell and scream, and he did. He was tough. But when I left there I felt that no matter what was thrown in my path in the future, I could deal with it. I had this belief or confidence that I didn't have before. It was a high-stress environment. There was a pressure to win, and a direct approach to things, that I had never experienced."

Looking at Grunwald's life in basketball, what is striking is how often he flirted with the NBA, and how often it turned on him. After the Celtics chose him in the eighth round of the 1981 draft, he went to their rookie camp in Marshfield, Massachusetts, expecting all the trappings and tradition of the first-class Celtics, with their championship banners, their fabled parquet floor and their long-time architect Arnold (Red) Auerbach. What he got instead were workouts on asphalt outdoor courts in baking heat and sleeping two to a cabin, dead flies on the single light bulb overhead. He brought few clothes with him, so he practised in the same shorts and T-shirt each day. "We'd pass the tennis courts on our way to practice, and Red and Larry Bird would be there playing tennis," Grunwald recalled of his brush with the legends.

After a week, Auerbach told Grunwald he wouldn't be staying on for the main training camp, but offered a small consolation that made him laugh. "Next time you see Bobby Knight, tell him he's full of shit," Auerbach said. "He shoulda played you more."

The experience had soured him on the game, and he turned down a chance to go to Europe to play for a club team in France. Instead, he later went to work for Winston and Strawn, Chicago's largest and oldest law firm, with ties to the Republican Party going back nearly a century. It was there that the NBA found him again. Peter Bynoe was a W & S client, and Grunwald was given his file when Bynoe was heading up a group negotiating to buy the Denver Nuggets. After the sale went through, Bynoe was impressed, asking Grunwald to be the team's general counsel. He jumped at the chance, phoning Dore and crowing, "Hey, it took me a while, but I made it. I'm in the league."

The Nuggets were indeed in the league, but in name only. They were a franchise in chaos. Trades were made and players signed without the owners' knowledge. In Grunwald's first year there, the Nuggets went through four general managers and four team presidents. They never stopped losing from there, and when Bynoe sold them four years later, Grunwald left. Now he was drifting, and going through what he would later call the most difficult time of his life as he dealt with the death of first his mother and then his father. He worked for a Denver law firm, then shifted to a company that sold pay-per-view television shows. "The only thing we made money on was soft-core porn, boxing and the WWF," he said. "I dealt with a lot of the porn promoters and marketers. The WWF lawyers were the sharpest guys I've ever dealt with anywhere."

Grunwald was offered a piece of the business and would have taken it — "all the other guys there who did ended up making millions," he chuckles — were it not for a phone call from John Bitove. The brand-new owner of the Raptors was doing a background check on Isiah Thomas, phoning former teammates in the pros and college. They talked for a while. Before hanging up, Grunwald told Bitove to keep him in mind for any legal job that might be available.

Thomas was calling pretty soon after he got the job. In November 1994, a year before the Raptors started play, Grunwald was hired as Thomas's chief assistant, in charge of legal, contractual and salary-cap matters. For the first few months, before there were any player contracts to deal with, he sold luxury suites for an arena that was years away from being built. People barely noticed Grunwald at all until Thomas left, and there he was, sitting up on stage next to owner Allan Slaight, being introduced as the new general manager of the reeling Raptors and not quite believing what he was hearing.

"There was a rift," Slaight said, alluding to the chasm between him and Thomas. "As of this morning, the rift is gone."

Grunwald's neck snapped around as if he had been rear-ended. He looked at Slaight for a second in horror, then back out at the Toronto media that were more interested in hearing Isiah Thomas horror stories. The prevailing opinion was that the Raptors were broke down and busted. And here was this tall, gangly fellow with a pronounced limp, wearing glasses — this was the saviour?

"Once Isiah was gone," Stoudamire said, "that showed me in my mind that there wasn't no commitment to winning. That left no basketball minds in the front office, and there wasn't even no attempt to go out and get another basketball mind.

"It's a code red on the Raptors. The word is out, and it ain't a good word."

Carlos Rogers, who also went to Portland in the deal, called the Raptors "CBA" in comparison to the Blazers, referring to basketball's long-time minor league. Even Grunwald wondered. As they walked out of the television studio, he turned to radio reporter Elliotte Friedman. "How do you think I'll do?" he asked.

The uncertainty wasn't limited to his job. Grunwald's marriage had ended in divorce after nine years. He was seeing less of their two children, Gabe and Emma. His older brother, Gary, his only sibling, was bouncing in and out of trouble in Seattle. With their parents gone, Grunwald was trying to administer long-distance care for his brother, diagnosed as schizophrenic as a young adult and alternating between institutional care and living on the streets. "Those were pretty difficult times for me, let alone what was going on with the team," he said.

Grunwald's immediate problems in basketball had to do with those 1997–98 Raptors, who were bleeding badly. Darrell Walker, Damon Stoudamire, Walt Williams and just about everybody else had no interest in continuing. "The thing that was really mind-boggling was how people just folded up the tent," Grunwald said. "It was a bad, bad time."

At the end of that season, Grunwald took the microphone in front of the departing crowd at Maple Leaf Gardens. It was a Raptors tradition to end the season with this kind of address, if a third-year franchise could be said to have a tradition. Honesty and credibility had never been part of the custom, however. After the first season, John Bitove had promised the crowd an NBA championship with Oliver Miller jumping centre, a truly laughable assertion. A year later it was Isiah Thomas's turn, and he gushed about the nucleus of the Raptors, including Stoudamire and Marcus Camby.

In each case, all of them would soon be on their way out of Toronto. When it was Grunwald's turn after that pathetic third season, he apologized and promised the crowd that changes would be made, that they would be better. The crowd responded with profound boos. They were sick of this kind of talk.

When Grunwald was inducted into his East Leyden High School hall of fame a couple of years later, it was a video of this moment that he chose to show the audience. If you can handle the bad times, he said, then the good times will come.

"I knew it was going to be ugly but it wasn't the hardest thing I ever had to do," he said. "I've faced some real-life hard things before. The death of my parents, the breakup of my marriage. Those are hard things."

And now, in the winter of 2001, those hard times had led to good times. Or at least better times, because there was always something to fret about. Grunwald remains a fan and media favourite. More than anyone else associated with the franchise, he is the Raptors lifer, having escaped the taint of close association with Thomas. He has escaped any wrath for losing McGrady, his biggest mistake, or trading away Christie and getting little in return. After all, he has stayed through the good and the bad times. And he is now one of us, a Canadian.

On the wall of his office, Grunwald has put up some framed mementos. There is a picture of a circus elephant dunking a basketball, part of a show he attended with his children. There is a photo of Assembly Hall, home gym of his Hoosiers. There is a letter from David Stern notifying the Raptors that their final payment had been received and the team was now officially an NBA partner. There is a team picture from the 1998–99 season, when Carter arrived and it all began to turn around, autographed by every player and coach, with an inscription "from Butch Carter."

The quiet, brainy guy in the background isn't in the picture. He can't quite get used to being recognized, sometimes under the most unlikely conditions.

"Mr. Grunwald!" says the man standing outside Union Station. "Good luck with the season!"

Grunwald does a double-take, walks over to shake his hand. The man is shivering, his beard is smeared with dirt and snow, and he is begging for change. Grunwald drops a loonie into his box as thanks for his interest. As he walks away, he turns to his lunch date: "You never know. He might be a season ticket holder one day."

CHAPTER 10

April 2001 :

In the Mecca

There are rare moments that approach poetry, or ballet, or maybe both, the combination defying the stark blackboard logic that is so much a part of the pro game. This was one of those moments: a play that lasted just a couple of seconds but would draw Vince Carter's eyes later.

He was putting the ball on the floor and, surprise, finding space in the painted area extended out from the basket. There was a sliver of daylight and he was free by perhaps a quarter of a step from the Latrell Sprewell shadow that had followed him around for the past five working nights, and suddenly Carter was rising up into the air as former Raptor Marcus Camby stepped out to meet him and began his matching ascent.

Carter looked trapped, as if he had committed one of basketball's cardinal sins in leaving his feet without knowing what he was going to do with the ball. Camby had blocked Carter's last shot, a three-pointer, giving the

Knicks and their habitual sellout crowd of 19,763 an emotional lift; they leaned forward again, anticipating another get-outta-here swat.

And still Carter hung in the air. He looked to the side, extending the ball in his right hand to pass when he saw Dell Curry prowling uncovered along the edge of the three-point line, then abruptly pulling it back when New York's Charlie Ward made a move to close that space.

Gravity began to claim Camby, but Carter still levitated. He squirmed and squared his hips and finally, gracefully, pushed the ball off his fingertips toward the basket. "I felt all awkward and I just threw it up," he would say later. "The only thing I remember thinking was just, 'Phew, please go in.' You look at it later and say, 'Man, that's nice.'"

For years, Madison Square Garden had been known colloquially as the mecca of the pro game. It was the oldest working arena in the NBA, and for just about any player it was a stage they had dreamed about running over, perhaps even conquering, since they started having dreams of the game.

This particular Vince Carter runner fell through the net with a soft whoosh. And for just a second, Madison Square Garden felt like Market Square Arena in February 1999, or the Sydney Superdome in September 2000: another stunned crowd, another masterpiece, another moment of, Did you see that?

This was the deciding Game 5 of a playoff series matching the Raptors against the battle-scarred Knicks, who hadn't been knocked out of the NBA's first round in 10 years. This was the same cauldron that had cooked Carter and the Raptors the year before. It was also a place that treated them roughly once again in the opening game of this series.

For the Raptors, everything had changed, as only pro sports can in the span of just 12 months — a new head coach and staff, one roster makeover and then another, and just four regulars back from the group that had been swept 3–0 by the Knicks in 2000 — and yet it looked so similar to start. On Carter's first drive to the basket, New York tough guy Kurt Thomas was waiting underneath the basket, welcoming him back to the playoffs by emphatically blocking his first shot and putting him on the floor. Carter sat up, felt for the back of his head and shot an imploring look up at referee Joe DaRosa, who turned away. No foul.

The Knicks' strategy in containing the Raptors was the same as the one they'd used the year before: stop Carter. Sprewell, a former first-team NBA all-defensive player, would handle the primary chores and would get consistent, aggressive double-team help. If Carter did make it to the basket, Thomas had just told him what he would find there.

The Raptors had closed the season well. They won 14 of their final 20 games to come back to this same spot. But Game 78, in Detroit, in which they blew an 18-point lead and a chance at the no. 4 seed and home-floor advantage against the Knicks, underlined how fragile a coalition they remained.

In Game 1 of these playoffs, they had looked ill at ease, an unsteady, irritable bunch anything but ready to change history. Up in the stands, Grunwald was showered with spitballs from a quartet of giggling teenagers who put away their pea-shooters only after the mild-mannered GM flashed his temper at them. When Charles Oakley ripped Lenny Wilkens and his staff for "lackadaisical" preparation — the coach gave them an easy day after the regular season ended, and didn't hand out the Knicks scouting reports and strategy until a day later — it was as if the fractures were already showing.

Carter attempted 22 shots in the 92–85 loss, and made just five of them. It was barely better than his 2000 debut, a 3-for-20 night. The subheadline in the *New York Times* called it "Another Clunker from Carter." He missed his first seven attempts, forcing shots from outside or short-arming the ball when he did get in close. In truth, Sprewell was defending him outstandingly. But the taunts were already starting. "That's some weak shit!" was one from the crowd, and on the floor Mark Jackson would soon be whispering in Carter's ear, Carter arching an eyebrow as if he wasn't quite sure whether it was the medium or the message that was so rattling.

"You never think Mark would even say a word on the court," said Carter. "But throughout the game he was like another guy, like somebody else. I kind of enjoyed it after a while. But it surprised me."

When Carter stood at the free-throw line with seconds to go before halftime, he front-rimmed his first attempt, smiled and muttered out loud, "What's going on?"

Antonio Davis walked to his side. "Vince, *everything* is going on." Davis used to grow concerned whenever he saw Carter smiling. "It means he's not serious, he's not focused enough," he said. But now he saw a worried frown. "Usually you see him out there smiling a little bit and enjoying what he's doing. I didn't think he enjoyed it tonight."

Like Oakley, Davis wondered whether Carter had the grit to make it through his NBA baptism, now in its third season, with so much expected, so much to gain and now so much to lose. Over in the New York dressing room, the Knicks were openly disdainful of the Raptors' star: "Vince Carter — No Heart!" shouted twelfth man Rick Brunson, who didn't play much but certainly could talk.

Carter had heard similar jeers, and worse, from the bench of the Miami Heat during two critical late-season games, and he had responded with two of the best all-round efforts of his career, which translated into two Raptors wins.

But this was the more intense world of the playoffs, and that much was plain as the Raptors readied for Game 2. They were down 0–1 and were in danger of losing any chance in the shortened five-game series of the NBA's first round. Carter's status as the league's brightest young light was on the verge of extinction, too, when he walked away from his teammates in the lay-up line before that Game 2. He leaned over on his haunches and talked to the man seated courtside wearing a no. 8 Knicks jersey, the remains of his pregame meal spread on a greasy piece of wax paper on his lap, an orange Knicks towel draped over the Knicks cap on his head. Spike Lee, unquestionably the Knicks' most high-profile supporter, was talking from his $1,500-a-night chair. Eight minutes before the biggest game of his career so far, and Carter was courting Lee for his upcoming inaugural summer all-star game in Toronto.

After a couple of minutes, Carter nodded his head. He gave Lee's fist a bump and returned to the floor.

Mission accomplished, and so it continued all night long. The Raptors beat the Knicks — manhandled them, actually, winning by 20 points. Carter's jump shots fell. He wasn't saying much, refusing to answer the media's questions about himself, continuing to insist that it was a team game, ignoring the absolute truth of the NBA playoffs: that a team will rise or fall on the back of its star player. Part of that blindness was programming, going as far back as his high-school days, when he was reluctant to enter dunk contests because he didn't want to be branded a show-off. But even so, he was listening to the critics, Oakley murmuring after that Game 1 nightmare that Carter had to make shots if the Raptors were going to win.

When he returned to Toronto for Game 3 at supercharged Air Canada Centre, and promptly coughed up another horrid shooting night in a second loss, he had to listen some more.

Lenny Wilkens tried to soothe him with an old chestnut regarding Bob Pettit, his St. Louis Hawks teammate from nearly 40 years before. It was standard NBA stuff, about shooters bringing themselves out of the doldrums by shooting more, but it again pointed out the generational divide between this soft-spoken, game-hardened coach and a young player who had barely an idea who Pettit was.

Davis at times grew tired of the Carter adulation and the notion that Carter was the leader and the catalyst who cast everyone else in shadow. But he also understood that if this Raptors team was a band, then he was the one who had to supply the steady bass line to Carter's dazzling but erratic solo guitar. He looked at Carter as one would look at a prodigy. "He's watching and he's listening," Davis said. "All these games are tests for him, just like you're going to class and figuring out you did your homework wrong. Next time you do it better and you pay more attention to certain things."

If there was a Raptors' opposite to Carter in natural talent, it was Davis, a power forward playing centre — and playing the best basketball of his career in what could be his last hurrah in a Raptors uniform. He had told his teammates throughout the season that he was considering opting out of a contract that would have paid him $7 million for the coming season and $8 million the next. He figured he was worth more than that on the open market, and he was no doubt correct. An all-star game berth — hell, he started (eastern conference coach Larry Brown being an admirer of his lunch-bucket approach, going back to their days in Indiana) — and his performance in these playoffs were merely the latest steps forward in a career that was among the more unlikely in the NBA. Davis had been so little regarded as an NBA rookie, drafted in the second round by Indiana, that the Pacers told him to go away to Europe and work on his game. Now, at 32 years old, he had gone from ugly duckling to swan, calling the shots as the Raptors' inside complement to Carter.

It was a long time coming. Davis had known his share of setbacks and real tragedy, going back to his childhood in Oakland. As a teenager, he was shocked when his mother, Alice, told him about his father. He'd never know him, having grown up with a stepfather who married his mother when Davis was five. Davis went searching for his natural father, found him, kindled the relationship and was trying to learn something about him, as well as himself, when his father was stabbed to death during a brawl outside an Oakland bar.

"I was 16, and it was a very hard time for me. At the time, I was really trying to reach out to him. I think that's why I am the way I am with my kids now. All those questions that I had — I want to be there for them when they have the same ones."

He started at Texas–El Paso after high school, UTEP coach Don Haskins giving him some simple advice. "He taught me about being a defender," said Davis, "and said as long as you can do that, you'll stay in the game. That stuck with me through my career."

The Pacers saw the long-term potential, even as Davis went to Greece, then Italy. Finally, at 25, he made the big club, becoming a solid role player but never breaking through, and then, in 1999, asking Pacers GM Donnie Walsh to trade him to some place where he could be a starter. The playoffs that spring had been Davis's worst nightmare, his foul on a Larry Johnson three-point shot in the last second leading to a rare four-point play and a one-point Knicks win over Indiana. The Pacers would lose that series, and that foul had lingered in Davis's mind ever since.

Until now, that is. Davis had fully flowered in Toronto. He complained about the cold and the taxes, and he worried about his family — his wife, Kendra, who missed home, and their twins, A.J. and Kaela — but accomplished everything he could have hoped. Even if he couldn't help but notice the differences between his blue-collar background and Carter's blue-chip.

"Nothing came easy for me, but it was like any job, getting a promotion when your time came," he said. "I think it's better that way. It must be tough to be always looked on as the best, and expected to be the best."

Vince Carter was finding that out. After a poor Game 3, the Raptors trailed 2–1 in the series, and he had shot a combined 10 of 43 in the two defeats. Such numbers could worm their way inside a player's head. So, too, could the voices of the critics lining up to take their shots. In a TV studio in Atlanta, Charles Barkley was merciless. As the halftime analyst for the TNT network broadcasts, Barkley had become a hilarious, often politically incorrect antidote to the usual television blather. Late in the season Barkley had dismissed Carter: "It's half-man, half-amazing. Or as some folks call him, all offence, no defence." Now, with Carter struggling, Barkley zeroed in. "Vince is playing like a girl," he said. "He played like a girl last year and he's played like a girl so far in this series. They put him on TV every week, they made him a superstar — now play like one and quit whining and telling me it's a team game."

Charles Oakley had no time for Barkley. The two were sworn enemies from their playing days, when they pushed and shoved and at times punched one another. But like Barkley, Oakley wasn't going to let Carter off the hook. After Game 1, he had said of Carter, "He's got to play better, point-blank." Speaking to reporters before Game 4 in Toronto, Oakley challenged Carter in his strongest language to step up his game. Oakley wasn't playing all that well himself, but as a co-captain he took it upon himself to speak up. If Davis was the good cop, then it was Oakley's turn to play the bad version.

"All the plays go through Vince. The focus on Vince has been there all year. You can't shy away from it now," said Oakley. "This is the time you have to step up and be a man about it, you know? When they made the Dream Team, he went — all 12 of us didn't go. When they do commercials, we don't go, he goes."

Oakley knew exactly what he was doing. Vince Carter's upbringing and his background at North Carolina made this whole role of team leader particularly difficult for him to get used to. As soon as he took it, he would shake it off. Even as Oakley lowered the boom, Carter continued to talk about it being a team game, he was only one man, etc. Carter's entire NBA career had progressed like this. As he climbed higher and the heat grew more intense, he would step back and wait until someone pushed him forward. Carter's internal engine was contemporary, ice-cool, egalitarian; Oakley's was old school, running hot and emotional, with a clear sense of hierarchy.

"I don't want any of these guys to think I'm coming out to play for Vince," said Carter. "I don't see this as a one-man show. When I put on my uniform, it says Toronto Raptors, not Vince Carter."

And: "When you get into the 'playoffs,'" he said, gesturing with his fingers to mark the quotation marks, "that's when it's the big games in your life — and they are. But why go out there and do something different? I've been doing it this way all my life. We got there as a team and that's how we're going to excel — as a team. Regardless of the way I played, if Antonio or Alvin or Oak or anyone else don't play the way they did, we don't win."

But Carter didn't tune out Oakley's comments. Just before Game 4, he approached Oakley and told him simply, "I see where you're coming from." Oakley nodded back. It was all Carter felt he needed to say. And for Oakley, there was the satisfaction that his point had been made.

The only one to react adversely was Michelle Carter, in a TNT half-time interview. "Ironically, the people who are doing the most talking are the people who are not doing their part tonight. But I'll just leave it at that," she said, referring specifically to Oakley, who was indeed having a miserable time of it. Carter and Oakley were both angry that Michelle had been interviewed at all, since they saw this as their own affair. As it was, the network interviewed her three times over the course of the series, more than they did Wilkens.

It was quite the little soap opera, and Carter shrewdly noted how his mother and Oakley were alike, even when they were at cross purposes. "They're much the same," he said. "They get their point across. That's how they do it. A mother like mine, hey, some mothers aren't like her, she's definitely going to say something."

Oakley shook his head and again wondered about the mettle of the young star for whom he was expected to ride shotgun. "He's a mama's boy. He's very sheltered," he said. "This league is about toughness. Or at least it used to be."

Such talk bothers Carter, but typically he did not make an issue of it. Michelle did. "I do smother him sometimes," she said. "He and his brother Chris have shared a very sheltered life. But what were the alternatives? As for me, I am a strong-willed person, but I wasn't always this way. At 25 years old, I was a doormat. I let people walk all over me."

The Jordan comparisons laid out on Carter earlier in his career had made Oakley shake his head some more. They were so different, these two, and Oakley would be the one to know. He broke into the NBA with the Chicago Bulls in 1985. Jordan, coming off his Rookie of the Year season when Oakley arrived, would be first his teammate then his friend.

"Vince needs the crowd to get him going," Oakley has said. "Michael brought it into the building with him every night."

If ever there were two more different individuals in the Raptors locker room, Oakley and Carter were them. Carter is perhaps the most important figure in Raptors history, and by extension in the NBA's tenuous Canadian experiment. But Oakley, with his 37 years and his honour code and his work ethic, is not far behind. He has been a substantive complement to Carter's sizzling act. It is no surprise that when Wilkens took over, these two became his co-captains. As the playoffs progressed, the pressures were telling on both.

For three years in Toronto, Oakley had served as Carter's icebreaker. He cleared paths. He dove into the laps and the popcorn boxes of the front-row toffs, picking up a spray of beer into the bargain. He delivered meaty forearms into the chests of whoever in the opposing jerseys was unfortunate enough to get in his way. His glower could melt Arctic ice. Playing in front of an audience raised on the lick-'em-in-the-alley, lick-'em-on-the-ice hockey tenets of Conn Smythe, Oakley had become one of the most popular of Raptors. He played many roles, but tough-minded enforcer is the one that the paying customers love to see on game nights.

Riding shotgun was nothing new. He did the same for Jordan in Chicago. He was a subordinate to Patrick Ewing in New York. In each place, he put off his own demands for the holy trinity of NBA stardom: the limelight, the shots and most of all, the money. Oakley took a financial hit from the lockout bigger than any other NBA player, his $10-million salary — a "balloon payment" at the end of his contract, part of the old rules that had since been revised — cut by almost half. When Toronto offered him more than anyone else could in the summer of 1999 — three years at $18 million — he accepted it after checking other locales.

"He's a very smart player," says Brendan Malone, who as an assistant coach with the Knicks got to know Oakley very well. "He studies the opponent, he knows the opponent better than most. And he can't tolerate people who shortcut the game."

All of these things have given Oakley a jaded, world-weary attitude. And when he looks toward Carter, all he sees is what might be, rather than what is. Shortcuts, rather than the sweaty, hard road he himself travelled.

"He could be so good," Oakley says of Carter, "but he has no hunger for the game. I wonder if he'll play anywhere near 10 years in the league. I wonder if he wants it. He settles for what's easiest, putting up jumpers instead of taking the ball to the basket."

Carter hates this kind of talk. And if anyone could be accused of favouring his own agenda over the team's, Oakley would be the one. He had missed four games during the season for suspensions, first for slapping the Clippers' Jeff McInnis on the top of the head during a morning shootaround. Their confrontation stemmed from rivalry over a woman in Charlotte, North Carolina, whom Oakley had dated and McInnis was interested in. McInnis made the mistake of phoning the woman when Oakley was visiting her. Oakley got on the line and warned him to stay away, and the argument escalated from there.

When Oakley ran into NBA disciplinary chief Stu Jackson at the all-star game, his message was typically stoic and idiosyncratic. "I didn't cry about it," he told Jackson. "You did what you had to do. I took it. That's the way it is. I ain't no bitch."

When he threw a basketball at Tyrone Hill during a pregame shootaround in April there was another suspension, this time for one game. Oakley claimed that Hill owed him money from a crap game two summers before. Wilkens indulged him, keeping him in the starting line-up rather than putting him on the bench like before.

Oakley had been transformed in at least one way when he moved from the Knicks to the Raptors. He had become one of the game's grumpy old men, but not at all one of its grand old men. Five teams called Grunwald before the trade deadline to ask about Oakley. Miami, the Lakers, Minnesota, Phoenix and Orlando were interested, but Grunwald wasn't returning any of it. He was used to Oakley's act, had even felt his barbs personally. "He's a lawyer first," Oakley said of Grunwald.

"Sometimes, he's scared." But Grunwald wasn't about to move him on just yet. Besides, it wasn't as if Oakley's irascible, contrarian nature was a recent development.

"He always was a brooder," said Tim Donovan, the Knicks' former public-relations man. "Now it seems like the only difference is everyone is listening to him."

Indeed, if there was a league award for griping, Oakley would be in the running every year. "He'd even complain about the food on the team plane," chuckled Malone. "'Who cooked this roast chicken?' he'd say. 'It's terrible.' Once, we got him a German chocolate cake, his favourite, for his birthday. But there was coconut around the edges. 'What's this white stuff?' he said. 'What's this stuff doing here on my cake?'"

In Chicago with the Bulls, Oakley had received his first crash course in NBA ethos — who got the ball and who didn't; who was expendable and who wasn't. "If I wanted to shoot, I had to go get the ball," he said. "It makes you a better rebounder, but not a happier person."

Halfway through his rookie year, Jordan took Oakley to the all-star game. The two were inseparable, cruising between the events in Dallas in a stretch limousine. For Oakley, who had gone to unheralded Virginia Union after being lightly recruited out of high school, it was like going to the Emerald City.

At the same time, he was obliged to carry luggage for the veterans. But in his second year, when Doug Collins had replaced Stan Albeck, Bulls rookie Brad Sellers refused to carry Oakley's bags. Oakley went off on Collins for letting Sellers get away with it. Ask Oakley about the incident now, and he levels his most withering insult on Collins: "Arrogant," he says. There's little wonder, then, that he has no patience with the NBA's kiddie corps of incoming players.

The Bulls shocked Jordan by trading Oakley to New York in the summer of 1989. He was a popular Knick and loved New York, but by 1998, he was deemed expendable again. Despite misgivings from Jeff Van Gundy and the rest of his staff, the Knicks dealt him to Toronto for Marcus Camby, in a classic experience-for-youth swap.

And here he was, still without a championship for his long career, and not getting any closer in this Raptors dressing room, where there were the Oakley Rules for game-day behaviour: turn off your cellphones; no music; game tapes only on the big-screen TV; no food.

Mentor, den mother, conciliator, businessman, aging hipster, culinary boss, president of the locker room ... Oakley played different roles, whether he was helping patch up McGrady's and Carter's wobbly relationship early in the season or cooking up a mess of pasta at the team's annual dinner for sponsors.

When Oakley said that 60 per cent of NBA players smoke pot, it set off predictable alarm bells at the league office. At his Yorkville condo, the phone was ringing all day. Four times the league called him, including a blistering verbal blasting from Horace Balmer, the NBA's chief of security.

"They keep saying, Do you have any proof?" said Oakley, whose preferred night-time substance was a Cosmopolitan. "I don't have any proof. I told them that. But I know. You would know. I don't know why anyone would ever smoke a joint anyway in the NBA. Just a little slip-up and you could blow it all."

But ask him about steroid use — Matt Geiger and Don MacLean were suspended and fined after testing positive to those drugs this season — and he shakes his head. "No, I don't know about that, I don't see that. Ain't a lot of that going on as far as I see. But the other stuff, the pot smoking, oh yeah. It's all over the place."

This was Oakley the rebel, rattling the cage of the establishment and enjoying every minute of it. Controversy had followed him throughout his career, even outside the bounds of the NBA and the basketball court. In 1991, he was charged with assault, disorderly conduct and public intoxication. The charges were dismissed. He was also charged with battery, after allegedly punching a woman in the face when she refused to have sex with him and his girlfriend. These charges were also dismissed. These brushes with the law and numerous league suspensions added to his reputation as a tough guy.

But Oakley had his soft side too. He sent boxes of clothes to young high school and college players who couldn't afford them. At a camp he used to put on in the Alabama neighbourhood where he was raised, he spotted a skinny kid with enormous desire and not a whole lot of ability. Oakley managed to line up a junior college and then a college scholarship for Ben Wallace, who would eventually become one of the league's top rebounders this season. And when Malik Sealy of the Minnesota Timberwolves was killed in a May 2000 auto accident, Oakley was a pillar of emotional and financial support for Sealy's widow, Lisa.

His world was all about the honour code, and Oakley was never afraid to wear the black hat. His public challenge of Carter was just another illustration.

"It bothered some of my friends that he would say that, but not me — I know how Oak is," said Carter. "He's different. He took me under his wing day 2 [of my first training camp] and said, 'I'm going to help you here: I'm going to criticize you, I'm going to be in your ear, but I'm going to make you better.' Everybody seems to forget that. Maybe they laughed about it then, but now that I'm established, they hear it again and they're surprised.

"People tend to forget I'm still in my third year. I'm a young guy still learning."

Carter rose to the occasion. He got the external prod he needed from an Air Canada Centre crowd of 20,282, and Davis would supply the grit. The Raptors came out wearing purple headbands as a token of team togetherness, a year after Dee Brown and Doug Christie had worn the same accessory as an act of defiance. They rolled over the Knicks, Carter looking as if he was enjoying the game again. He had 32 points, but he also did the other things that marked a complete player, precisely the stamp of approval he had been looking for since he came into the league. He drew fouls and got to the free-throw line, he rebounded the ball, he got active on defence, gambling and making steals, he set a couple of hard picks for his teammates. Mostly, though, he made everyone around him better, the rushing earlier in the series having given way to a more clinical approach, Carter drawing extra defenders, then finding his teammates for open shots.

Perhaps Oakley's words had an effect, or perhaps it was just as Davis had said, that he needed to go through the exam a couple of times before he got the answers right. But if Oakley was right on with his be-a-man posturing, so too was Carter: he needed help from his teammates, and he got it.

"The outcome still would have been the same," said Carter. "I didn't know about Oak's comments until shootaround that morning, but I knew when I woke up that morning that I was prepared. Hey, I was mad [about Game 3] like everybody else. I knew I had played bad, and it was time to step up."

Oakley had been on him before, during the season, but, said Carter, "this was different because he put me into one of those big situations. It was the playoffs. He wants to win. Maybe to wake me up, that's the way he had to get it done."

Two nights later in New York, playing in one of those win-or-go-home situations the league's commercials trumpet, Carter was floating in the lane. Davis was battling underneath. Oakley was fighting his tiring legs, following bad turnovers with nasty screens, making two or three solid plays that no one but people like Brendan Malone see and appreciate for every one bonehead mistake that's apparent to everybody in the building. Everybody was doing their part, and at the other end Sprewell was doing his, almost single-handedly keeping the Knicks close.

And in the final minute, with the Raptors up by a scant basket, Carter was putting up another shot from outside — just off, but he had followed it in and was there, elevating in an eyeblink for the putback. It was as if the stake had been driven into every attending New Yorker's heart. The Garden began to empty, and Davis struck the killing blow, a jumper set up by a Carter pass out of a double-team as the shot-clock expired.

The Raptors had gone through one of those ordeals by fire and come out tougher at the end, none more so than Carter. He'd won a personal battle inside his head as much as with his legs and his shot and his scoring, growing more accustomed to the star's role and the Knicks' pressure, eventually making them pay for it with tired legs and open shots for his teammates.

"This solidifies him as a star," said Wilkens. "Every great young player needs to get over the hump."

"Like Charles said, I had to bring it," Carter said, as close as he would come to admitting his own importance. "We did it together. We actually put a complete game together. We erased what had happened the year before. Nobody was going to remember that."

Fittingly, Carter was the last one to leave the court. He was still out there doing interviews when Chris Childs burst into the locker room. The former Knick had been inserted into the starting lineup to replace Morris

Peterson after Game 1 and had played emotionally and mostly effective-ly. He grabbed every morsel of satisfaction he could from this win over his old team in his old building.

"In the mecca! In the mecca!" Childs chanted over and over, and one by one the rest of them joined in with him.

"It was so emotional, and everybody was showing a lot of love for everybody else, it reminded me of a bunch of high-school guys in the state tournament," said assistant coach Brian James. "It seemed like a lot of pressure had been lifted. There was such a sense of relief, because peo-ple had pointed at this series and said if we don't get out of it, the season is no good. The players felt that way, too."

They were still repeating the chant when Carter finally walked in, and it died away, replaced by steady applause for this young man.

He clapped back at them. Usually the coolest and quietest, he went around the room, hugging each one of them and nodding and liking the sound of Childs's chant so much he couldn't stop from repeating it again and again.

In the mecca, he had delivered.

Time and Distance

So, what's up with Vince? That's been the big question since the day he arrived in Toronto.

At first, we wanted to get a sense of who he was, what the sport is all about, how easy he makes it look. Easy enough for anyone to appreciate what he does on the basketball court — even an audience unschooled in basketball, even an audience somewhat defensive about accepting it. There is still a sizeable minority among the hockey-first masses who simply refuse to get it and wear their indifference like a badge of honour, but their numbers are shrinking. When Carter showed up at a Leafs playoff game, his appearance on the scoreboard screen drew a huge round of applause from the Old Toronto hockey audience.

In the larger sense, though, Carter bridged that divide as effortlessly and gracefully as an uncontested lay-up. Raptors attendance topped the 20,000-a-night mark during the 2001 playoff season — perhaps his neatest and certainly his most important crossover.

After just over two years and three seasons, there appears little doubt that Carter has set a hook in Toronto. The NBA in the spring of 2001 is a business that has batted .500 in its attempt to expand beyond its own provincial boundaries, making the likelihood of further international expansion someday, to Europe and Asia perhaps, little more than a pipe dream. The percentage is based on the bare facts of the scorecard: Toronto yes, Vancouver no. The Grizzlies were pulling up stakes, readying to move to Memphis, as the Raptors finished their sixth season. Around the league, Toronto was still a foreign outpost — but now it was one to be considered, when a couple of years ago the very notion was outlandish.

It was mixed success, but in a global marketplace of flatlining numbers for the NBA, the only place where the numbers were actually rising was Canada. For that phenomenon, the credit goes to Carter. Still, there was disbelief and an ongoing sense of angst as the summer of 2001 beckoned. What's up with Vince? Is he staying? Is he going? What happens next?

One thing is certain: Vinsanity is dead. Probably it was inevitable, part of the requisite story arc that accompanies celebrity in this age, from the glorification to the flame-out. Charles Oakley has said it more than once, looking across the locker room at the latest one to be given the "Next Jordan" label: "Hype is like a kite. It goes up. It comes down."

Coming home from Sydney with a gold medal and a newfound sense of belonging, Vince Carter would make perhaps the first independent decision of his professional basketball career. As he turned 24 years old, he began pulling in the line on that kite. Instead of embracing the spotlight, he backed away from it, mistrustful of its glare and wary of its heat.

The Next Jordan? Along with Vinsanity, it was on his personal scrap heap as 2000 turned over. While Carter stayed purposefully low-key, Tracy McGrady's star rose spectacularly, and Allen Iverson and Kobe Bryant overtook Carter at the top of the league's jersey sales ticker.

All of that matters very little to Carter. What he wants for himself appears to be a contradiction. There is the basketball at the highest level. But he also yearns to remain a "nice guy" living a "normal life." In a league full of rough, tough, streetwise pros, here was a young man who by everyone's account had been a good kid, never in trouble, bouncing a basketball with his brother as they followed their mother around on her daily errands. Here was a young man who at 11 years old found himself out in front in the 100-yard dash, only to slow up and cross the line with another student, sharing the prize with him — because his mother wanted him to. Here was a young man who cried as a teenager when someone stole the cap he bought from the local sporting goods store in Daytona, the one with the logo from Michigan, during the Fab Five days of Chris Webber and Jalen Rose and Juwan Howard, men he would later line up opposite.

"He couldn't believe anyone would steal it," recalls Michelle Carter. "He saved up all his money, $17.50, to buy that hat, then he left it on a bleacher bench while he played a game and someone took it. It crushed him.

"Vince wants to be liked. More than anything, he wants to please people. But I think that's starting to change. I think he's beginning to realize that you can't please people all the time."

He's still that kid, though. A little wiser, a little less trusting — but still a nice guy. In sports, however, they say nice guys finish last.

"I remember when I was first drafted and was getting ready for my first training camp, telling myself that once this day started, I could easily get caught up in the hype," he says. "I never wanted to do that. I thought it would be hard, but it's not.

"This is something I love doing. I've gotten to be famous, to be recognizable to a lot of people, and that's a great feeling. But just because of who I am, I like to be in the background. I like to sit back. My goal in life as far as basketball is to be as normal as possible, if that makes sense."

It would appear to be an impossible balancing act. But Carter has taken his career one rung at a time, even if so many have expected more and demanded more. He has his endorsements and off-court income that, as of the spring of 2001, are scheduled to earn him $35 million over the next five years. There is his charitable foundation, the Embassy of Hope, which has branched out to include a Canadian arm and a bigger Toronto presence in with the first summer all-star game in 2001. Carter dreams of running his own restaurant someday, of owning businesses, of winning a championship. And keeping it low-key.

"To whom much is given, so much is expected." That aphorism was sent along to Carter by his agent Merle Scott when the pressure to perform was at its highest in the spring of 2001, when his ability and cool were being questioned in so many quarters, including his own locker room.

It will never stop, even if Carter hopes for a break as he does it his way. Once the Knicks were out of the way and it was the Philadelphia 76ers and Allen Iverson providing the opposition, Carter was playing it his way. This meeting with the 76ers didn't carry the same hefty baggage that accompanied that first series, with its sense of relief and progress so evident at the conclusion. But it would go to a seventh and deciding game, the ultimate pressure situation in sports — and Carter would show just how far he would go to pursue that goal of normalcy.

Game 7 would be the longest day — and the end to his longest year to date. It would come down to a matter of numbers: two seconds, about 22 feet, over 20,000 at the First Union Center watching, and one man.

This is the way it works in sports, especially basketball. From an expansive 48 minutes at the start to mere seconds that can stretch out like an eternity at the finish, the long journey comes down to short strokes. For Carter, that journey began with a 7:15 a.m. wakeup call in Chapel

Hill, N.C., and culminated with this moment 13 hours and nearly 1,000 miles later in Philadelphia.

It was a most unconventional way to prepare for a playoff game. A two-hour meeting on the previous Friday night, after the Raptors forced Game 7 with a win at the Air Canada Centre, finalized the plans. Just about everyone in the room, including Wilkens, Grunwald, Tanenbaum and even Scott, had reservations. But Carter and his mother were insistent: he would go to Chapel Hill to make an appearance at his class of 2001's commencement ceremony, fulfilling a promise he had made to her on the highway to North Carolina in August of his freshman year. And then he would play in Game 7.

Wilkens worried about the vagaries of weather and mechanics. Tanenbaum volunteered his private plane for the flight to Chapel Hill and on to Philadelphia. Grunwald arranged for another plane in Chapel Hill, standing by with a mechanic just in case.

With rain threatening at Kenan Stadium, Carter and 2,900 others marched into the end-zone seats at Kenan Stadium wearing their Carolina-blue gowns. He stood close by the exit ramp, with his old Tar Heel teammates Max Owens and Brendan Haywood sitting just a few seats away. He waved down below to his graduation party: his girlfriend, Yvonne Lopez, his friend Nikki Riggsbee, his mother, Michelle, Scott and Tanenbaum with his wife, Judy.

At the centre of his small circle of intimates is Yvonne, with whom he has kept up a long-distance relationship for two years. Nikki remains a close friend from North Carolina days. Joe Giddens and Cory Brown, two friends from Daytona Beach, come up to Toronto to visit regularly.

Someone who has been missing from his life in Toronto is his brother Chris, who prefers to stay in Daytona, away from the whirlwind that surrounds his older brother. For the two brothers, coming to grips with their contrasting lives has been difficult, at times impossible.

"I know he hears it from everybody: 'You've got to do this, and do that,'" says Carter. "I don't want to stay in his ear. Sometimes we have these heart-to-heart, hurt-your-feelings conversations. It's just to make him realize his potential. As he was growing up, he was a great brother. He's heading in that direction now.

"I told him it's always there, the opportunity, he never has to worry about not having a job — but he has to do it for himself first. I think he's starting to understand that. Once he shows he wants to do better, to be somebody, life will be easier for him.

"I think he got caught up in that 'Just because my brother's doing this, I don't have to do anything. I can just wait for him to give me this and that.' My family doesn't operate that way, not at all."

This is part of Carter's apprenticeship and makes him more wary. That nice-guy persona pegs him as a chump in some quarters, and of course he knows that. "Some people take advantage of that, take advantage of who you are."

Putting his graduation on an equal footing with the most important moment of his career was a controversial moment in the guys-will-be-guys world of sports, where transgressions are tolerated as long as you win. To some, including the *New York Times* editorial board, Carter was a hero. To others, like his old Olympic teammate Ray Allen, he was selfish.

He had gone to each player and explained what he was doing and why. Some of them shook their heads but weren't about to criticize. Around the league, there was a lot of that going on. To leave your team the night before the seventh game of the playoffs? It just wasn't done. Carter was expecting some negative media reaction, and couldn't care less. He was dismayed to read of Allen's criticism. But what he cared about most was his team.

To Carter, this was normal. This was "the right thing to do."

"Walking in there, it was almost the same feeling I had walking in for the opening ceremonies of the Olympics," he said. "I think I was mesmerized — I felt like I finally made it, I'm in the Olympics. And when I walked into that stadium for graduation, it was the same: I finally made it. I saw a lot of the friends I went to class with, hung out with, some of the guys on the team, one of my best friend's roommates. We sat together. We laughed."

Carter could have come back later in the year, to the December ceremony, but the moment he wanted was this one: a last commune with these friends, turning the page on this chapter in his life, just like everyone around him was doing. Even if his day job was so different than everyone else's who crowded around him, passing over their programs and their mortarboards to be signed. Hey, it certainly was different than the NBA, where the autographs are scribbled hastily on bubblegum cards or caps or jerseys, or even an admiring woman's breasts.

It didn't last long. Less than an hour later, he was on his way out of the stadium. He wouldn't take the gown off until he was back on the plane, the same one that had brought him from Toronto the day before, after Raptors practice.

One of Carter's self-criticisms is an acknowledgment that, sometimes, he doesn't prepare enough, instead relying on sheer physical prowess to get him through. But in this case, he was locked in and it all came off without incident. Even the rain held off, and as the Raptors were sitting down to have their pregame meal at a Philadelphia hotel, Carter strode in. On time, just as if he were coming down from his room.

"I walked in there like it was a normal day," he said. "I was glad. A lot of these people, and maybe these guys, they probably thought, 'He won't be back till game time.'"

After the meeting was over, each player came over and congratulated him. And then it was down to the usual business, in this case an excruciating evening of playoff basketball, all of it coming down to this final moment: a one-point Philadelphia lead, Toronto ball out of bounds with two seconds to go, and the entire First Union Center crowd going bonkers.

In the timeout, Lenny Wilkens conjured the play out of the thin, last-minute air that can choke players and spectators alike. This is what coaches are paid to do: Wilkens quickly marking out the patterns and the responsibilities in black on the white greaseboard. All the zigs and zags and cuts and screens led to the inevitable, to what Wilkens had dreamed of when he took the job, to what everyone in the arena knew was going to happen: seventh game, Vince Carter with the ball, final buzzer going off.

"I felt like I had the play written all over my face," Carter said. "I walked out there, and it was like it was broadcast to the world. It was great."

It was supposed to be. When the Raptors and the Philadelphia 76ers entered their playoff series, it was hyped as a matchup of two young NBA superstars in Carter and Sixers guard Allen Iverson. Iverson was awarded the league's Most Valuable Player award during the series. Iverson's jersey had surpassed Carter's at midseason as the league's top seller, in the wake of his MVP trophy at the all-star game and his remarkable generalship in leading the Sixers to the top rung of the eastern conference. It was a remarkable transformation in a number of ways: Philadelphia's head coach Larry Brown had had enough of Iverson over the summer of 2000, and the 76ers traded him away only to have the deal broken. In the fall of 2000, before the season, Iverson's homophobic gangsta rapping on his upcoming CD had him in trouble with the league hierarchy, Sixers management, a number of gay-rights groups and the NAACP.

Put these two together on the same floor over the course of a play-off series and it was like the proverbial matchup of fire and ice. Iverson's blinding speed, fearlessness and scoring ability was a formi-dable package, but his heart and passion were equally apparent to even the most casual observer. Carter, meantime, had shed some skin of his own in the victory over the Knicks. He was the cool choirboy next to Iverson, but just as capable of explosion and getting used to this play-off pressure.

And so they went, the Raptors stealing Game 1 as Iverson outscored Carter 36-35. Game 2, and Iverson dropped 54 on the Raptors. Game 3, and it was back to the Air Canada Centre and back to Carter, raining an NBA record eight three-pointers by halftime, on his way to a 50-point night. By Game 4, with the Sixers looking utterly spent, still it was Iverson who left the floor taunting the Raptors with cries of "Bring it!" The semi-finals stretched to the seven-game limit with another Iverson eruption, 52 points in Game 5. Carter came back with 39 in Game 6, in front of a home crowd that tickled the spine all night long.

In three short years, Toronto fans had grown into a smarter, more passionate group that through these playoffs numbered 20,000 strong each night. As the crowd gave it up for the Raptors during the playoffs, there were signs that Carter was giving it back to them. He motioned for noise, and they responded. He was growing more comfortable putting forth his opinion on personnel moves and making his voice heard in the locker room.

His future in Toronto has been a constant source of speculation. But as this Raptors team began to play better in the second half of the season and into the playoffs, the small group of intimates around him were see-ing a growing sense of comfort.

"If I was a betting person, I would say Vince is going to stay in Toronto," says Michelle Carter. "I don't want to say that to him, I don't want him to make any decision based on my feelings. It's his call. Toronto is a good city for him, a good situation. There was a time earlier where there was a sense of 'What are the Raptors doing?' They've turned that around."

Even among the skeptics in the Toronto dressing room, chiefly Oakley, Carter's turn against the Knicks was opening some eyes. Oakley wasn't about to back down on his assertion that Carter lacked "the hunger." But Carter, who once would have put that down to one man's opinion, wasn't going to agree.

"I think I proved that I have that," he said. "I don't worry about that. Everybody approaches it a little different. Some guys have a scowl on their faces, they mean-mug the whole game. I don't. I still think we accomplish the same things.

"I might approach it a little different than Oak, because Oak's a guy who doesn't like to have fun, he's down to business. I do the same, but I like to be calm. I like to be relaxed, to have fun. I don't like to be uptight. That's not me."

There are moments, though, when Carter's concentration level on the floor drops. He senses it, too, and asks for patience. "I'm a little hard on myself when I don't start off well," he said. "I get down on myself, and I'll tell myself not to shoot the ball, or I'll doubt myself and I'm out there trying to aim instead of just letting it go.

"I've learned enough that I don't let every little thing bother me," says Carter. "I think I'm focused on what I want to accomplish, regardless of any grief, or disagreements, or the way I played. I do realize I'm not going to make everybody happy."

The play was simple. Dell Curry, once a baseball pitcher with a 92 miles-per-hour fastball and good enough to be drafted by the Baltimore Orioles, would inbound the ball. Carter would dive down off an Oakley screen. With the 76ers in their "White Defence" — switching on everything — the Raptors hoped to get a mismatch, with Carter the first option on the wing and Antonio Davis second choice inside.

They got what they wanted, Tyrone Hill jumping out on Carter, who received Curry's deft bounce pass around seven-footer Todd MacCulloch. There was presence of mind, Carter pump-faking to get Hill up in the air. The 76ers forward kicked out his leg as he flew at Carter, who ducked under for a clear look at the basket, albeit balancing a little awkwardly on one foot.

Make the shot, and Carter's day goes down in history. He had had a decent game, not making his usual percentage of shots, but also finding his teammates for good looks, playing good defence then lapsing on some plays. Some would blame the outcome on the graduation trip, but it sure looked like Carter out there, and it looked like the smart, physical, fundamentally sound Sixers in the opposing shirts.

"I was comfortable," said Carter. "I've been there before. It was what you live for."

The horn sounded as the ball was just off his fingertips. He needed 22 feet. He shot maybe three inches more. The ball hit the far side of the iron and bounced up and out. It was over.

As he walked off, a few fans heckled. "You should've stayed in college four years!" one yelled, and others in the rough-and-tumble Philadelphia crowd applauded.

His year was over, along with the first phase of his career, the arc from nova to this steady, pulsating star. Pro athletes tend to be narrow-minded and egotistical — they have to be, to get where they are, sports being the ultimate in Darwinian arenas. Not Carter.

"For some, that's how they got here," he says. "I understand that. Sometimes I think maybe I should be like that. But I can't — that's not who I am."

Who is he? League saviour, dunking machine, Prince Vince, Air Canada. Take your pick. They're roles and labels he never asked for and seems vaguely uncomfortable with.

Who he is, or at least who he wants to be, is a rare mix of low-key and high-wattage. If he can pull it off, it may be the neatest trick of all.

ACKNOWLEDGMENTS

This book is the product of 73 interviews and the personal (sometimes painful) memories of covering the Raptors in Toronto since they began operations in late 1993. None of it would have been possible without the initial support of my employers and colleagues at the *Toronto Star*, particularly sports editor Steve Tustin and managing editor Mary Deanne Shears, who readily granted my request for a six-month leave of absence and even let me come back to the job after Mary Ormsby sparkled in my stead.

Among the Raptors who put up the most with my nagging, I am indebted to Jim LaBumbard, Matt Akler, Mark Dottori, John Lashway and Laura Leithe. Glen Grunwald never failed to open his door to me, Jacquie Allinson never failed to go the extra mile and Lenny Wilkens was as gracious as ever in enduring my inquiries past time. At the NBA offices, Terry Lyons, Brian McIntyre and Andrea Grumet deserve thanks and mention for their usual brand of professional courtesy and help. Around the league, some of my longtime faves like David Benner in Indiana, Brian Kirschner and Karen Frascona in Philadelphia, Joel Glass in Orlando, Ray Ridder at Golden State and Tim Donovan at Miami went beyond the call, as did Bill Bevan and Bill York of the Pacers' crew.

Here at home, Merle Scott, Dave Haggith and Kathryn Mertens of IMG always came through. Michelle and Vince Carter proved that very busy people can be good and gracious people, too, and the same goes for Ann Smith of Vince's Embassy of Hope Foundation.

Among my friends in the media, special mention and thanks goes out to Bill Magrath of SBN, New Yorkers Dave D'Alessandro, Chris Sheridan and Mike Wise, Rob MacLeod and Mike Grange of the *Globe and Mail*, Bill Harris and Craig Daniels at the Toronto *Sun*, Dave Feschuk at the *National Post*, Paul Jones and Susan Antal at TSN and Chuck Swirsky and Jack Armstrong of The Fan 590. At the *Star*, Doug Smith, Jennifer Quinn and Mary O. were always helpful. I am also indebted to the fine work published in *Sports Illustrated*, the *New York Times* magazine, *Esquire*, *Newsweek*, the *Saturday Evening Post* and *Ebony*, some of which found its way in here, or at least pointed me in the right direction. As far as research assistants, I couldn't have found a better pair than Sasha Johnston and Jessica Simone.

As for those interviewees, thanks to all. To those who asked their names not be used, I have honoured that request wherever possible.

When I first approached Doubleday Canada about this project, I was overwhelmed and a little surprised by their enthusiasm, given that books on pro basketball in this country have been few and far between. Maya Mavjee and Brad Martin never wavered in their support. But the heavy lifting fell to my editor, Meg Taylor, whose shots always beat the buzzer and who, I'm told, added a purple no. 15 Carter jersey to her Casual Friday wardrobe.

Finally, for putting up with the vagaries of a sportswriter's schedule for all these years — and then for enduring my act for six successive months at home in Toronto, surely a record — there has been the love of my life, Pauline, and our girls Nicole and Jessica. Home game or away, they've always been there for me.